# Constructing Global Civil Society

*Also by David Chandler*

BOSNIA: Faking Democracy After Dayton

FROM KOSOVO TO KABUL: Human Rights and International Intervention

RETHINKING HUMAN RIGHTS: Critical Approaches to International Politics
(*Editor*)

# Constructing Global Civil Society

## Morality and Power in International Relations

David Chandler
*Senior Lecturer in International Relations,*
*Centre for the Study of Democracy,*
*University of Westminster, UK*

First published 2004 by
PALGRAVE MACMILLAN
Houndmills, Basingstoke, Hampshire RG21 6XS and
175 Fifth Avenue, New York, N. Y. 10010
Companies and representatives throughout the world

PALGRAVE MACMILLAN is the global academic imprint of the Palgrave Macmillan division of St. Martin's Press, LLC and of Palgrave Macmillan Ltd. Macmillan® is a registered trademark in the United States, United Kingdom and other countries. Palgrave is a registered trademark in the European Union and other countries.

ISBN 1–4039–1322–6

This book is printed on paper suitable for recycling and made from fully managed and sustained forest sources.

A catalogue record for this book is available from the British Library.

A catalogue record for this book is available from the Library of Congress.

10   9   8   7   6   5   4   3   2   1
13   12   11   10   09   08   07   06   05   04

Printed and bound in Great Britain by
Antony Rowe Ltd, Chippenham and Eastbourne

*For Bonnie and Harvey*

# Contents

# Acknowledgements

This book would not have been possible without the support and patience of my wife Bonnie. I am well aware that it is not merely our own 'free time' that gets consumed in the process of writing a manuscript but often also that of our partners. I also need to thank Tara and John in London who made possible and pleasurable my long distance working and living arrangements, after my move to Westminster.

I would like to thank the Nottingham University politics MA students attending my course on NGOs, from where the idea for this book arose, and the Westminster University international relations MA students at the Centre for the Study of Democracy with whom I have developed the themes of global civil society and international relations over the last couple of years.

I am grateful to CiSoNet, the European civil society research network, funded under the European Community Framework 5 programme, for inviting me to take part in the programme workshops and conferences, where many of the themes here received their first airing. I would also like to thank the convenors of panels at the Political Studies Association and the British International Studies Association in 2003, as well as the organisers of seminars at University College London, Birkbeck, Kings, Lancaster, Sussex and Aberystwyth where the themes were also developed.

I am also grateful for the support, ideas and guidance from colleagues at the Centre for the Study of Democracy, including John Keane, Chantal Mouffe, Richard Whitman and Jon Pugh, as well as the assistance from many other friends and associates, including Michael Pugh, Daniele Archibugi, Nicholas Wheeler, Alex Bellamy, James Heartfield, Gideon Baker, John Pender, Dominick Jenkins, Gemma Collantes Celador, Frank Füredi, Philip Hammond, Michele Ledda and Vanessa Pupavac. Where my views have gained from their input and where I have decided to ignore their good advice will be clear from the text, for which, of course, I take full responsibility.

Chapter 2 is an amended version of 'Constructing Global Civil Society' in G. Baker and D. Chandler (eds) *Global Civil Society: Contested Futures* (London: Routledge, forthcoming 2004). Chapter 3 is an amended version of 'Culture Wars and International Intervention: An "Inside/Out" View of the Decline of the National Interest', *International*

*Politics*, Vol. 41, No. 3, forthcoming 2004. Chapter 4 is an amended version of 'The Responsibility to Protect: Imposing the "Liberal Peace"?', *International Peacekeeping*, Vol. 11, Special Issue, forthcoming 2004. Chapter 7 is an amended version of 'New Rights for Old? Cosmopolitan Citizenship and the Critique of State Sovereignty', *Political Studies*, Vol. 51, No. 2, 2003, pp. 339–356.

# 1
# Introduction

Today there is a growing consensus that morality is returning to the study and practice of international relations. This optimism is grounded in the belief that the nation-state, which long held a central position in the international order, has been increasingly side-lined by new international actors, orientated around more universalist beliefs and motivations. In particular, the world's states are held to be squeezed from 'above' by institutional frameworks, understood to presage the growth of new forms of global governance, and from 'below' by a myriad of non-state actors and networks, which operate on both a domestic and an international level. The boundaries of sovereignty, once seen to clearly demarcate a geo-political map of the world, now seem to be much more 'fuzzy' at the edges and to represent little to those seeking to understand the mechanisms shaping the international order in the 21st century. Instead of state interests being the determining factor in world affairs, it appears the debate is increasingly opening out to encompass more and more voices. At every level it seems new approaches are being taken to decision-making and at the heart of this process of change has appeared a new actor, an actor whose precise shape and contours may be indeterminate and disputed, but whose presence is not: global civil society.

Global civil society is seen by many analysts as an extension of the rule of law and political community, *societas civilis*, beyond national boundaries. For its most radical advocates, global civil society is about political emancipation, the empowerment of individuals and the extension of democracy. Mary Kaldor, for example, argues that the end of the global conflict of the Cold War 'allows for the domestication of international relations and the participation of citizens, and citizen groups at an international level' which was previously the preserve of governments (Kaldor 2003:13). For John Keane, 'brand new democratic thinking – implicit in the theory of global civil society – is required' in the face of the growing lack of accountability of global governance (Keane 2003:126).

Over the last fifteen years it appears that the international realm has been transformed, no longer the sphere of violence and competition of the 'war of all against all', the international is the sphere of transnational values and transnational actors increasingly able to influence and overcome the selfish and narrow interest of national elites. Analysts of global civil society argue that a new normative and ethical international agenda demonstrates the waning influence of the sovereign state pre-occupied with national concerns. For Jean Grugel: 'The global civil society approach represents an overt attempt to blend normative theory with international relations.' (Grugel 2003:275) Along similar lines, Kaldor asserts: 'The new meaning of civil society offers expanded possibilities for human emancipation.' (Kaldor 2003:143) While for John Clark, 'the time is ripe for "ethical globalisation" morally underpinned by new activist citizens' networks' (Clark 2001:18).

This book has two main aims. Firstly, it seeks to analyse how international relations theorists have sought to understand the political impact and workings of global civil society. In this respect it differs from many books on the subject. It is not a study of global civil society per se. There is no attempt to strictly define or to empirically document the rise of global civil society nor to comprehensively survey the role of global civic actors in various domestic and international institutions. Neither does this book seek to establish a set of normative claims for global civil society or to interpret the collective demands of this society in a prescriptive set of normative rules and practices. The project is a more modest one, to seek to understand why and how the concept of global civil society has captured the imagination of journalists, politicians, academics, radical activists, and policy advisors from across the political spectrum.

The second aim of this investigation is to investigate the apparent happy coincidence that just as it seems that domestic politics is entering a terminal decline, with falling voting figures and widespread disillusionment with the political process, the international sphere should become suddenly seen as filled with the dynamic promise of radical change. Today it appears that everyone is an internationalist. Every campaign group, political party, NGO, government and local authority is busy making international links and 'making a difference' at an international level. Why is it that the international sphere holds such an attraction for individuals and groups involved in politics? For some cynics it is merely the foreign junkets and chance to travel on per diem expenses which draws the attraction of our globalised political classes. For others, it is the new openness of the post-Cold War world, with less barriers to travel and fewer visa restrictions (for some at least). For others, it is the cheapness of air travel and mass communications which have encouraged global consciousness and new broader political horizons.

In the past, domestic and international political activism were closely correlated. However, today the decline of domestic political engagement and the rise of international activism appear to have marched hand-in-hand. This book seeks to investigate whether an analysis of global civic thinking can furnish any insights into this political conundrum.

## Global civil society

Global civil society theorists cover an increasingly wide range of perspectives and views, including constructivists, critical theorists, normative theorists and postmodernists. All of these approaches focus on the break between old forms of 'citizenship' tied to the nation-state and new forms of moral and political community. All the theorists locate global civic actors as the source of moral action and their break from conventional state-based politics as the strategic basis for radical political change. One concept which captures the importance of global civil society is the idea that it 'signifies the domestication of the international' (Kaldor 2003:78). The international sphere was once dominated by *realpolitik* and the 'struggle for power', while the domestic sphere was seen as the sphere of ethical and normative concerns of 'the good life'. Today, in contrast, it is held that the sphere of power and contestation has been 'colonised' by the domestic sphere of ethics and civility. For global civil society theorists, it is non-state actors which are held to have overcome the empirical and ethical divide between the domestic political realm and the international.

### The empirical case

For many commentators, 'Power Shift', the title of Jessica Mathew's article in *Foreign Affairs* (Mathews 1997), aptly sums up the seismic shift which has taken place in international relations since the ending of the Cold War. Rather than the end of the Cold War resulting in a shift in power relations among states, there is alleged to be a 'novel redistribution of power' away from states towards global civil society. The most important empirical trend since the end of the Cold War is alleged to be that of the development of a global civil society because it brings with it emancipatory alternatives and new ways of doing politics and of establishing political and moral communities. As Ann Florini states: 'The state system that has governed the world for centuries is neither divinely ordained nor easily swept away. It is, however, changing, and one of the most dramatic changes concerns the growing role of transnational civil society.' (Florini 2001:30)

The number of international NGOs had grown from 176 in 1909 to 28,900 by 1993 (CCG 1995). The early 1990s witnessed a huge increase in the number of non-state actors involved in international policy. The number of development NGOs registered in the OECD countries of the industrialised 'North' grew from 1,600 in 1980 to 2,970 in 1993 and their total spending doubled, rising from US$2.8 billion to US$5.7 billion. In the 'South' the growth in the registered number of NGOs was even more impressive, for example, figures for Nepal show an increase from 220 in 1990 to 1,210 in 1993, in Bolivia, from 100 in 1980 to 530 in 1993; and in Tunisia, from 1,886 in 1988 to 5,186 in 1991 (Hulme and Edwards 1997b:4).

Mathews argues that we are, in fact, witnessing a historic reversal of the steady concentration of power in the hands of states, which began with the Peace of Westphalia in 1648. So much so that 'increasingly, NGOs are able to push around even the largest governments' (Mathews 1997:53). In another hugely influential article in the same journal, Lester Salamon, Director of the Institute for Policy Studies at Johns Hopkins University, claims that 'we are in the midst of a global "associational revolution" that may prove to be as significant to the latter twentieth century as the rise of the nation-state was to the latter nineteenth' (Salamon 1994:109).

Descriptively there can be little doubting the dramatic rise in non-state actors in international affairs, nor the dramatic collapse of a number of nation-states in the former Soviet block and in Africa. For commentators on the right of the political spectrum, this has been celebrated as symbolising the crisis of old statist solutions to development and the need to free global economic initiative from bureaucratic constraints (Salamon 1994; Fore 1993). The NGO sector has also been seen instrumentally as a crucial mechanism for opening up political space and challenging state regulation in the South (Salamon 1994). Analysts of NGO growth have acknowledged that the international agenda of neo-liberal economics and liberal democracy promotion was largely responsible for the 'associational revolution'. However, the initial fears of NGOs being discredited through their connections with international institutions have given way to a growing consensus on the unique values of the third sector as a vital regulatory and constraining actor, which can challenge the power monopolies and inequalities enforced and promoted by both the state and the market (Christenson 1997:732–3; Hulme and Edwards 1997c: 276–7).

Non-state actors are often held to have been central to the development of international policy on transnational questions, for example, to the abolition of slavery, women's and workers rights in the nineteenth century, and the adoption and expansion of international norms and regimes on human rights, the environment, children's and women's rights and rights of minorities and indigenous peoples in the last century. Today, as transnational questions of human rights, the environment and international terrorism dominate the international agenda, it appears as if non-state actors of various kinds are becoming increasingly important players in international policy-making. Not just playing a major role in United Nations' forums but also in the policy-making of international financial institutions and governments (van Tuijl 1999; Edwards and Gaventa 2001; Wilkinson and Hughes 2002; Weiss and Gordenker 1996). For some commentators, progress in international affairs, from the development of human rights regimes, to the overthrow of apartheid and the ending of the Cold War, to the establishment of war crimes tribunals and the International Criminal Court, are all the product of human rights NGO initiatives and pressures (Korey 1999:152).

According to many political analysts, the growth of the non-state sector threatens the political monopoly of nation-states in international decision-making and reflects a growing alternative to states and the market; representing a 'third force' capable of empowering citizens and possibly transforming the international system itself. For Kaldor: 'The site of politics has shifted from formal national institutions to new local and cross-border spaces and this is, to a large extent, the consequence of global civil society activities.' (Kaldor 2003:148)

Over recent years there have been many landmark initiatives led by non-state actors, such as the campaign against breast-milk substitutes, targeted at Nestlé; the campaign to ban landmines, resulting in the Ottawa Land Mines Convention; the Greenpeace campaigns for Ogoni rights in Nigeria and against the dumping of the Brent Spar, both targeted at the Shell oil company; and the Jubilee 2000 campaign for debt-relief. Non-state actors have initiated parallel summits organised at UN conferences on the environment and women's rights, attended by thousands of NGOs, and have won greater involvement in World Bank and international financial institutional decision-making. For many analysts, the Seattle protests in 1999 demonstrated the potential for non-state actors to shape the international political agenda. John Gaventa, an influential authority, asserts that global civic actors have been successful in 'challenging power relations at multiple levels', from restraining the actions of international financial institutions and multilateral corporations to impacting on international treaties and conventions (Gaventa 2001:278–9). As one leading left commentator argues:

> The anti-globalisation movement is the first movement that represents a break with the 20th century and its truths and myths. At present it is the main source of politics for an alternative to the global right. When on February 15 [2003], 100 million people took to the streets, the *New York Times* referred to it as a second 'world power', a power that in the name of peace opposed those who wanted war.   (Bertinotti 2003)

## The normative case

There is little agreement about the precise definition of global civil society. For many commentators this is not of key importance as global civil society is an appealing concept less because of its empirical strengths, in capturing actually existing international relationships, than because of its normative or moral implications. Like the concept of human rights, few people would argue against the normative or ethical concept of civil society or global civil society. Even those who may dispute the existence of global civil society in practice would not argue against the use of the concept to highlight a positive normative goal or ideal (see van Rooy 1998:30; Kumar 1993:388).

There are three dominant answers to the question, posed in the opening paragraphs, of the grounds for the growing consensus advocating the need for developing and recognising global civil society and the attractiveness of global civic activism itself. They are that the concept of global civil society captures three aspects of global progress in recent decades: firstly, the extension of political community, as international politics is no longer seen as a political sphere limited to the narrow national interests of states; secondly, that global civil society places a normative emphasis on human agency, rather than the economic determinism of the market and the conservatism of the 'end of history'; and finally, the role of global civil society in the extension of democracy, the recasting of decision-making processes beyond exclusive national boundaries. This book investigates each of these claims and suggests other, additional, explanations for the success of global civil society as an approach to both understanding and participating in political life.

## The extension of community

Global civic activism is seen as restoring collective values and morality as a counterpoint to the narrow individualism or political apathy reflected in the institutions of formal, state-based, politics. According to Richard Falk: 'globalisation from below extends the sense of community, loosening the ties between sovereignty and community but building a stronger feeling of identity with the sufferings and aspirations of peoples, a wider "we"' (Falk 1995:89). For Mary Kaldor, global civil society has emerged with the end of the Cold War and growing global interconnectedness, which has undermined the importance of territorial boundaries and spatial barriers, blurring the distinctions between regions and states. These interconnected processes 'have opened up new possibilities for political emancipation':

> Whether we are talking about isolated dissidents in repressive regimes, landless labourers in Central America or Asia, global campaigns against landmines or third world debt...what has changed are the opportunities for linking up with other like-minded groups in different parts of the world, and for addressing demands not just to the state but to global institutions and other states... In other words, a new form of politics, which we call civil society, is both an outcome and an agent of global interconnectedness. (Kaldor 2003:2)

For normative theorists, such as Andrew Linklater, the nation-state restricts the bounds of moral reasoning to the 'boundaries of political association' (Linklater 1981:27). Linklater argues that the obligations of citizens to states have acted as a historical constraint on the development of man's moral and political development. In an internationalised social environment the self-determination of the individual, man's capacity to 'participate in the control of his total political environment' is restricted by the territorial limitations of sovereignty. He argues that these political and moral limits are historically conditioned

(Linklater 1981:34). The solution is that of radical political struggle to resolve the tensions between the moral duties of men and the political duties of citizens through the 'actualization of a higher form of international political life [which] requires [a] radical critique of the state' and the formation of a broader, more inclusive community. (Linklater 1981:35).

The critique of the sovereign states system is simultaneously an argument for 'the widening of the moral boundaries of political communities (Linklater 1998:2). Ronnie Lipschutz argues that 'the growth of global civil society represents an ongoing project of civil society to reconstruct, re-imagine, or re-map world politics' (Lipschutz 1992:391). Richard Falk summarises the distance between current normative theorising of global civil society and traditional international relations theory:

> Realism, with its moral commitment to the pursuit of the national interest – or state interest as defined by political leaders...leads to the validation of warfare, the marginalisation of international law and morality, the privileging of the logic of economic growth at the expense of ecological sustainability, and the uncritical acceptance of the patriarchal heritage.   (Falk 1995:82)

The connection between global civil society and normative theorising sees non-state actors as key agents in expanding moral ideas and reconstituting the political. As Neera Chandhoke observes:

> ...global NGOs have become influential simply because they possess a property that happens to be the peculiar hallmark of *ethical* political intervention: moral authority and legitimacy. And they possess moral authority because they claim to represent the *public* or the *general* interest against official- or power-driven interests of the state or of the economy.   (Chandhoke 2002:41)

The subject matter of international life is no longer the apparently male-dominated questions of economics and war. Jessica Mathews, for example, argues that global civil society actors are better placed to address 'the "soft" threats of environmental degradation, denial of human rights, population growth, poverty, and lack of development' which are increasingly recognised as more important to international life than the traditional state concerns of the 'high politics' of security (Mathews 1997:63). It is also assumed that global civil society actors are better suited to transnational or global issues: 'Their loyalties and orientation, like those of international civil servants and citizens of non-national entities like the EU, are better matched than those of governments to problems that demand transnational solutions.' (Mathews 1997:63) Richard Falk similarly argues that: 'normative content can be introduced into global market operations only by the self-conscious and dedicated efforts of those social forces that [consti-tute]...globalisation from below' (Falk 1995:181). Both the need for and the existence of an international or global civil society has now gained a consensus. As John Clark summarises: 'Civil society is increas-ingly seen as a vehicle for injecting values and moral pressure into the global marketplace.' (Clark 2001:19)

*Human agency*

The second attraction of global civil society theorising is that it posits the need for radical human agency in distinction to the economic determinacy and perceived market dominance of globalisation theory. As Naomi Klein reported from the first annual World Social Forum in Porto Alegre, Brazil: 'Many people said they felt history being made in that room. What I felt was something more intangible: the end of the End of History.' (Klein 2002:193) By challenging the 'end of history' thesis, which suggests the end of radical alternatives to capitalist liberal democracy, global civic advocates reaffirm the potential for change (Heins 2000:37).

It is now apparent to many commentators that realist theories of international relations did not just reflect division and conflict, they were also responsible for reproducing it. Given the assumption that ideas and norms structure identities and practices, realism becomes, in Alexander Wendt's words, a 'self-fulfilling prophecy' rather than merely an ideological justification (Wendt 1992:410). Critical theorists such as Robert Cox and Andrew Linklater also argue that realist theory has helped to reproduce the very structures that it argued were immutable (Cox 1981:128–9; Linklater 1998:21). As Richard Falk notes, interna-tional theory of 'political realism' has directly reflected elite attitudes:

> The realist mindset...forecloses the political imagination in several respects: it dismisses moral and legal criteria of policy as irrelevant for purposes of explanation, prediction, and prescription; it grounds speculation on an assessment of relative power as perceived by rational, even ultrarational, actors, essentially states, and is there-fore unable to take account of passion, irrationality, and altruistic

motivations as political forces, or of the impacts of non-state actors.   (Falk 1995:37)

The struggle against realist theory, with its privileging of state agency and rationalism and its limited vision of international progress, is held to be central to the success of the global civil society project:

> ...the horizons of politics are self-fulfilling: if the main agents of political action are confirmed realists, then a realist land-scape results. If the visionary convictions of dedicated exponents of global civil society hold sway, then a more humanistic landscape results.   (Falk 1995:43)

Indicative of the current vogue for global civil society approaches is the fact that in many international relations undergraduate textbooks realism's focus on plural and conflicting interests is considered to be neither of value as an explanatory nor even a descriptive analysis. As Nicholas Wheeler and Alex Bellamy outline: 'Realism purports to describe and explain the "realities" of statecraft but the problem with this claim to objectivity is that it is the realist mindset that has constructed the very practices that realist theory seeks to explain.' (Wheeler and Bellamy 2001:490)

The difference between liberal or idealist thought today and these currents in the inter-war period is that these ideas are not based merely on philosophical assertions of a moral cosmopolitanism but on what are perceived to be powerful existing international trends and social forces highlighting the importance of human agency. For example, Margaret Keck and Kathryn Sikkink argue:

> The problem with much of the theory in international relations is that it does not have a motor of change, or that the motor of change – such as state interests, or changing power capabilities – is impoverished, and cannot explain the sources or nature of interna-tional change... Classic realist theory in international relations has not been useful for explaining profound changes, such as the break-down of the Soviet Union and the satellite states in Eastern Europe, the end of slavery, or the granting of women the right to vote throughout the world.   (Keck and Sikkink 1998:213)

For many writers, the end of the Cold War domination of super-power rivalries and the process of globalisation has opened up the possibilities for an overdue alignment of political realities with moral principle. Today the emphasis of constructivist, critical and normative approaches on non-state actors and the norms and ideas they are held to promote, offers a way of understanding the world which puts human agency at the centre. The politically active individual can, does and historically did, make a difference. The struggle for progress is thus often portrayed as one waged by non-state actors against governments. Falk writes, for example: 'The realist mindset is most strongly present among elites. In civil society, ideas about truth, decency, and destiny have always held sway.' (Falk 1995:41) This injection of human agency, and the understanding of international structures as transient, is seen to reflect both an empirical and a normative challenge to the dominance of states.

Globalisation is considered to be the central problematic of international relations today. The neo-liberal perspective of the end of politics and domination of the free market, with states powerless to shape economic and social policy, is often posed as the backdrop which makes necessary the agency of global civil society and a restoration of the political on a new basis:

> Civil society is a process of management of society that is 'bottom-up' rather than 'top-down' and that involves the struggle for emancipatory goals. It is about governance based on consent where consent is generated through politics. In a global context, civil society offers a way of understanding the process of globalisation in terms of subjective human agency instead of a disembodied deterministic process of 'interconnectedness'. (Kaldor 2003:142)

## The extension of democracy

The normative project of global civil society is held to be a potential challenge to the non-democratic structures of global governance emerging in the wake of globalisation and the end of the Cold War:

> What was new about the concept, in comparison with earlier concepts of civil society, was both the demand for a radical extension of both political and personal rights – the demand for autonomy, self-organization or control over life – and the global content of the concept. To achieve these demands, the new civil society actors found it necessary and possible to make alliances across borders and to address not just the state but international institutions. (Kaldor 2003:76)

For Mary Kaldor, global civil society expands the sphere of 'active citizenship' referring to 'growing self-organization outside formal political circles and expanded space in which individual citizens can influence the conditions in which they live both directly through self-organization and through political pressure' (Kaldor 2003:8). Similarly, James Rosenau asserts that 'citizens now have many more avenues along which to pursue their interests' and 'a multitude of new points of access to the course of events' (Rosenau 1992:285). Richard Falk argues that global civic resistance from below similarly goes beyond the limitations of state-based politics:

> ...global civil society [movements]...carry the possibility of an extension of the movement for democratisation beyond state/society relations to all arenas of power and authority... It is not a matter of insisting upon a confrontation with the geopolitical leadership, but of expressing an overriding commitment to join the struggle to shape emergent geogovernance structures in more satisfying directions and orientating normative order at all levels of social interaction...   (Falk 1995:35)

Rather than states being the location of democratic politics and contestation of 'the good life', the international sphere is the location of 'democratization from below through the articulation of radical and new forms of transnational citizenship and social mobilisation' (Grugel 2003:263). For the advocates of actually existing global civil society, transnational campaigning is part of the new form of global governance which is an improvement on the past. Leading NGO analyst, Michael Edwards argues:

> This form of governance is messy and unpredictable, but ultimately it will be more effective – by giving ordinary citizens a bigger say in the questions that dominate world politics... For citizens of non-democratic regimes, transnational civil society may provide the only meaningful avenue for voice and participation in decision-making.   (Edwards 2001:4)

Mary Kaldor expands on the new mechanisms created through global civic action:

> Global civil society does provide a way to supplement traditional democracy. It is a medium through which individuals can, in princi-

ple, participate in global public debates; it offers the possibility for the voices of the victims of globalisation to be heard if not the votes. And it creates new fora for deliberation on the complex issues of the contemporary world, in which the various parties to the discussion do not only represent state interest.   (Kaldor 2003:148)

Having established that the most important social struggles need to take place on the international level, global civil society advocates argue for the reform of governing institutions. Jean Grugel identifies two dominant global civil society approaches, the radical and the liberal, which fix the international as the sphere of democratic struggle (2003: 275). The radical approach of bottom-up global civic action and the liberal approach of top-down cosmopolitan democratic governance will be considered in Chapters 6 and 7.

By way of introduction, the rest of this chapter provides a brief historical recap of the development of international relations theorising with regard to questions of morality and power in the international realm in order to better appreciate the claims of global civil society theorists. The next sections then break down the theoretical approaches to global civil society which will be considered in this book and outline in more detail the chapter contents which follow.

## Morality and power in international relations

The dominant perspectives in the study of international relations during the Cold War, realism and neo-realism, stressed the structural limitations of the international environment which prevented the realisation of normative visions of radical change. These approaches placed much less emphasis on normative and ethical values than present day global civil society theorists and emphasised the importance of power relations more.

As explored below, international theorists today condemn the 'amorality' of Cold War international relations theory, which is alleged to have merely stressed the interests of power. This is a rather one-sided re-reading of the discipline. Rather than stressing the importance of power and self-interest as the single guide to action, international relations theorists were largely preoccupied with the problem of war. In the wake of two world wars – which were waged under the banner of universal principles, rather than national interests – for many theorists, as long as the world remained geo-politically divided, universal ethics were to be cautioned against as potentially destabilising and dangerous. Yet, rather than highlight the historical links between realism, the rejection of universal ethics and the advocacy of peaceful co-existence, today, traditional international relations theorists are portrayed as if they were advocates of power, injustice and war. This way of representing Cold War realism downplays the earlier theorists' concern with the abuse of power at the same time as portraying today's normative advocates as the only commentators in the field concerned with peace and justice.

For E. H. Carr, one of the founders of the modern discipline of international relations, writing in 1939, with the world of empire crumbling and another world war starting between the major powers, it seemed obvious that the use of universal moral claims reflected an increasingly divided world, where ethics were used to justify and further the particular interests of powerful states (Carr 2001:71). Carr was not arguing against the existence of ethics and morality in international relations, merely that power could never be taken out of the equation when dealing with international politics, and that vast power inequalities even more starkly undermined any 'harmony' of collective interests in the international sphere than in the domestic arena. For Carr, those who argued that states could consistently act morally, either ignored the factor of power or unconsciously perceived the interests of their own state as the same as those of international society more broadly. The fact that morality could not be disassociated from power meant: 'Theories of international morality are...the product of dominant nations or groups of nations.' (Carr 2001:74)

Hans Morgenthau, the author of possibly the most influential book in Cold War international relations, *Politics among Nations* (1993), first published in 1948, drew out clearly the problem of ethics in the international arena. He highlighted the development of international norms in inter-state relations and how morality restrained state actions in the modern age (1993:225–35). However, his work, like Carr's, emphasised how politics and power limited these moral restraints on international behaviour, rather than their absence. Morgenthau argued that universal ethics were a threat to world peace and the international order and, like many of today's normative critics, he suggested that international morality had deteriorated with the rise of the modern nation-state and democratic rule (1993:235–41). For Morgenthau, the shared community of interests, reflected in 'natural law' upheld under the rule of European aristocracy, had fragmented into the distinct national interests of modernity. The conflict between universal loyalty to the interests of humanity and particular loyalties to the state was solved by:

> ...pouring, as it were, the contents of a particular national morality into the now almost empty bottle of universal ethics. So each nation comes to know again a universal morality – that is, its own national morality – which is taken to be the one that all the other nations ought to accept as their own.  (Morgenthau 1993:242)

Rather than the conflict between European powers being constrained by shared moral beliefs and common values, the two world wars had revealed the dangers of competing ethical systems in a divided world. Whether war was waged under US President Woodrow Wilson's 'crusade for democracy', or the universal aspirations of Soviet Bolshevism or German National Socialism, claims to global moral principles were a barrier to peaceful co-existence. For Morgenthau, even with the best intentions, US attempts 'to impose its own principles of government upon the rest of mankind' would fail in the face of inevitable compromises of power or the unintended consequences of their actions (Morgenthau 1993:247–9; 48–9).

The concern with ethics of these early realist thinkers was abandoned, particularly in US academic circles, as international relations theories increasingly took on a more abstract or behaviouralist approach, highlighted in the systems analysis of Morton Kaplan in the late 1950s and the later structuralism of Kenneth Waltz (Kaplan 1957; Waltz 1979). The main challenge to these approaches was through the revival of liberal theory in the mid-1970s. However, it is important to note that this was not a critique of the amorality of realist approaches, but rather of the limitations of their focus on states as sole actors and on the centrality of military conflict. As Robert Keohane and Joseph Nye – authors of *Power and Interdependence* (2001), the leading critique, published in 1977, – stressed, their problem with realism had an empirical, not an ethical, basis. They felt that more elements needed to be brought into the analysis in order to understand US economic decline, growing forms of post-war international cooperation and the development of international norms reflecting and reinforcing this. The self-interest of states was still the primary concern and there was no conception of ethically critiquing state practice as morally unconstrained. The 'historical sociology' of Keohane and Nye offered an alternative methodology to realist analysis but not an ethical or normative critique (Keohane and Nye 2001:ix).

Outside the US, the behaviouralist approach was rejected by advocates of the 'English School' of international society, theorists who maintained the importance of ethical and moral considerations in international relations. These theorists similarly warned of the dangers of universal morality as a threat to peace. Martin Wight's extensive historical treatment of international theory followed Morgenthau in stressing the militarism and threat of conflict involved in the espousal of ethical universals. To Wight's historical mind, the early universalists of the Hellenic world, such as Alexander the Great and later Roman emperor Marcus Aurelius, were cosmopolitan empire-builders who easily conceived of their interests as at one with universal right (Wight 1991:83–4; see also Brown 2002:41). Wight saw ethical universals as as much a threat to international norms of law and diplomacy, established in international practice, as a pure focus on power and national interests would be. Shaped by the totalising experiences of fascism and communism, pluralism was high on the international agenda of Cold War international relations theorists. For the 'English School', international society was seen as neither a sphere of self-interest and anarchy (as in the abstract schema of neo-realists) nor as one of shared interests (as it was for early liberal theorists).

International society theory received its clearest theoretical expression in Hedley Bull's *The Anarchical Society* (1995), first published in 1977. Bull stressed the shared normative rules that made the international system a 'society of states' rather than a system of anarchy. Nevertheless, in fact particularly because of his emphasis on the importance of moral norms, Bull argued that the disparity of national interests and inequalities of power meant that normative pluralism was the building-block of the social order internationally. Any attempt to bring in universal values could only lead to conflict and instability and serve the interests of the most powerful states (Bull 1995:74–94). Bull also criticised ethical theorists who searched for models of world unity, such as Richard Falk, arguing that the job of academics was to attempt to understand the world rather than campaign to change it: 'there is greater danger in the confusion of description and prescription in the study of world order than in drawing too sharp a distinction between them'. (Bull 1995:266; xviii) In the mid- and late-1980s some theorists in the English School tradition challenged the 'pluralist' focus and advocated a more universalist 'solidarist' approach emphasising the importance of individual rights (see, for example, Bull 1984; Vincent 1986; Wheeler 1992). This shift laid the basis for the later development of constructivist approaches and a return to the mainstream of normative theorising with the end of the Cold War (Wendt 1999:31–2; Dunne 1995).

Until the late 1980s almost every text book on international relations took for granted the separation between the international and the domestic realms. While ethics and moral values were held to play a central role in domestic politics, power and strategic interests were assumed to be at the heart of international questions. Over the last fifteen years the traditional divide between the domestic and international spheres has been problematised. The realist assumption of the permanence of the institution of state sovereignty has been treated to wide ranging sociological and historical critiques which have suggested the transient and contingent nature of the sovereign state system.[1]

Today, there is a new consensus that the realm of morality has expanded and the old distinctions between the domestic and the international no longer apply. This shift in thinking has resulted in a growing attention to the prioritisation of ethical or moral approaches in international theorising. Philip Allott, for example, argues that traditional international relations theory was based on Machiavellism, 'the overriding of general moral duty by *raison d'etat*', a paradoxical 'morality of immorality' (Allott 1999:34). For Allott, this privileging of power politics over morality meant that international relations theory tended to be innately conservative and uncritical:

> Machiavellism was...a calculated negation of a long tradition which conceived of values that transcend the power of even the holders of the highest forms of social power. Those ideas – especially ideas of justice and natural law, but also all those philosophies which speak of 'the good' or 'the good life' – were transcendental and aspirational and critical in character; that is to say they were conceived of as an *ideal* which could not be overridden or even abridged by the merely *actual*, and in relation to which the actual should be oriented and would be judged. The ideal makes possible a morality of society.   (Allott 1999:35)

In contrast to realist approaches to international relations that have been accused of justifying the status quo, the ethical advocates of global civil society set out a radical agenda of criticism. Ken Booth asserts that the narrow focus on the political sphere of state interests and inter-state rivalry in international relations theory had become a barrier to developing new approaches which could address the problems of the international arena: 'What is needed must have *moral* at its centre because the fundamental questions of how we might and can live together concern values, not instrumental rationality.' (Booth 1995:110) He argues:

> To my mind the twenty-first will be the century of ethics, and global ethics at that. What I would like to see is a shift in the focus of the study of international relations from accumulating knowledge about 'relations between states' (what might be called the 'dismal science' of Cold War international relations) to thinking about ethics on a global scale.   (Booth 1995:109–110)

Andrew Linklater similarly argues that international relations theory needs to develop a 'bolder moral standpoint' (cited in Wheeler 1996:128). Richard Falk suggests: 'reorienting inquiry into the character of world politics, injecting moral purpose at the centre of our evaluative procedures; international relations is a social construction, and its normative emptiness is not a necessity' (Falk 1999b:191). It would appear that the shift in theorising about power to theorising about morality has mirrored the shift in ontological focus from states to global civic actors.

## This book

Global civil society theorists have two core concerns: firstly, explaining and describing empirical change in the international sphere – the construction of an actually existing global civil society – and secondly, the pursuit of a normative project of political change, through the promotion of global civil society norms, values and practices. As Mary Kaldor notes, despite the ambiguities involved in the concept of global civil society, all versions 'are both normative and descriptive'. Writers and advocates are both describing 'a political project i.e., a goal, and at the same time an actually existing reality, which may not measure up to the goal' (Kaldor 2003:11). For Kaldor and other commentators, such as Jean L. Cohen and Andrew Arato, global civil society is not only an attempt to understand the world, it is also 'a contemporary emancipatory project' (Kaldor 2003:27; see also Baker and Chandler forthcoming).

The definition of global civil society and theorists' approach to the nation-state differs between commentators, with most empirical and some normative approaches including (Western) states as members of global civil society while most normative approaches tend to exclude the formal political sphere from their considerations. However, there is a key theme uniting all the global civil society frameworks to be considered here: the underlying emphasis on extending the boundaries of moral community and the political autonomy of individuals. All the approaches seek to reconsider the relationships between the universal and the particular in a post-sovereign world. They do this through the ethical or moral problematisation of traditional views of sovereignty and the related concepts of state sovereign equality and non-intervention.

While seeking to highlight the inter-relationship between empirical and normative approaches to global civil society, this book deploys a similar division between actual existing global civil society and global civil society as a normative project. It is divided into two parts. Part I analyses the empirical case for a new form of global politics and Part II considers the normative or moral case.

Part I deals largely with constructivist theorists of international relations who are generally concerned with explaining international change and developing empirical frameworks of enquiry. Constructivism is the broadest and most mainstream approach of global civil society theorising, which sees morality constraining power through new mechanisms of international interaction, whereby non-state actors pressurise states to act in more morally-enlightened manner. Constructivists argue that states, especially Western states, have redefined or reconstructed their identities and interests, becoming part of a new post-Westphalian moral agenda.

Chapter Two outlines the key constructivist approaches at the heart of global civil society analysis in mainstream international relations theory. Constructivism would seem to offer many insights into post-Cold War policy developments such as the promotion of ethical foreign policy or the high profile privileging of individual human rights concerns over the rights of sovereignty; developments which appear to go against the self-interest of states. The development of constructivist frameworks of global civil society are traced with a focus on the processes through which it is argued non-state actors increasingly shape international policy. The chapter concludes with a discussion of whether constructivism is better able to explain and grasp these international changes than rationalist or realist alternatives.

Chapter Three broadens the discussion, considering the weakness of rationalist and realist approaches and forwarding an alternative framework for understanding the decline of the national interest and the increased attention given to the role of non-state actors. The chapter considers the problems of winning international legitimacy for humanitarian intervention and the 'war on terror'. It suggests that the apparent difficulty of governments externally projecting their self-interests in their foreign policy may have more to do with problems of clarifying and cohering a sense of political mission at home than with the influence of non-state actors operating in global civil society.

Chapter Four brings power relations back into the constructivist equation, focusing on the interplay of power and morality in discussions of international intervention. The bulk of the chapter discusses the report of the Independent International Commission on Intervention and State Sovereignty, *The Responsibility to Protect*, which uses a constructivist framework to address the clash between the traditional right of state sovereignty and the modern right of international intervention. The problems of achieving the consensus aimed at by the international Commission highlight that rather than moral norms restricting the powerful there is instead a much more ambiguous relationship between morality and power in 'actually existing global civil society'.

Part II considers the normative claims for global civil society as a project of emancipation. It will be suggested that normative theorists draw heavily on the work of Jürgen Habermas, establishing the basis for non-essentialist norms and values through the discourse and practices of global civil society. In this analysis, the relatively autonomous realm of transnational public space has opened the way for the practice of global citizenship and the development of communicative ethics. In many ways, this 'associational revolution' is held to be developing the qualities and practical experience of global citizenship in the same way as Alexis de Tocqueville argued that voluntary associations provided vital 'free schools' for the development of the virtues of national citizenship (Tocqueville 1945:124). Many theorists, in fact, take the argument further, suggesting that the communicative ethics of the global sphere provide a new set of moral standards to guide international practices, independently of the mediation of interests through formal political processes which privilege states.

Normative theorists can be usefully divided into two main categories (which, however, are not entirely mutually exclusive). Firstly, post-liberal, critical, postmodern, radical or subaltern theorists whose focus is on the potential of new social movements and decentralised resistances to power to construct global civil society from the bottom-up (see, for example, Baker 2001; Kenny 2003; Otto 1996:128–136). Secondly, liberal cosmopolitans, whose focus is on international law, cosmopolitan democracy and structures of global governance, who

argue for the need for new post-Westphalian mechanisms of global regulation. In this approach, global civil society actors provide important
inputs to legitimise multi-levelled governance institutions, from the
local to the global.[2]

Chapter Five considers the Habermasian case for global civil society
as an ideal communicative realm based on the ethics of communicative rationality, pluralism and non-violence. The new global space for
politics opened up by global civil society is argued to herald a new way
of constructing political communities freed from territorial constraints.
The chapter concludes with an analysis of the strengths and weak-
nesses of this approach, highlighting the conservative underpinnings
of the communicative project.

Chapter Six surveys the critical and postmodern perspectives of
global civil society as radical resistance 'from below'. Central to this
project is the rejection of 'territorialized' politics dominated by the
nation-state; the key arguments are surveyed, highlighting why the
state is seen as both too strong and too weak to be a legitimate site of
democratic political struggle and why even isolated struggles and
protests are understood to be immediately global in their effect.
The chapter concludes by discussing whether it is possible to build
a global political community on the basis of the recognition of the
validity of individual autonomy, separate 'spaces' and a highly person-
alised morality which tends to question and undermine any collective
processes of democratic decision-making.

Chapter Seven engages with the cosmopolitan paradox, the
ambiguous notion of cosmopolitan or global citizenship, where individual rights are held to be capable of protection and enforcement
by international and transnational institutions, assumed to be
accountable to global civil society. While radical 'bottom-up' global
civil society advocates argue that sovereignty should be undermined
'from below', the liberal cosmopolitan perspective shares many of
their assumptions in the argument that sovereignty should be
limited 'from above'. These claims are discussed with particular ref-
erence to the role of global civil society. The chapter concludes with
an assessment of whether replacing the central authority of sovereignty with over-lapping jurisdictions increases or limits democratic
accountability.

Chapter Eight concludes the work, returning to the key claims for
global civil society raised in this Introduction to reassess whether the
norms advocated on behalf of global civil society extend or restrict
political community, whether the framework of global civil society

encourages human agency or passivity, and whether the 'bottom-up' and 'top-down' approaches to global civil society extend or restrict the possibilities for democracy.

# Part I

# Actually Existing Global Civil Society

# 2
# The Constructivist Thesis

## Introduction

Constructivist theories which developed in international relations in the early 1990s challenged the central theoretical perspectives in the academic discipline of international relations. During the Cold War and most of the history of international relations, the research agenda was dominated by rationalist approaches which subordinated morality to the interests of power. The constructivist framework challenges this emphasis on power and seeks to demonstrate that rather than power, it is norms and values which shape the behaviour of the majority of states. States may still wield power in terms of military and coercive might but the use of this power is not guided solely by amoral state interests. Rather, in the constructivist framework, power is constrained and state interests reshaped through international normative structures created by the multiple interactions of state and non-state actors in actually existing global civil society. Constructivist theorising in international relations today influences a wide range of differing approaches from liberal internationalism to critical theory and postmodernism.[1]

This chapter focuses on constructivist theory as it relates to empirical studies of global civil society rather than attempting to engage with constructivist thinking per se. The following sections outline briefly the developments leading to a shift away from more traditional international relations concerns of liberal institutionalism and towards transnational networks operating in global civil society. Then the explanatory strength of the constructivist approach in this area will be considered and finally some of the limitations will be raised, which will be drawn out further in Chapters 3 and 4.

## A new research agenda

Until the end of the Cold War, the dominant theoretical perspectives in international relations assumed the nation-state was the key actor and that it acted in the pursuit of pre-given national interests. There were a number of disagreements between commentators and theoreticians, regarding the nature of these interests and whether co-operation or conflict was the predominant means of attaining them. But, whichever perspective was followed, the assumption was that these 'self-interested' interests were themselves pre-given. The main debate in international relations was between neo-realists who focused on the limits of cooperation and the possibility of conflict and the neo-liberals who focused on the possibilities for cooperation and the limits to conflict (for surveys see Keohane 1986; Nye 1988; Baldwin 1993). For both sides, states were theorised as rational actors pursuing self-interested goals.

These approaches had three core assumptions. Firstly, that states were the key subjects, i.e., the main actors in international relations. Secondly, that the interest of states as rational actors was to maximise their power and influence, by pursuing their self-interests. Thirdly, that in the context of international anarchy, i.e., the lack of a world government, states had to pursue self-help strategies, limiting the nature of international cooperation and making the international sphere one of strategic interaction in which security concerns were paramount. The development of constructivist approaches challenged all three of these core assumptions.

### De-centring the state

Constructivist theory de-centres both the subject or active agent of international relations, the nation-state, and simultaneously the structural constraints of neo-realism. Rather than the structure of anarchy creating states and state interests – in which case the needs of 'power' constitute ideas and ideological constructions which further these interests – constructivists assert that understanding international relations in purely structural or 'instrumental' or 'rationalist' terms is inadequate. The structure of self-guided egoistic state-subjects operating in a world of self-help power politics is questioned. The relationship between the individual state and the society of the international sphere of relations is transformed. Rather than the immutable framework of anarchy creating the conditions of possibility and structural limitations, for state interaction and state interests, constructivists hold that state interaction creates society. States have mutually-constituted themselves as self-interested power seekers and in so doing have created and reproduced this particular form of international anarchy as a central feature of international political life (see further Wendt 1999:246–312).

Alexander Wendt was one of the first influential international relations theorists to take up a constructivist approach (however, see also Kratochwil 1991; Onuf 1989 and Katzenstein 1996). Wendt argues:

> ...states do not have conceptions of self and other, and thus security interests, apart from or prior to interaction... [Rationalist] claims presuppose a history of interaction in which actors have acquired 'selfish' identities and interests; before interaction...they would have no experience upon which to base such definitions of self and other. To assume otherwise is to attribute to states in the state of nature qualities that they can only possess in society. (Wendt 1992:401–2)

Wendt is still starting the analysis with nation-states as the subject of international relations, the central actor, but the subject is transformed in two contradictory directions. On the one hand, the state is freed from the structural constraints of neo-realism. As Andrew Linklater argues, constructionist thought highlights the importance of agency at the basis of normative international theorising, as the dominance of norms and values would be impossible without the presupposition that states and other actors have the capacity to overcome structural limitations on ethical action (Linklater 1998:19). But, the agency which constructivist frameworks give with one hand they take away with the other. The autonomy or subjective agency of the state is 'hollowed-out'. The subject is no longer a self-determining, self-interested actor but rather is constituted through interaction. It is 'inter-subjective knowledge' which constitutes the interest or identity of the subject rather than self-determined or structurally determined interests. It is this inter-subjective focus which distinguishes constructivism from the English School focus on the shared norms of 'international society' (see Bull 1995). Wendt explains the importance of this shift in perspective:

> This may all seem very arcane, but there is an important issue at stake: are the foreign policy identities and interests of states exogenous or endogenous to the state system? The former is the answer of

an individualistic or undersociologized systemic theory for which rationalism is appropriate; the latter is the answer of a fully socialized systemic theory.   (Wendt 1992:402)

Constructivism is a theory of change. Rather than seeing states as having pre-given interests or 'being exogenously constituted', i.e., having identities established outside of the international sphere, states and their identities and interests are understood to be constructed through the process of international interaction (Wendt 1992:392). In Wendt's famous phrase, 'anarchy is what states make of it'. If identity and interests are not pre-given but shaped through social interaction, identities and interests can change. For Wendt, the nation-state is still the subject of analysis but the focus has shifted towards the sphere of interaction rather than that of rational interests. Wendt saw this as an extension of neo-liberal theorising, freeing the study of the process of interaction, highlighted in regime theory, from the structuralist framework of fixed identities (Wendt 1992:393, 417; see also Kratochwil and Ruggie 1986; Finnemore 1996a, 1996b; Ruggie 1998; Haas 1999 and Wendt 1999:36). Some critics have questioned whether Wendt's work does in fact break with rationalist approaches (see S. Smith 2001:247; H. Smith 2000:15). Nevertheless, the logic of de-centring the state as the primary subject and prioritising regulative norms, established through interaction and ideas, laid the foundation upon which theories of actually existing global civil society were constructed. Once state actors were seen to intersubjectively constitute their interests and identities, the focus shifted to the role of transnational and international network activity in establishing and internalising these new norms.

## Identities and interests

Writing in the aftermath of the end of the Cold War, constructivist theorising which challenged the structural fixity of neo-liberal and neo-realist thought found a ready audience. As Christian Reus-Smit notes: 'the end of the Cold War undermined the explanatory pretensions of neo-realists and neoliberals, neither of which had predicted, nor could adequately comprehend, the systematic transformations reshaping the global order' (Reus-Smit 2001:216). It appeared that the study of states and state interests could no longer adequately explain international politics. Instead, the research focus shifted away from fixed identities and narrow material interests to one which emphasised the power of norms and ideas. As Jack Donnelly argues in his comprehensive study of realist approaches:

> Neorealism...cannot comprehend change. During the Cold War, this theoretical gap seemed acceptable to many. But when the Cold War order collapsed seemingly overnight, even many otherwise sympathetic observers began to look elsewhere – especially because the collapse was intimately tied to ideas...and processes...that were excluded by neorealist structuralism. (Donnelly 2000:31)

Wendt argued that it was not just the distribution of power that was important but also the 'distribution of knowledge', the intersubjective understandings which constitute the state's conception of its self and its interests. As an example he states that having a powerful neighbour in the United States means something different to Canada than it does for Cuba or that British missiles would have seemed more of a threat to the Soviet Union than to America (Wendt 1992:397). It was the interaction between states that shaped their identities and interests. Rather than power it was subjective conceptions that were important, therefore: '[I]f the United States and Soviet Union decide that they are no longer enemies, the Cold War is over.' (Wendt 1992:397)

The collapse of the Soviet Union, through implosion rather than military defeat, fundamentally challenged realist perspectives of state interests and the importance of military power and thereby facilitated the revival of more idealist perspectives of change – based on social interaction rather than material interests. As Wendt has stated, inversing the rationalist framework: 'Identities are the basis of interests.' (Wendt 1992:398) From a constructivist perspective, the end of the Cold War could be seen as a product of change in Soviet identity, interests and policy-making, which then provoked a shift in US policy towards the Soviet Union, breaking the circle of suspicion and hostility and creating a new framework of international cooperation.

Where rationalist approaches were based on the assumption that states pursued (relatively fixed) national interests, constructivist theorists argue that national interests should be seen as flexible and indeterminate. Thomas Risse and Kathryn Sikkink write:

> Actors' interests and preferences are not given outside social interaction or deduced from structural constraints in the international or domestic environment. Social constructivism does not take the

interests of actors for granted, but problematizes and relates them to the identities of actors.   (Risse and Sikkink 1999:8–9)

As Risse and Sikkink note: 'This new emphasis has resulted from the empirical failure of approaches emphasizing material structures as the primary determinants of state identities, interests and preferences.' (Risse and Sikkink 1999:6) They continue:

> We do not mean to ignore material conditions. Rather, the causal relationship between material and ideational factors is at stake. While materialist theories emphasize economic or military conditions or interests as determining the impact of ideas in international and domestic politics, social constructivists emphasize that ideas and communicative processes define in the first place which material factors are perceived as relevant and how they influence understandings of interests, preferences, and political decisions.   (Risse and Sikkink 1999:6–7)

In a fluid context where identities and interests are no longer constrained by material divisions, ideas become more important. If identities are no longer seen as fixed or given then, by fiat, there is much less of a barrier to a global moral outlook. Constructivists assert that the abstract theorising of a Rawlsian 'veil of ignorance' is then not so abstract after all (see further Chapter 5). If ideas are more important than military or economic power then moral agencies and actors such as international NGOs will be able to have a major influence merely through 'the power of persuasion' (Korey 1999).

### The global as a constitutive sphere

Wendt struggled to explain the cause of the radical change in Soviet identity, highlighted by Gorbachev's 'New Thinking', which, he argued, transformed the United States' conception of itself and its identity and thereby was held to have transformed the international system from one based on competition to one based on cooperation (Wendt 1992:420). The problem was that it did not appear that intersubjective relations, i.e., the international environment, had become more favourable. US policy towards the Soviet bloc was in fact more hostile than in the Cold War 'thaw' of the 1970s and, following the Soviet invasion of Afghanistan in 1979 and the breakdown of disarmament talks, commentators were discussing the emergence of a 'second Cold War' (Halliday 1986). In fact, as late as 1986 leading academics considered that: 'This conflict is permanent and global.' (Halliday 1986:264)

Wendt therefore argued that the shift in Soviet policy could only have happened through the Soviet leadership rethinking its own identity. In order to avoid this process contradicting the thesis that identities are created through interaction, psychoanalytic concepts were called for, to argue that this identity change was enacted through the Soviet Union 'altercasting its ego' to induce the West to act as if it had already taken on a new identity. This 'altercasting' was achieved through withdrawing from Afghanistan and Eastern Europe and implementing asymmetric cuts in nuclear and conventional forces (Wendt 1992:421).

Wendt's view of ideas overcoming structures and material interests was a liberating one for a discipline in a state of crisis, but his narrow confinement of constructivist methodology to the traditional field of international relations – the relations between states – was seen to be too restrictive. Instead, other strands of neo-liberalism were drawn upon, particularly the pluralist focus on the growing influence of non-state actors. Once it was established that old-fashioned instrumental politics, based on territorially restricted states, was the outcome of territorially-tied communicative processes, which led to the construction of competing interests, then the addition of non-state actors changed the picture. It was now argued that the growth of non-state actors in international affairs could be constituting a new type of non-instrumental dialogue and discussion where values and norms rather than instrumentality prevailed. The focus of attention on non-state actors tied in with the concerns of civil society theorists which focused on the generation of ideas and norms in the non-governmental sphere (Diamond 1994; Seligman 1992; Cohen and Arato 1992; Keane 1998).

Rather than Wendt's focus on the interactions between states, constructivist theory was extended to give a central role to non-state actors. It is at this point that the concept of transnational or global relations comes in, in distinction to international relations, i.e., relations between states. The international sphere is no longer seen as one in which states project their national interests, instead the process is reversed, through participation in international and transnational relations the national interests of states are constituted.

In this way, the end of the Cold War could be held not just to discredit realist approaches but also to provide compelling evidence of the role of non-state actors in the development of state 'identities' and interests. As Thomas Risse and Stephen Ropp argue:

...the turnaround of Soviet foreign policy as an enabling condition for the peaceful revolutions of 1989 resulted at least partly from the fact that the Gorbachev leadership was itself heavily influenced by Western liberal ideas spread through transnational actors and coalitions...the peaceful transformation [in Eastern Europe] was brought about by dissident groups in Poland and Czechoslovakia with the transnational human rights networks empowering and strengthening their claims.   (Risse and Ropp 1999:268)

The growth of international human rights norms over the last decade is held to be the leading example demonstrating the strength of constructivist approaches: 'because international human rights norms challenge state rule over society and national sovereignty, any impact on domestic change would be counter-intuitive' (Risse and Sikkink 1999:4). The assumption that human rights norms challenge nation-state interests therefore implies that norm changes cannot come through state agency but must mainly stem from the influence of transnational non-state actors. Even where states may use the normative rhetoric, such as human rights concerns, it is the influence of non-state actors which serves to prevent these from being used in a purely instrumental way.

Thomas Risse and Kathryn Sikkink argue that the 'process by which international norms are internalised and implemented domestically can be understood as a process of *socialization*' (Risse and Sikkink 1999:5). This process is seen to act independently of power relations. One example given by Risse and Sikkink is that of US foreign policy. They argue that the Reagan administration took a principled position in favour of democratisation but used it instrumentally as a vehicle for an aggressive assertion of US interests against left regimes, such as the USSR, Nicaragua and Cuba. However, the US establishment could not use the principled issue purely instrumentally because it was obliged to a minimal consistency and eventually actively encouraged democracy in authoritarian regimes which were loyal allies to the US, such as Chile and Uruguay. US interests changed as the 'principled issue' won out over the state's attempt to use the issue instrumentally (Risse and Sikkink 1999:10). In this way, constructivist theorists write about the 'power of principles' to overcome the instrumentalist purposes behind their initial adoption (Risse and Sikkink 1999:9).

The articulation of certain principled norms potentially changes the identity of the state itself. In *The Power of Human Rights*, edited by Risse, Ropp and Sikkink, the authors analyse 'the process through which principled ideas (beliefs about right and wrong held by individuals) become norms (collective expectations about proper behaviour for a given identity), which in turn influence the behaviour and domestic structure of states' (Risse and Sikkink 1999:7). The constructivist argument is that international society plays a powerful role in turning ideas (held by individuals) into norms (collective guidelines) and establishing norms as state practice. International society, rather than inter-state competition is crucial because: 'While ideas are usually individualistic, norms have an explicit intersubjective quality because they are *collective* expectations. The very idea of "proper" behaviour presupposes a community able to pass judgments on appropriateness.' (Risse and Sikkink 1999:7)

The constructivist 'turn' in international relations fundamentally lays open the previous assumptions of the discipline. The relationship between morality and power is inversed; no longer does Carr's dictum hold true that: 'Theories of international morality are...the product of dominant nations or groups of nations.' (Carr 2001:74) In today's globalised world, with the emergence of transnational linkages, committed transnational ethical campaigners are held to be capable of changing the identity, and thereby the interests, of leading states. What is crucial to this thesis is the socially constructed identity of the state actor rather than the alleged structural constraints, where ideas are understood to be merely a reflection of pre-given material interests:

> What I am depends to a large degree on who I am. Identities then define the range of interests of actors considered as both possible and appropriate. Identities also provide a measure of inclusion and exclusion by defining a social 'we' and delineating the boundaries against the 'others.'   (Risse and Sikkink 1999:9)

The non-instrumentalist assumptions made for global civil society rest heavily on the constructivist framework that assumes a connection between moral or ethical discourse and a power to shape identities and thereby interests:

> Moral discourses in particular not only challenge and seek justifications of norms, they also entail identity-related arguments. What I find morally appropriate depends to some degree on who I am and how I see myself... The logic of discursive behaviour and of processes of argumentation and persuasion rather than instrumental bargaining and the exchange of fixed interests prevails when actors develop collective understandings that form part of their identities and lead them to determine their interests... People

become convinced and persuaded to change their instrumental interests, or to see their interests in new ways, following the principled ideas.   (Risse and Sikkink 1999:13–14)

The constitution of an international community 'able to pass judgments on appropriateness' and therefore establish principled international norms does not depend on free floating norms and ideas but the impact of 'transnationally operating non-state actors', specifically the impact of 'principled-issue' NGOs or 'transnational advocacy networks' which diffuse 'principled ideas' and new 'international norms' (Risse and Sikkink 1999:4). Rather than states and inter-state arrangements being key to international change it is the action and linkages of non-state actors:

> ...the diffusion of international norms in the human rights area crucially depends on the establishment and the sustainability of networks among domestic and transnational actors...these advocacy networks serve three purposes... They put norm-violating states on the international agenda in terms of moral consciousness-raising... They empower and legitimate the claims of domestic opposition groups against norm-violating governments... They challenge norm-violating governments by creating a transnational structure pressuring such regimes simultaneously 'from above' and 'from below'.   (Risse and Sikkink 1999:5)

Where power and instrumentality are acknowledged to dominate the world of traditional inter-state politics, 'the power of principles' is king in the extended international sphere of actually existing global civil society where identity creation is driven by developing international norms and values (Risse and Sikkink 1999:9). Constructivist theorists posit the existence of a virtuous circle whereby global interconnectedness establishes a new sphere or new space for non-instrumental politics which potentially transforms the actors engaged in it. As Martha Finnemore states:

> [S]tates are embedded in dense networks of transnational and international social relations that shape their perceptions of the world and their role in that world. States are socialized to want certain things by the international society in which they and the people in them live.   (Finnemore 1996a:2)

This new sphere, which includes both states and non-state actors engaged in communicative action, is often termed global civil society.

For leading global civil society theorist Mary Kaldor, global civil society theorising is less about defining which organisations or institutions are included or excluded than about understanding 'the global process through which individuals debate, influence and negotiate' with centres of power (Kaldor 2003:79). The presumptions of actually existing global civil society turn those of realism on their head. Rather than self-interested and self-directed subjects, states now become bearers of international values and socialised by international society. An instrumentalist power-seeking government, institution, association or individual engaging in norm-orientated debate in the global civic space will eventually emerge with a new and better identity and a broader, less exclusive, view of their 'interests'.

## The explanatory framework of constructivism

The area where most theoretical analysis has been undertaken to substantiate constructivist claims has been in the impact of new international norms in changing policy in non-Western states. Network theory has been one of the most important developments in linking change in state policy to the activity of non-state actors in global civil society. Keck and Sikkink argue: 'network theory links the constructivist belief that international identities are constructed to empirical research tracing the paths through which this process occurs' (Keck and Sikkink 1998:214–5). Network theory builds on the work of theorists, like Paul Wapner, who have emphasised the new nature of non-state campaigning groups, seeing them not as traditional lobby or pressure groups, organised around changing state policies, but as 'political actors in their own right' (Wapner 1995:312). He argues:

> [T]he best way to think about transnational activist societal efforts is through the concept of 'world civic politics.' When activists work to change conditions without directly pressurising states, their activities take place in the civil dimension of world collective life or what is sometimes called global civil society.  (Wapner 1995:312)

Rather than pressurising the state through traditional means, new social movements and activist networks rely on the power of information and ideas. They are engaged with transnational society beyond the boundaries of the state as well as lobbying states (see further Melucci 1985; Habermas 1981; Offe 1987).

## The 'boomerang' approach

Probably the most cited example of constructivist explanations is the boomerang theory where non-state actors are credited with achieving change through mobilising international pressure. Margaret Keck and Kathryn Sikkink in their path-breaking work *Activists beyond Borders* (1998) argue that the shift to international concerns with human rights practices can be explained by studying the emergence of transnational advocacy networks which instigated and sustained this international value shift (Keck and Sikkink 1998:ix). According to these writers: 'The new networks have depended on the creation of a new kind of global public (or civil society), which grew as a cultural legacy of the 1960s.' (Keck and Sikkink 1998:14)

According to Keck and Sikkink, transnational advocacy campaigns have shifted the balance between states and individuals in need of support through the 'redistribution of knowledge':

[I]n a world where the voices of states have predominated, networks open channels for bringing alternative visions and information into international debate. Political scientists have tended to ignore such nongovernmental actors because they are not 'powerful' in the classic sense of the term. At the core of the network activity is the production, exchange, and strategic use of information... When they succeed, advocacy networks are among the most important sources of new ideas, norms, and identities in the international system. (Keck and Sikkink 1998:x)

Keck and Sikkink argue that the space for alternative voices to be heard provided by transnational networks challenges the domination and control of states. The 'boomerang process' occurs through these non-state channels of information: 'Voices that are suppressed in their own societies may find that networks can project and amplify their concerns into an international arena, which in turn can echo back into their own countries.' (Keck and Sikkink 1998:x) This boomerang effect blurs the boundaries tying nation-states and their citizens as these citizens can now join transnational networks which give them a voice and capacity to alter state policy. As Ann Florini asserts:

For a large number of people whose governments are less than fully democratic (or less than fully responsive to the needs of those citizens unable to make large campaign donations), transnational civil society may provide the only meaningful way to participate in decisionmaking.   (Florini 2001:39)

Keck and Sikkink emphasise the non-rationalist aspect of transnational advocacy networks, the key agents of global civil society:

> Advocacy captures what is unique about these transnational networks: they are organized to promote causes, principled ideas, and norms, and they often involve individuals advocating policy changes that cannot be easily linked to a rationalist understanding of their 'interests.'   (Keck and Sikkink 1998:9)

They also stress the importance of the strategic use of information in mobilising international allies which can bring pressure on their states from outside. They term this 'leverage politics' and argue: 'By leveraging more powerful institutions, weak groups gain influence far beyond their ability to influence state practices directly.' (Keck and Sikkink 1998:23) The most important international allies are, of course, other states. In diagrammatic shorthand they describe the boomerang pattern: 'State A blocks redress to organizations within it; they activate network, whose members pressure their own states and (if relevant) a third-party organization, which in turn pressure State A.' (Keck and Sikkink 1998:13) As Risse outlines, the constructivist thesis is focused on the development and implantation of international norms. The relationship of global civil society to state power is an ambivalent one though, one which relies on some states to impose norms on other states: 'transnational civil society needs the cooperation of states and national governments. To create robust and specific human rights standards [and]...also needs states for the effective improvement of human rights conditions on the ground.' (Risse 2000:205)

Clearly the constructivist analysis does not ignore the role played by states in international change. In fact, the role of the Western state is central to the success of the work of non-state actors. 'Bypassing the state' and mobilising in the international arena only works if other states or international institutions are willing to take up the call. The new space which is created and the new possibilities depend as much, if not more, on the activity of states than they do on non-state actors. The key to the success of the 'boomerang' is the relative power of the states involved in the equation. Power is crucial to the success of principled-issue campaigns, as Keck and Sikkink state: 'The human rights issue became negotiable because governments or financial institutions connected human rights practices to military and economic aid, or to bilateral diplomatic relations.' (Keck and Sikkink 1998:23) Ideas and values may be necessary but they are by no means sufficient:

> In the United States, human rights groups got leverage by providing policy-makers with information that convinced them to cut off military and economic aid. To make the issue negotiable, NGOs first had to raise its profile or salience, using information and symbolic politics. The more powerful members of the network had to link cooperation to something else of value: money, trade, or prestige.   (Keck and Sikkink 1998:23)

The imbalance of power would appear to be essential to the 'boomerang' theoretical approach. American citizens concerned about the death penalty, for example, would probably have little success persuading principled-issue networks to get governments to cut off military and economic links. This would appear to be a one-way process which can only work where target states are 'sensitive to leverage' and dependent on economic or military assistance (Keck and Sikkink 1998:29; see also Burgerman 1998). The 'boomerang' can only work against non-Western states. As Chetan Kumar notes the 'right circumstances' for the likely success of global civil activism in effecting the removal of 'nasty dictatorships' necessarily include 'a specific interest on the part of a major power capable of using force' (Kumar 2000:136). As Martin Shaw argues: 'the activists of globalist organisations, such as human rights, humanitarian and development agencies, make a reality of global civil society, by bringing the most exposed victims among the world's population into contact with more resourceful groups in the West' (Shaw 1994b:655). However, rather than emphasise the power side of the equation, constructivists choose to emphasise the role of global civic actors. Some, such as Susan Burgerman, explicitly shift the focus away from states. She argues:

> The research program on transnational issue networks is designed to capture the increasingly complex webs of nonstate actors who participate in other people's politics without resorting to the power base of either their own government or that of the target state.   (Bugerman 1998:908)

The implication is that this intervention 'in other people's politics' is not based on power but morality, the power that some states wield over others merely demonstrates the influence of network activists in lobbying states other than their own. The implicit assumption appears to be that because some states are more moral than others, small groups which are too weak to influence their own states can influence other (more morally aware) states and persuade these states to 'leverage' their own one. The boomerang perspective assumes firstly, that it is 'principled' non-state actors that set the agenda and, secondly, that they can do this because the states with the most leverage are also the most open to moral appeals. Burgerman terms network activists 'moral entrepreneurs' to highlight the fact that their strength and influence stem from the content of their ideas rather than the political or economic weight of their supporters (Burgerman 1998:909).

Keck and Sikkink argue that 'perhaps the best example' of transnational advocacy politics was the ability of the human rights network to use the human rights provisions of the 1975 Helsinki Accords to pressure the Soviet Union and the governments of Eastern Europe to change (Keck and Sikkink 1998:24). The weakness of East European dissident groups and state restrictions on political activity meant that they were forced to rely on external institutions to legitimise them and strengthen them domestically. As Kaldor notes, the turning point in the creation of the current concept of global civil society was the 1975 Helsinki Accords which established the Conference on Security and Cooperation in Europe (CSCE), later formalised as an organisation, the OSCE, under whose auspices the domestic policies of East European states came under international monitoring arrangements. The Helsinki Accords established a process whereby in exchange for recognition and economic aid from the West, East European states were pressurised on human rights questions. This process encouraged the formation of small dissident groups of intellectuals such as Charter 77 in Czechoslovakia, KOR (the defence of workers) in Poland and the Democratic Opposition in Hungary (Kaldor 2003:54–55).

But this example demonstrates the centrality of state action, and many would argue the instrumental rational interests of Western states in pressing for 'regime change'. The mechanisms set up under the CSCE were a direct reflection of Cold War rivalries. For example, the human rights monitoring forum, the Human Dimension Mechanism, was used overwhelmingly by Western states against Eastern Bloc states, with only one example where intra-bloc concerns were raised (see Chandler 1999:62–3). Human rights concerns would appear to have been used instrumentally by Western powers. In fact, this process continued in the OSCE's double-standards of intervention in East

European states over minority rights, while ignoring concerns of recognition of minorities in Western states (see Heraclides 1992; Barcz 1992; Zaagman and Zaal 1994). While there may have been a concurrence of interests between powerful groups of Western states and weak opposition groups in Eastern Europe, there seems little evidence that the Western states involved went through any change in their 'identities' and their interests seemed relatively fixed.

Clearly, the 'boomerang' assumptions are open to question. Was it really primarily a matter of available information and skilled lobbying which enabled human rights groups to persuade the US to cut aid to some states but not to others (see, for example, Chomsky 1999)? Why should it be assumed that it is the 'less powerful' members of transnational networks, the NGOs, which set the agenda for the more powerful members, states and international institutions, to act on? Questions of this sort led to a refinement and development of the 'boomerang' model into the later 'spiral' model.

## The 'spiral' model

The 'spiral' model develops the 'boomerang' approach to address the issue of power inequalities and how these relate to the power of communicative norms. The 'boomerang' model was successful because weak groups with superior information skills were held to be capable of mobilising more powerful alliances to pressurise states. The 'spiral' model expands this analysis to argue that the exercise of international coercive power should not detract from the communicative emphasis, because even if coercion is used initially, it is never decisive. The power of ideas and the communication of information is more important in the long run as these ideas are not just accepted through being externally imposed but become seen as representing the genuine interests of the states concerned through new identities created by the process of discussion, campaigning and information distribution.

In this refined version of the constructivist analysis, states and interstate institutions operate in a much more symbiotic relationship in an international context shaped by the demands of transnational and domestic non-state actors. Risse, Ropp and Sikkink describe the 'spiral' model as a five stage process.

Phase One: The activation of the network. Transnational advocacy networks raise the issue of (in)actions of the domestic state. Information required for an international campaign against the 'target' state will normally be provided through at least some minimal links between domestic opposition and the transnational network (Risse and

Sikkink 1999:22). According to Burgerman: 'domestic organizations provide their transnational counterparts with a channel into the national political arena, a justification for meddling in national affairs' (Burgerman 1998:916).

Phase Two: The transnational network gets to work lobbying international human rights organisations and Western publics and governments. Western governments are persuaded through moral calls reminding them of their own 'identity' as promoters of human rights and public 'shaming' should they refuse to take a stance consistent with international treaties or ethical policy declarations (Risse and Sikkink 1999:22–4).

Phase Three: Tactical concessions by the target state which 'depends on the strength and mobilization of the transnational network' and the vulnerability of the norm-violating government to international pressure (for example, dependency on external military or economic aid). At this point the target state is responding largely by using instrumental and strategic reasoning: 'Norm-violating governments tactically adjust to the new international discourse in order to stay in power, receive foreign aid and the like.' (Risse and Ropp 1999:273) International pressure creates or strengthens local networks and empowers and legitimises their demands. The 'transnational network serves to help, creating space for the domestic groups and amplifying their demands in the international arena, creating pressure 'from above' and 'from below' (Risse and Sikkink 1999:24–8). It is often only at this stage that international human rights norms 'start resonating with domestic audiences' (Risse and Ropp 1999:272).

Phase Four: The target state accepts principled ideas and they gain 'prescriptive status'. This involves the ratification of international treaties, the institutionalisation of new norms and acknowledgement of the validity of criticism (Risse and Sikkink 1999:29–31). Even in this stage national governments still need to be 'continuously pushed to live up to their claims and pressure from below and "from above" continues' (Risse and Sikkink 1999:33).

Phase Five: Rule-consistent behaviour is the final stage of the socialisation process when international human rights norms are 'internalized' (Risse and Sikkink 1999:31–33). Risse and Ropp argue that at this stage:

...we find that a different logic of interaction incrementally takes over and at least supplements strategic behaviour. The logic emphasises communicative rationality, argumentation, and persuasion, on the one hand, and norm institutionalisation and habitualization, on the other. We feel that social constructivism, which endogenizes identities and interests of actors, can accommodate this logic more easily...    (Risse and Ropp 1999:273)

The progressive role of Western states, and their coercive influence, is implicitly assumed in the 'boomerang' model. The 'spiral' model argues that the importance of coercion is limited to the initial stages of the process until target states open up the decision-making process to involve domestic non-state actors then the force of debate and persuasion changes the identity and interests of the target state.

## The limits of constructivism

The empirical focus of constructivism is on why non-Western states follow the principled-issue agenda but there are three core assumptions made by the constructivist analysis which are never satisfactorily engaged with. Firstly, the assumption that the 'principled-issue' agenda is established by non-state actors rather than states. Secondly, there is an assumption that this shift towards ethical policy-making reflects the power of ethical norms rather than the power of material interests. The third assumption is that global civic actors can convince Western states to pursue an ethical agenda despite the fact that, unlike in the empirical case studies of non-Western states, they are without the powers of external coercion which could open up the process of communicative dialogue. These questions are considered further in the following sections.

### The power of networks?

The first key empirical evidence which constructivists use to justify the argument of the influence of actually existing global civil society is the increase in numbers of NGOs and campaign groups in parallel with the shift in foreign policy and development of ethical norms in international relations. John Keane scathingly describes this methodological approach as the 'numerical theory of global politics', whereby a quantitative model, derived from counting up the number of non-state institutions and rates of growth, is alleged to demonstrate their influence (Keane 2003:95). We learn from the statistics that the linkages between international NGOs have increased 35 per cent from 1990 to 2000 and that while there were 13,000 international NGOs in existence in 1981, there were 23,000 in 1991 and 47,000 in 2001 (Anheier, Glasius and Kaldor 2001a:5; Anheier and Themudo 2002:194–5). One study of global civil society provides 90 pages of statistical tables charting the growth, density and participation in global civil society (Anheier, Glasius and Kaldor 2001b:231–322).

Since 1989, the collapse of traditional foreign policy concerns which shaped international institutions around the Cold War has led to a new language and new methods of doing international relations. Mary Kaldor notes that states and international institutions are 'more receptive to individuals and citizen groups outside the corridors of power' (Kaldor 2003:79). This is undoubtedly the case. However, the correlation between NGOs and non-state actors' international engagement with states and international institutions and specific policy-changes is hard to quantify (Burgerman 1998:913–4; Keck and Sikkink 1998:202; Forsythe 2000:168–78). Firstly, it is difficult to establish criteria for which policy success can be measured. For example, should the criteria be located at the level of policy statements, or of written policy or only consider more substantial outcome changes? Secondly, it is not easy to link the action of NGOs to specific policy outcomes. Even in a particular case study, multiple factors are at play in the development of government policy, let alone the success or failure of its implementation (Hubert 1998). For example, commonly referred to interests in US politics such as the 'tobacco lobby', the 'Israeli lobby' or the 'China lobby' have all seen their influence wax and wane in different periods with no obvious connection to their own campaigning (Forsythe 2000:173).

In the early 1990s few NGO analysts saw the increasing links between NGOs and states and international institutions as part of a shift towards a more ethical, normative agenda. While constructivist theory gives primary importance to non-state actors many empirical studies suggest that the impact of NGOs and non-state actors on the policy choices of international institutions and Western states is minimal. Until recently, NGO activists rarely saw themselves as occupying positions of power or influence and NGO-based analysts were often bemused by the idea that they could be dictating terms in the relationship. In fact, they counselled against the exaggeration of their success and influence (Hulme and Edwards 1995; 1997a).

For many commentators, neo-liberalism and structural adjustment policies were creating a welfare crisis that necessitated further Western engagement in welfare through non-state agencies in the late 1980s and early 1990s (de Waal 1997a:49–64; van Rooy and Robinson 1998). In this context, there was concern that the NGOs were being incorporated into serving the interests of international financial institutions promoting the neo-liberal 'new policy agenda'. Leading authorities saw the shift towards the voluntary sector as potentially problematic and one which could see NGOs risk losing their distinctive moral legitimacy, derived from their independence and connections with those most in need (Edwards and Hulme 1995; 1996; Clayton 1996).

Much of the critical work on global civil society argued that institutions imposing the neo-liberal agenda promoted civil society as an apolitical form of welfare administration independent of and opposed to the state. This process undermined state authority and contributed to a 'crisis of governance' in many non-Western states (de Waal 1997a:55; Duffield 1996, 2001; Onishi 2002; White 1999:319). The civil society realm was one of regulation, 'of stability rather than struggle, of service provision rather than advocacy, of trust and responsibility rather than emancipation' (Kaldor 2003:22; see also the excellent analysis in Hearn 2000). Critical analysts, such as John Clark, argued that official agency funding had resulted in the 'puppetisation' of NGOs (Clark 1991).

However, in the late-1990s, there was a shift away from a narrow emphasis on economic development and towards more comprehensive forms of external regulation. Under the 'post-Washington consensus' international financial institutions highlighted the need for poverty reduction and emphasised the importance of social capital, giving civil society organisations a central advocacy role. This shift from service to advocacy led some theorists to see that NGOs could potentially have a limiting effect on international financial institutions, as advocates of those traditionally excluded from policy-making (Edwards 2001:2; Brown and Fox 2001).

The empirical studies, however, suggest that the vast majority of NGOs have to operate on the terms of states and international institutions and that, where there is engagement in policy-making, this is on highly unequal and selective terms (see for example, Scholte 2001; Lister 2000; Najam 1996; Hudock 1999). Paul Cammack's work on the World Bank concludes that the bank has created a set of discursive devices and channels of consultation which aim to promote local input from developing countries, 'country ownership' in the bank's terminology, but which are, in reality, highly coercive (Cammack 2002). The World Banks' own internal publications make clear the hierarchy involved, stating that 'consultations' with civil society should not be confused with 'negotiations' or with 'a shared control over outcomes' (World Bank 2000:8).

As Cammack argues, the World Banks' holistic approach to regulation, highlighted by the 1999 launch of its Comprehensive Development Framework and detailed Poverty Reduction Strategy Papers, mean that rather than acting as 'the mother of development' it aspires to be the 'mother of all governments', preventing, rather than facilitating, policy autonomy in developing countries (Cammack 2002; see also Pender 2001, 2002; Tusie and Tuozzo 2001; World Bank 2001). The fact that the World Bank is actively involved in establishing NGOs and community-based organisations (CBOs) in order to assist in pushing through its projects, that Western governments are increasingly using NGOs as conduits for overseas aid and development funds, and that non-Western governments are setting up their own NGOs to access these funds, suggests that if any empirical correlation exists between NGOs and power hierarchies it is just as likely to be a positive one (Alkire et al 2001:4, 29; Tusie and Tuozzo 2001:112; White 1999:313; *Economist* 2000).

Traditional political theorising would suggest that NGO lobby groups would have less influence on state policy-making than that of traditional interest groups such as mass membership organisations, like trade unions, or business interests (Forsythe 2000:169). As Mary Kaldor notes: 'The weakness of both "new" social movements and NGOs is that although they have widespread moral authority, they are largely composed of an educated minority and they lack the capacity for popular mobilization.' (Kaldor 2003:100) Without a large or concentrated membership, which could threaten the electoral chances of political candidates or the financial resources to affect party financial contributions, it would seem that small groups of NGO lobbyists are in a weak position either to influence the policy of their own government or that of foreign governments.

However, constructivist case studies nearly always correlate the numbers and activities of non-state actors with the success of certain policies which have been lobbied for. It is easy to do case studies which retrospectively study a certain policy adoption, for example, the Ottawa Land Mines Convention, but even then few analysts focus on the role played by governments or actually study the impact and implementation of their select example (for a useful study of the landmines campaign see Scott 2001; also Florini 2001:34). The focus is on the success stories, and history is then read backwards to substantiate how global civil society works, for example, how the environmental lobbyists managed to influence the World Bank over certain projects in the developing world, rather than why they failed to influence US policy and prevent the US rejection of the Kyoto accords, or how the human rights movement managed to influence US foreign policy on Latin America, rather than how they failed to influence it regarding

Turkey, Saudi Arabia and Indonesia. Figures and estimations for the success of global civil society vary widely, but few would argue that 'success' goes beyond selective concerns and issues.

The advocates of a constructivist approach argue that the selective approach to the empirical information is implicitly valid because they are identifying an emerging context in which decision-making takes place. For critical theorists, anxious to accentuate the positive and 'encourage confidence' in popular initiatives, a one-sidedness in analysis is not problematic. Richard Falk, for example, argues: 'In this spirit, an emphasis is placed on positing the reality of "global civil society" and of accentuating transnational extensions of democratic and non-violent forms of governance.' (Falk 1995:44) However, there is a danger that the normative theorising of critical theorists can undermine the pretence to objectivity and 'explanation' of constructivists. Ronen Palen, for example, argues that the claims of constructivists are inevitably exaggerated by their normative aspirations:

> [Constructivism] effectively conflates a methodology with a theory...general theories of interactionist order cannot provide an explanation for the specificity of an *order*... Theirs is a phlegmatic society – a harmonious society based on laws and norms... [W]hy are there variations in social constructions?... When...constructivism...is used as a theory of international relations, it exorci[ses] any form of social critique from the narrative. It tells us that while neorealists think that world politics are 'mean and nasty', in fact it is not.   (Palan 2000:592–3)

Attempting to force the empirical facts into the constructivist framework has meant that an increasingly flexible methodology is often employed. Starting from the assumption that new social movements and 'principled-issue' NGOs are shaping the moral and political agenda means that traditional methods of doing and theorising politics come under question (see, for example, Wapner 1995:318–20). The lack of clear material influence of NGOs is held to demonstrate that it is their ideas which are crucial and that the methods of influencing state policy must be much more mediated.

As Wapner notes: 'one must focus on the political action per se of these organizations and trace its world significance and interpret its meaning independent of the argument about relative causal weight' (Wapner 1995:320). Rob Walker similarly argues that: 'It is futile to gauge the importance of social movements without considering the possibility that it is precisely the criteria of significance by which they are to be judged that may be in contention.' (Walker 1994:672) The increasingly subjective methodological approach taken by many theorists has undoubtedly led to an exaggeration of the influence which these new social movements can wield. In the words of Colás:

> Such primarily descriptive accounts tend to conflate the self-proclaimed aspirations and objectives of international social movements with their *actual* impact, thereby falling into the trap of an excessively subjectivist and therefore one-sided view of the... international social world. (Colás 2002:65)

## The power of principles?

The key to the success of constructivist theorising, despite its empirical limitations, is the argument that the evidence of the existence of global civil society and of its influence cannot plausibly be denied because there has been an undisputed shift towards ethical foreign policies. As two contributors to a leading international relations textbook assert: '[W]hat emerges from a study of state practice in the 1990s, is that it is not states but an emergent global civil society that is the principal agent promoting humanitarian values in global politics'. (Wheeler and Bellamy 2001:490)

The core assumption is that because non-rationalist or non-instrumentalist campaigning in global civil society challenges the traditional norms of sovereignty the society of states would be opposed to it: 'Because many of these campaigns challenge traditional notions of state sovereignty, we might expect states to cooperate to block network activities.' (Keck and Sikkink 1998:36; 203) There is an assumption that without the work of non-state actors in global civil society the human rights agenda would not be possible. As leading constructivist Kathryn Sikkink argues: 'Realism offers no convincing explanation for why relatively weak non-state actors could have an impact on state policy or why states would concern themselves with the internal human rights practices of other states, especially when such concern interferes with the pursuit of other state goals.' (Sikkink 1993:437)

A strange irony, at the heart of constructivist theorising about the relationship between morality and power in actually existing global civil society, is that it implicitly relies on a prior acceptance of the realist understanding that states only act in a narrowly conceived self-interest. As Keck and Sikkink argue: 'for states to act, either the values in question must plausibly coincide with the "national interest" or the government acting must believe (correctly or not) that the action is not costly (or at lest that it is less costly than not acting)' (Keck and Sikkink 1998:203). It is only this assumption that states will pursue national interests that enables constructivists to confidently assert the influence of global civil society on foreign policy decision-making.

This of course begs the question, 'Why, if principled-issues are those of the powerless rather than the powerful, will these principles be the guide to state action and policy-making?' This is where non-state actors are alleged to play a crucial role in acting as the 'conscience' of Western governments. Principled-issue networks 'transform state understandings of their national interests, and alter their calculations of the costs and benefits of particular policies' (Keck and Sikkink 1998:203).

Risse and Sikkink argue that relations of power, while existing, are not adequate to explain the normative shift in the policy of leading Western states. In fact, the mere existence of a shift from the pursuit of 'national interests' to ethical norms and values is argued to vitiate any power-politics explanation:

> This approach would need to explain, however, why great powers change their positions on which norms they choose to back. For example, why did the United States move from a position, before 1973, in which human rights were seen as an inappropriate part of foreign policy to a position in which human rights formed an important pillar of US policy by the 1990s?   (Risse and Sikkink 1999:35)

Historically, NGO and lobby groups can be found to have promoted ethical and normative concerns before these were taken up by Western governments. This is a strong prima facie argument to suggest that principled issue campaigners led the shift in government approaches. Keck and Sikkink argue that it is the work of principled-issue activists which has transformed the agenda rather than states: 'We argue that individuals and groups may influence not only the preferences of their own states via representation, but also the preferences of individuals and groups elsewhere, and even of states elsewhere, through a combination of persuasion, socialization, and pressure.' (Keck and Sikkink 1998:214) But how can constructivism explain the shift from governments ignoring these lobby groups to their alleged wielding of substantial influence in international institutions and Western governments? The relationship of influence is normally presented as non-state actors using the opportunities of ethical policy for their own advantage, these groups 'were able to take advantage of this new openness as well as the ways in which the new language of global civil society legitimised their activities' (Kaldor 2003:79). There is little question that the international agenda has been transformed but doubt remains as to whether the moral actors of global civil society or new needs of states and international institutions are driving the process.

The analysis by Hans Peter Schmitz of transnational activism and change in Kenya and Uganda illustrates the double-edged nature of the constructivist account as does the work of David Black on South Africa (Schmitz 1999; Black 1999; see also Klotz 1995). Schmitz and Black both assume that the shift from Western governments ignoring Amnesty International and other transnational organisations to acting in concert with them illustrates how 'continued transnational mobilization *eventually* had important effects on governmental foreign and domestic policy decisions' (Schmitz 1999:40). Starting from widely publicised abuses of human rights in the early 1970s, they find that 'it is puzzling that it took so long for these widely available reports to affect a significant change' in international policy (Schmitz 1999:42). However, by the late 1980s and early 1990s, 'finally, the efforts of the human rights network to socialize the international public by means of moral consciousness-raising and persuasion had some effect' (Schmitz 1999:49). This change in international policy of leading Western states, particularly the US, towards South Africa, Kenya and Uganda is held to have been 'preceded and caused by the activities of the human rights network' which over twenty-five years socialized the donor governments into the human rights discourse and led them 'to reinterpret their "national interest"' (Schmitz 1999:73–4; Black 1999:95).[2]

Similarly, Risse and Sikkink argue that it is only relatively recently that international financial institutions such as the World Bank and the International Monetary Fund have imposed human rights conditionality as a basis for financial and economic development aid. Their answer to the question of the dynamic behind this process is a clear cut one:

> If Western donors start coordinating foreign aid or the World Bank attaches 'good governance' criteria to their structural adjustment programme, these changes in policies might well result from network and INGO activities... Only if it can be shown empirically that pressures generated by great powers and/or international financial institutions are the most significant factors in

the domestic-transnational-international link to induce sustainable human rights improvements...would this constitute a challenge to our model.    (Risse and Sikkink 1999:36)

Here the weight of evidential argument is placed on the rationalists to demonstrate that the power of states rather than global civic actors as the most significant factor. The constructivist story could easily be read (and written) the other way around. Rather than a rationalist analysis being forced to explain the shift towards normative values the constructivist approach could be asked the same question: 'Why now?' The fact that principled-issue campaigns had little success in the Cold War period could be used to argue that the recent shift towards normative approaches could have little to do with the work of these worthy activists.

The constructivist approach raises the question 'why now?' against the rationalists but has no convincing answer. Risse and Sikkink admit that, according to their analysis, 'there is no obvious reason' why between the mid-1980s and the mid-1990s there was a transformation in the prescriptive status of human rights norms (Risse and Sikkink 1999:31). They state that, considering the differing domestic structures of the states studied, 'the convergence around the dating of prescriptive status is puzzling unless there is an international process of socialization underway. Yet, why does international norm learning appear in the period 1985 to 1995?' (Risse and Sikkink 1999:31) As critics of constructivism point out:

> It is, of course, one thing to begin from the premise that ideas and norms are the principle agent of change; it is an entirely different proposition to demonstrate the inherent necessity of this to be the case, and in addition outline the specific form by which the 'construction' of the international environment, on its opportunities and constraints, takes place.    (Palan 2000:577)

Risse and Sikkink offer two possible conclusions. Firstly, that norm socialisation takes time and therefore we are witnessing the fruition of a gradual process of dialogue and socialisation which has stretched from the end of the Second World War to the present. Alternatively, they suggest that there may be a change from quantity into quality, in that all the relevant international social structures, institutions, norms and transnational networks, needed to be in place for the process to be effective. In regard to the latter possibility, they assert that: 'Not until the mid-1980s were all parts of this structure fully formed and dense – with the increasing number of human rights treaties, institutions, NGOs, increased foundation funding for human rights work – and human rights had become a part of foreign policy of key countries.' (Risse and Sikkink 1999:31) This conclusion is surprising seeing as the end of the Cold War, a major event in precisely the period of the shift in values and the 'realignment of the geostrategic interests of major states', is ignored in this account. Some analysts, who agree with the empirical detail of Risse and Sikkink's accounts, argue that this was a vital 'permissive condition to explain the deployment of human rights enforcement mechanisms' (Burgerman 1998:918). However, if geo-strategic interests were to be accepted as changing before the shift in moral concerns this would seem to fundamentally weaken the constructivist case.

It would appear that the weakness of the realist approach – of theorising international change – seems to be just as much as a problem for constructivist approaches. While constructivism can describe changes in values and interests it cannot easily explain why such changes occur or why one norm rather than another should become widely accepted (see further, Heartfield 1996a:18–24; Florini 1996:363). Inter-subjectively created identities are not free-floating. The constructivist rejection of essentialism or foundationalism and grand-narratives rules causality beyond the contestation of ideas out of court. Unlike the perspective of earlier critical theorists, such as Robert Cox, who criticised the conservatism of neo-realist approaches, any wider social or political analysis of why particular ideas are prevalent at particular times or the interests behind them is impossible (Cox 1981). In this context, ideas are simply good or bad. Ironically, what started as an intellectual current at least partially influenced by critical theory has arguably now become thoroughly uncritical (Reus-Smit 2001:215).

## The power of communication?

Just as constructivist theory needs an agent in global civil society, global civil society needs constructivist theory to substantiate its claims to influence. A leading example of the power of ideas and small campaign groups to influence state identity and interests, is often held to be that of the 1989 transition in Eastern Europe. But how exactly were small dissident groups responsible for the fall of the mighty Soviet empire in Eastern Europe? Mary Kaldor writes:

It was the many small holes that penetrated the Cold War structures, said Jan Karavan, the former Czech Foreign Minister...that helped to undermine the whole edifice... [T]he endless negotiation and pressure on officials...did eventually begin to influence 'insiders' who contributed to the non-violent nature of the 1989 revolutions. 'It is like water dripping on a stone,' one official told me... It helped to undermine the ideology of the regimes. Above all, it helped to influence the 'new thinking' of the Gorbachev regime.   (Kaldor 2003:69)

The collapse of the East European Soviet regimes is simultaneously used to substantiate the relevance of constructivist theory and the importance of global civil society connections. As Kaldor states: 'Those who studied Eastern Europe "from above", who studied economic trends or the composition of politburos, failed to predict the 1989 revolutions.' (Kaldor 2003:70) Yet the argument is an entirely negative one. Where is the evidence that even those involved in the process on behalf of civic groups actually thought that their action and ideas were the engine of change rather than a product of the process itself? Kaldor herself admits that 'the dissidents did not expect to take power; all their writings suggest that they envisaged anti-politics and the parallel *polis* as long-term strategies for transformation' (Kaldor 2003:76).

The strength of this negative argument is that despite the power inequalities and the apparent lack of clear mechanisms of influence, the new ethical agenda nevertheless develops bringing with it a transformation of the existing system. As Palan astutely notes, where constructivism is useful is in the problematisation of the conception of power and interests as understood within the realist framework. However, 'what we end up with is privileging 'ideas', devoid of human experience, over power and interests as conventionally understood' (Palan 2000:590).

For leading constructivist theorists, states which put power and interests before norms and values need external pressure (of bad publicity or sanctions) to enter the sphere of norms and human rights values. However, once they have started 'talking the talk' external pressure and strategic bargaining gives way to the process of '*argumentative discourses* in the Habermasian sense' of global civil society (Risse and Sikkink 1999:12–13). Rather than power and instrumentality 'socialization through moral discourse emphasizes processes of communication, argumentation, and persuasion' as, rather than self-interest, 'actors accept the validity and significance of norms in their discursive practices' (Risse and Sikkink 1999:13).

This faith in communicative practices inevitably leading to moral or ethical outcomes unfortunately leads many constructivist theorists to avoid focusing on state-non-state actor relations as they are currently constituted and instead to project their normative visions into the future. Kaldor argues that the fact that international institutions and leading Western states have even used the term 'global civil society' is a positive factor: '[T]he neoliberal version of the concept, despite its shortcomings, has legitimised the term and provided a conceptual platform on which civic activists...can gain access to the centres of power.' (Kaldor 2003:146–147) It is the norms which become the focus rather than the power relations which currently influence their usage. The crucial point for constructivist claims is that even if non-Western and Western states initially take up principled-issues to serve their own instrumental interests, the fact that these norms are publicly endorsed *may* then lead to policy changes in the future. For example, Jean Grugel highlights the importance of norms in response to criticisms of token consultation measures taken by international financial institutions. Grugel argues that opening up the World Bank and other agencies to scrutiny by civil society actors 'would mark a highly significant step in the democratisation of the post-Bretton Woods institutions':

> If the notion that supra-territorial agencies have similar democratic responsibilities to those of governments is accepted, then it will be hard to return to the *status quo ante*. Putting the genie back in the bottle will prove difficult, if not impossible. With this in mind, an impressive array of civil society actors – including business fora, religious organisations, NGOs, think tanks, labour associations, community groups and women's organisations – now target the governance agencies on a daily basis. (Grugel 2003: 272)

Keck and Sikkink argue that their constructivist approach does not ignore or downplay the importance of power, political struggle and instrumental interests, but that the initial adoption of principled policies for instrumental reasons incrementally changes the identity of the state actor. They argue:

> Modern networks are not conveyor belts of liberal ideas but vehicles for communicative and political exchange, with the potential for mutual transformation of participants... The importance of this *process of mutual constitution* is particularly relevant for considering issues of sovereignty, about which significant differences may exist

among network members... Northerners within networks usually see third world leaders' claims about sovereignty as the self-serving positions of authoritarian or, in any case, elite actors. They consider that a weaker sovereignty might actually improve the political clout of the most marginalized people in developing countries. In the south, however, many activists take quiet a different view... It is over such issues that networks are valuable as a space for the negotiation of meanings... this process of negotiation within the emergent cosmopolitan community is not 'outside' the state. Instead it involves state actors in active reflection on state interests as well. (emphasis added) (Keck and Sikkink 1998:215–6)

Where network theory falls down is in establishing how the process of the 'mutual constitution' of the network, so crucial for the argument that ideas are more important than power, is established. Firstly, the non-Western state which is the target of the principled-issue network is presumably excluded, at least initially. Additionally, as the principled-issue network involves non-Western state activists, Western activists and Western states and international institutions, in what way can the power relations be overcome for the *mutual* transformation of the participants according to communicative precepts?

The detailed case-studies are essentially those which study the impact of intervention in the policy-making processes of non-Western states, in effect rewriting the imposition of an external Western agenda as a product not of shifts in the balance of state power internationally but of NGO activism and the values of global civil society. As Ronen Palen astutely notes:

The distinction between constructivism and materialism...becomes a dichotomy between the politics of norms and law, on the one hand, and the politics of self-help and coercion, on the other. Constructivist idealism then becomes an assertion about the primacy of norms and laws in both domestic and international politics. So that, to paraphrase Wendt, the superstructure indeed is able to counter the material base of power. The result is that in the name of social theory, Wendt manages to remove traces of 'materialist' interest from the analysis of international order. (Palan 2000:578)

What could be seen as the imposition of external regulatory intervention is instead interpreted as the expansion of communicative moral norms, which appear to be legitimated by the success in imposing them:

> When a state recognizes the legitimacy of international interventions and changes its domestic behaviour in response to international pressure, it reconstitutes the relationship between the state, its citizens, and international actors. This [is the] pattern, by which network practices instantiate new norms... (Keck and Sikkink 1998:37)

The reshaping of power relations is portrayed as the extension of international morality and the institutionalisation of new norms. Constructivist global civil society theorists do not just uncritically accept Western state coercion, in the service of an interventionist ethical foreign policy agenda, but even claim that Western states themselves are reluctant to undertake such action. The ethical or moral foreign policy agenda is instead held to indicate the strength of actually existing global civil society. This agenda is seen to be part of a virtuous circle as nation-state policy in this area further contributes to the influence of non-state actors, as they will acquire additional 'leverage' over policy-making. Implicit in the constructivist argument is the assumption that the only gain for Western states is norm-related one, i.e., their national interest in being seen as a 'good international citizen'.

## Conclusion

The growing power of Western states and international institutions appears as the power of norms or the influence of global civil society. This is because the human rights discourse, raising human rights or individual rights above sovereignty, is seen to be a progressive one that challenges states and puts forward a new and positive agenda.

As we have seen, there are two central assumptions at the heart of the constructivist account. Firstly, the thesis that states need to be pressurised to accept the new ethical agenda and, secondly, that the acceptance of a new understanding of limited sovereignty and more interventionist norms is the product of dialogue not power. Both these assumptions are held to demonstrate the importance of ideas, of moral and ethical dialogue, over the importance of power relations.

Firstly, it is always argued that the ethical agenda is a threat to state interests per se, rather than to specific states, on the assumption that the struggle to advance global ethical values, which inevitably question state rights of sovereignty, is a goal which could only be pursued by ethical non-state actors in global civil society. In which case, the success of these campaigns illustrates the power and influence of these actors and the importance of information and ideas.

Secondly, there is an assumption that the transformation of post-Cold War international relations has been a product of communicative dialogue between state and non-state actors. This is reflected in the view that the shift from the power and influence of nation-states to that of non-state 'moral entrepreneurs' has involved a renegotiation of the importance of sovereignty. The idea of sovereignty as an inter-subjective shared understanding leads to the conclusion that ideas and understandings have been transformed rather than power relations. Instead of a more hierarchical world we have a more moral world.

In the following two chapters these claims will be dissected in more detail. Chapter 4 will consider the 'renegotiation' of sovereignty. The following chapter addresses the rise of non-state actors and the decline of 'national interests'.

# 3
# The Decline of 'National Interests'

## Introduction

Today the key actor in international relations, the nation-state, appears to have lost the capacity or will to pursue its self-interest defined in terms of power. Commentators from a variety of theoretical perspectives argue that the most developed nation-states increasingly see themselves as having moral obligations to international society.[1] The key theoretical framework for understanding the international sphere, that of state interest, not only central to realism but also to the rational choice perspective of neoliberal frameworks of international co-operation, appears to have lost its explanatory power. Rather than states and national interests shaping the direction of policy it appears that there is a new agenda set by non-state actors, whether it is the normative values and transnational concerns of the 'principled-issue' campaigners of global civil society or, more recently, the threats to security from terrorist networks such as al-Qaeda.

There is a new consensus, expressed most clearly by global civil society theorists, that the foreign policy of leading Western powers cannot be understood through considering nation-states as egoistic actors pursing narrow self-interest. Since the end of the Cold War, major states have increasingly stressed the importance of ethics and values in the shaping of international goals and have intervened internationally on the basis of 'other-regarding' concerns such as human rights and international justice. Many commentators have understood this shift to 'value-led' or 'ethical' foreign policy through a constructivist approach to the question, viewing this value shift as a response to international pressures of global civil society networks and new cosmopolitan constituencies.

This chapter instead suggests that the shift away from the articulation of national interests and the drive to defend 'values', particularly through international intervention, can be understood as products of and responses to the domestic political malaise at the heart of Western politics, regularly referred to in the US as an outcome of the 'Culture Wars'. The term 'Culture Wars' is a short-hand expression for the struggle against the relativist challenge to cohering national values and community goals, held to have resulted in 'the loss of respect for authorities and institutions' (Himmelfarb 1999:20). The neo-conservatives in the United States have sought to overcome what they see as the debilitating effects of 1960s counterculture through re-establishing 'American moral values' through foreign and domestic policy initiatives.

The interest here is not so much the cultural struggle itself, rather the consequences of this well documented concern that 'there is no common purpose, or common faith', which reflects a lack of shared framework of meaning and sense of socio-political purpose connecting Western states and their citizens (Bell 1975:211). The inability to establish a shared socio-political vision of what 'the nation' stands for – the lack of a strong 'idea of the state' in Buzanian terms – has meant that Western powers find it difficult to formulate a clear foreign policy or to legitimise the projection of power abroad in terms of national interest (Buzan 1991).

The rest of this section outlines the breadth of today's 'post-national consensus' and the limited critical appeal of theorists who seek to reassert the importance of national interests and *realpolitik* in the international sphere. Rather, it suggests that issues of subjectivity play an important explanatory role in the making of foreign policy (see further, Campbell 1998a). The following sections highlight the difficulties which Western elites face in articulating and projecting a national vision, both domestically and internationally, and consider how this difficulty has been reflected in and compounded by the international framework established through support for humanitarian intervention and the war on terror. If this is the case, then today's focus on the power and influence of global civil society and the actions of non-state actors, may mistake cause and effect.

### The post-national consensus

As considered in Chapter 2, the constructivist approach rejects the 'outside/in' approach of understanding national interests as structured through the logic of anarchy, suggesting that national interests and identities are contingent and socially constructed (for example, Wendt 1992). Nevertheless, these interests are still constructed in the international sphere itself, even if states do have the potential to make and to act on alternative identity 'choices' (Wendt 1992:419). While the domestic political framework and institutional structures play an important role it is generally held to be a secondary one. It is transnationally operating non-state actors which are the active agents of change, diffusing 'principled ideas' and 'international norms' related to human rights and transnational justice (Risse and Sikkink 1999:4). It is in response to this changed international context that states are generally understood to have been driven to reshape or redefine their identities. The largely instrumental use of 'principled ideas' during the Cold War is held to have given way to the institutionalisation of new practices in the international sphere, sustained by the pressure of transnational human rights networks 'from above' and supported by civil society pressure 'from below' (Risse and Sikkink 1999:34).

Today, there is a broad consensus around this approach, stretching well beyond writers and commentators who would consciously place themselves in the constructivist framework. Liberal internationalists argue that power is not exercised in the old way. Influential US liberal theorist Joseph Nye, for example, argues that the traditional distinction 'between a foreign policy based on values and a foreign policy based on interests' should be rejected (Nye 2002:138). Nye writes that the challenges of the 'global information age' have required the redefinition of national interest (Nye 2002:136). *The Responsibility to Protect* report, from the high-level International Commission on Intervention and State Sovereignty, considered in more detail in the following chapter, asserts the consensus view that nation-states are not forced 'by systemic or structural factors' to pursue narrow interests, but are free to make moral choices (ICISS 2001b:129).

The challenge to the idealist focus of constructivist theorists in international relations comes in part from defenders of realist and rationalist frameworks which emphasise explanations based on power-interests (see below) but most influentially, from within normative theorising itself. The debates are between cosmopolitan universalists and communitarian, republican strands with the compromise position of a 'thin' cosmopolitanism. The mainstream academic case for defending realism is increasingly a normative one, couched in moral terms. Barry Buzan, for example, affirms the 'powerful, and often neglected, normative attraction' of realism, which values ideological and cultural diversity, political independence and

economic decentralisation (Buzan 1996:62). For republican and communitarian theorists the social bonds of political community cannot
encompass territories which are too large or too diverse, undermining
aspirations towards a global moral and political realm (see for
example, Walzer 1995; Brown 1995, 2002; Kenny 2003; see also
discussion in Linklater 1998:46–76).

The view of the end of national interests has attained a broad
consensus from radical postmodernists and left-leaning academics
to senior British diplomats. Michael Hardt and Antonio Negri, for
example, argue that Vietnam was the last attempt the US made to
play an imperial role, pursuing its national interests 'with all the violence, brutality and barbarity befitting any European imperialist
power' (Hardt and Negri 2001:178). But the defeat in Vietnam
marked a passage to a new regime of genuine internationalism. For
these radical critics, the 1991 Gulf War illustrated that the US had
now become 'the only power able to manage international justice,
*not as a function of its own national motives but in the name of global
right'* [emphasis in original]. Sussex professor, Martin Shaw, argues
that rather than the imperialism of national interest, the projection
of Western power since the Cold War has been 'post-imperial'; a
moral response to crises provoked by non-Western powers which still
seek to pursue territorial claims and the narrow interests of power
(Shaw 2002).

Leading European Union and former British government policy-
advisor Robert Cooper argues that major Western powers are 'postmodern' imperialists, no longer asserting any national interests of their
own:

> A large number of the most powerful states no longer want to fight
> or conquer. It is this that gives rise to both the pre-modern and
> postmodern worlds. Imperialism in the traditional sense is dead, at
> least among the Western powers.   (Cooper 2002:14)

Cooper writes that we now live in a 'postmodern world, *raison d'état*
and the amorality of Machiavelli's theories of statecraft, which defined
international relations in the modern era, have been replaced by a
moral consciousness' (Cooper 2002:13). If there is a 'national' interest
that is seen as respectable today it is the 'national interest in being, and
being seen to be, a good international citizen...regularly willing to
pitch into international tasks for motives that appear to be relatively
selfless' (ICISS 2001a:72).

## The realist response

Constructivists have been criticised for ceding too much ground to realist theorists in terms of their focus on state interests. In fact (as considered in Chapter 2), the similarities are the source of the strength of constructivist theory. Constructivist theory implicitly accepts the realist claim that states are power-seeking and interest-pursuing goal-directed actors. The point at which they depart from orthodox realism is in the assertion that now these interests have been shaped, or 'constructed', through an inter-subjective engagement with other states and non-state actors in global civil society. The theory is anchored around the empirical claim that state interests have changed, particularly as illustrated in the shift towards ethical foreign policy, prioritised by leading states and institutions since the end of the Cold War. The constructivist argument is essentially that ethical foreign policy does not serve traditional interests of power and aggrandisement and that therefore the 'identity' and the 'interests' of major Western states have been changed. As Ronen Palen notes:

> A legitimate, if not illuminating critique of IR constructivism would simply be to say that constructivists are empirically and methodologically wrong: that in the last analysis 'ideas' are not the principal force of order and change in the international system; that material factors and material interests override the primacy of normatively constituted practices. (Palan 2000:576)

The response of critics seeking to defend a traditional realist or rationalist approach has, in fact, been to essentially counterpose an allegedly 'materialist' realism to the 'idealism' of the constructivists. Perhaps because of the inherently ideological nature of this project, it would appear that the few defenders of national interests or narrow rational instrumentality as a guide to understanding the international sphere are marginal critics from the left. Alex Callinicos, for example, argues that the US is still an imperialist power pursuing national interests and that international co-operation stems from the need to contain and structure the conflict and competition inherent in international capital (Callinicos 2002). Peter Gowan similarly asserts that behind the drive for economic globalisation lies traditional US imperialism (Gowan 1999). The 'realist' view of timeless competition for power appeals to commentators who wish to argue that the ending of the Cold War has made little difference to the operation of capitalism and the power inequalities implicit in the world market.

For many critics on the left, the talk of postmodern imperialism, human rights and cosmopolitan justice is merely the latest in a long line of moral justifications for national interests. For Noam Chomsky:

> 'the new interventionism' is replaying an old record. It is an updated variant of traditional practices that were impeded in a bipolar world system that allowed some space for nonalignment... With the Soviet deterrent in decline, the Cold War victors are more free to exercise their will under the cloak of good intentions but in pursuit of interests that have a very familiar ring outside the realm of enlightenment.   (Chomsky 1999:11)

The most common critique of global civil society theorising from the political left has been that it is part of the neo-liberal offensive, de-legitimising the state, which in the non-Western world acts as a vital locus of opposition to international capital, and enhancing the power of pro-market groups and elites (for example, Beckman 1993, Gowan 1995; Marcussen 1996; Hearn 1999; Roniger and Güneş-Ayata 1994; Abrahamsen 2000).

In the post-1945 retreat from Empire, non-Western states won the formal rights of political and legal equality and the new 'constitution' for international society, the UN Charter, guaranteed the collective rights of sovereignty and self-government against intervention from major powers. In this context, it is undoubtedly true that ethical inter-nationalism has reflected, and to some extent legitimised, the rewriting of the rules of the international order, facilitating a return to Great Power intervention and the overturning of the political gains of the post-colonial period (Chandler 2000b; considered further in Chapter 4). However, the collapse of the Cold War balance of power and shift to a unipolar world under US domination would suggest that the protections of the UN framework of 1945 would no longer have withstood the post-1989 realignment of power, regardless of how this was legitimised after the event.[2]

Rather than simply asserting the existence of power-political competition, it would seem more challenging to ask a question rarely posed by the critics of 'humanitarian' wars and 'postmodern imperialism' – 'Why is it that national interests appear to have been so roundly rejected?' Even in the 'war on terror' the US has continually asserted that it was not acting out of purely national concerns. For example, the invasion of Afghanistan was promoted as an act of concern for the people of the region. When President George W. Bush announced the start of the bombing campaign on 7 October 2001 he presented it as one in aid of the 'oppressed people of Afghanistan' rather than an entirely legitimate action of self-defence in response to an attack on American national symbols of economic and military power. Rather than emphasising national interests, Bush stressed America's humanitarian aims:

> As we strike military targets, we'll also drop food, medicine and supplies to the starving and suffering men and women and children of Afghanistan. The United States of America is a friend to the Afghan people, and we are the friends of almost a billion worldwide who practice the Islamic faith.   (Bush 2001b)

Even the avowedly hawkish National Security Strategy, issued in September 2002, seems remarkably 'soft' in its humanitarian emphasis on nation-building with the assistance of NGOs. On the one hand, the US writes a blank cheque for the exercise of power in its declaration of a unilateral right to strike pre-emptively before threats materialise. Yet, on the other, it pledges to 'continue to work with international organisations such as the United Nations, as well as non-governmental organisations, and other countries to provide the humanitarian, political, economic, and security assistance necessary to rebuild Afghanistan' (US 2002).

The realist critics take the national interests behind foreign adventures as a given. This chapter suggests that it is not straightforward to challenge the constructivist assumptions of the global civil society theorists at the level of the empirical counter-assertion of material interests. That, in fact, there is more to the rejection of 'traditional' national interests, than merely government PR spin. Constructivist approaches reflect the dominant change in international relations since the Cold War, the apparent decline of power politics or *realpolitik*. In these circumstances, it is not surprising that more idealist frameworks of analysis should become increasingly dominant.

The strength of support for global civil society theorising, that emphasises ideas rather than power relations, is in part a reflection of real changes in the process of articulating states' national interests. Critics from the left tend to ignore the central facet of the post-Cold War world – the problem that Western powers have in presenting and projecting a coherent national interest. This study contends that the projection of power abroad is more a response to the difficulties of negotiating national goals and aims, than a straightforward projection of these pre-given interests.

What is new about the international climate today, and theoretical representations of it, is the rejection or down-playing of national interests. The constructivist framework, which posits the existence of an international society of state and non-state actors engaged in a dialogue over norms, depends, as we have seen in Chapter 2, on the assumption that states have been forced to reject fixed national interests. The ending of the Cold War in itself need not have undermined realist approaches. The collapse of Soviet power could have been understood as a product of ideas or as a product of the material factors of power or through different combinations of the two. It is factors outside the international sphere which have contributed to the revival of idealist thought which minimises the importance of power relations.

## Constructivism and decolonisation

One example, to highlight this, is that the constructivist understanding of the ending of the Cold War is generally read back to understand other major transitions in the international system. Particularly important in this context is the rewriting of the history of decolonisation. The decolonisation process is today neither seen as a product of political struggle for independence nor as a product of the consequences of inter-Western rivalries which did much to discredit the idea of empire. The struggle of independence movements and the experience of fascism and the world wars are taken out of the picture to argue that it was largely a matter of normative value change on behalf of Western powers themselves, which led to decolonisation. The decolonisation process is seen as a product not of the discrediting of the legitimacy of Western power but of new normative ideals of sovereignty and equality which were developed and then projected abroad by the West:

> A hundred years ago, most Westerners considered it not merely acceptable but right that they exercise imperial control over almost all of Africa and most of South and Southeast Asia.... [D]ecolonisation radically reshaped the map of the world... These fundamental changes in the actors in international politics had little to do with changes in the distribution of capabilities... Change has occurred not in the relative balance of military resources between great powers, or between weak and powerful states, but in norms and practices relating to sovereignty and intervention, under the influence of changing ideas of national self-determination and the meaning of sovereign equality.   (Donnelly 2000:143–5)

Robert Jackson captures this well in his argument that the new sovereign states were 'quasi-states' created by Western powers' recognition of the moral claims of Third World independence, rather than a recognition of power and capacity. For Jackson: 'What has changed is not the empirical conditions of states but the international rules and institutions concerning these conditions.' (Jackson 1990:23) The argument being that, since the 1960s, the moral argument has moved on and that Western powers now have recognised the importance of universal claims of human rights and the need for intervention.

Sovereignty as an internationally-constituted normative social construct becomes in this way constituted by actually existing global civil society, as expressed through the policy changes of Western powers. Critics of this perspective, for example, Alejandro Colás, take issue with Jackson and other constructivist thinkers for ignoring the role played by social movements and political actors, both in the colonial states and the colonies, which forced the withdrawal of empire. Rather than a discourse of ethics, this was, for Colás, a political struggle for power and independence against colonial rule. For Colás, the key to decolonisation was not a growing normative awareness of Western powers, but rather the factor of revolutionary struggle for national liberation which put these new norms on the agenda (Colás 2002:132–4).

However, a second, and much less commented upon factor behind the establishment of the post-war order of sovereign political equality was the crisis of confidence within Western ruling elites. The legitimating ideas of Western elite rule, of natural hierarchy, class and race, were discredited by the fascist experience and the confidence of the British elite was badly shaken by the collapse of their Asian empire in World War II, with the fall of Singapore in February 1942, followed by the loss of Burma and Malaya (see Füredi 1994, 1998; Chandler 2000b). The informal 'white consensus' that had regulated international affairs and the coherence and confidence of Western elites was severely shaken. This defensiveness led to compromises in both domestic and international spheres, producing the welfare state consensus in Western Europe, and the UN system of sovereign equality internationally.

The key point is that the UN system and new norms of nonintervention did not reflect pure material power-relations, but neither did they represent a new consensus driven by a demand for increasingly progressive ethical norms. The weakness of these norms can be seen in the rapidity with which they have crumbled in the post-Cold War context, highlighted by the return of Western paternalism (see Bain 2003). In many respects the system of sovereign equality was a by-product of a collapse of Western elite confidence in its ability to project power internationally, rather than a positive ethical shift or a result of power relations changing.

In Chapter 4 it will be suggested that today's rolling back of sovereign equality and the renegotiation of the social construction of the meaning of sovereignty has to be seen in the context of changing power relations internationally. The following sections of this chapter focus more on the question of Western elite confidence and suggest that the one ideological support which was salvaged in the wake of World War II, that of nationalism, became increasingly problematic in the years that followed. From this perspective, post-Cold War attempts to maintain domestic political legitimacy and elite coherence can be understood as major factors in the shift towards ethical and normative concerns internationally. Just as the birth of the UN system cannot be explained purely by power relations or by ethical ideas, it suggests that the decline of this system, and the reshaping of international affairs today, cannot be understood solely in realist terms, as the product of US power (or Great Power rivalries), or solely in constructivist terms, as a result of shifting international normative values.

## Culture wars

The majority of commentators adopting a liberal or constructivist framework today tend to reproduce the 'outside/in' approach of structural realism in attributing the shift away from national interests to changes in the international sphere. In place of the external structure of anarchy imposing a uniformity of decision-making it is asserted that the external development of 'principled-issue' constituencies and a globalised cosmopolitan consciousness compels nation-states to adapt to a new international environment. Rather than deriving new national 'identities' or interests from international pressures, this chapter emphasises the possibility that international interventions can be driven by a domestic process of constituting and defining national interests. There has been a long tradition of thought, since Kant's essay on *Perpetual Peace*, which considers the impact of domestic political institutions and national identity in shaping the projection of power internationally (for example, Doyle 1986; Müller and Risse-Kappen 1992). However, less has been written about the use of international activism abroad in the attempt to forge a national identity at home.[3] Let us consider the two most interventionist powers, Britain and the US.

At the domestic level it appears that political power can no longer be exercised in the traditional way. Governments are increasingly seen to be less important or influential. There is increasing cynicism and doubt over government and politics, demonstrated by falling turn-outs at the polls, declining party memberships and lower viewing figures for the nightly news. Even General Election victories, the defining point of the domestic political process, no longer bring governments a sense of authority or legitimacy. This was clear in the contested victory of George W. Bush in the 2000 elections, which turned on the question of the 'hanging' chad in Florida. However, the problem of deriving legitimacy from elections is a much broader one, not directly connected to concerns of manipulation or even to voter apathy. In the British elections in 2001 Tony Blair achieved a land-slide second term mandate, the government had little political opposition to speak of either in the British parliament or in the country at large, yet there was no sense of a connection to the general public or of a political project which could engage society.

No matter the size of the parliamentary majority, without a political project, which can give meaning to government actions and the passing of legislation, governments appear weak and ineffectual. Domestic policy decisions, whether in education, health, transport or policing, appear to be short-term or knee-jerk responses bereft of any long-term aims. Without an ideological context, policy is liable to be reversed or undermined at the first sign of funding difficulties or problems in implementation. Rather than 'modern' politics where the state had a political programme or project which promised to transcend the present, to take society forward, today, governments are caught in a 'postmodern' malaise. There appears to be no vision or project which can give government a sense of mission or purpose. In this context, domestic policy-making is caught in the 'everlasting present' where legislation is passed to deal with crisis-management and policy-making is contingent on events rather than shaped by government.

Without a sense of purpose or mission, governments lack coherence and credibility. In this context, foreign policy can be a powerful mechanism for generating a sense of political purpose and mission (Chandler 2003a). While the end of the Cold War has highlighted the domestic political malaise which makes government coherence and political vision difficult, it is important to note that the problems are rooted in a lack of confidence of the Western political elite which has deeper historical roots. Hardt and Negri, for example, note that Vietnam marked the 'point of passage' away from the confident pursuit of US national interests (Hardt and Negri 2001:178). After Vietnam, US power could no longer be projected with moral certainty. The American establishment no longer had a belief in their 'manifest destiny'.

However, the 'postmodern' state was born not in military humiliation in the Far East but in the disintegration of the moral certainty of US national interest at home. The lack of consensus over Vietnam reflected the lack of collective identification with US 'national' interests. Of the two million young men called up for the military draft an unprecedented 139,000 refused to serve. As Christopher Coker astutely notes, it was not the failure of intervention in Vietnam in itself that made the assertion of US national interests problematic, but the domestic response to the war. Reflecting broader social trends of individualisation or, in Ulrich Beck's terms 'reflexive modernisation', the decay of traditional social bonds and values meant that the nation-state could no longer be seen as an end in itself (Coker 2001:154–5).

The 'postmodern' shift was a product of a lack of confidence in the innate superiority of the American way of life. The US establishment's defeat in the 'Culture Wars' of the late 1960s and 1970s corroded the old certainties about truth, justice and the American way. Everything about the past was called into question as American history was increasingly seen as tainted by racism and colonialism. Since Vietnam, dissent became respectable and there could no longer be a 'grand narrative' about US identity or 'national interest'. The Cold War framework served to minimise the postmodern domestic 'crisis of meaning', the lack of confidence of the American establishment in any great project. The end of moral certainty in the justness of the projection of US power meant that American intervention abroad could no longer find legitimacy in a clearly expressed 'vision of the future', instead it was 'reduced to managing the present' (Coker 2001:157). Rather than acting in national interests, the US rejected any positive project for the claim to be a 'subject-less' world policeman.

The end of the Cold War, and the removal of restrictions on an increasingly activist foreign policy, created the possibility for the US establishment to use the international sphere to reverse the defeats of the Culture Wars, to lay to rest the 'Vietnam Syndrome'. The attempt to regain a sense of mission was strengthened by the restored sense of national pride in the aftermath of 'victory' in the Cold War. This restoration of American mission was initially articulated in the moral language of human rights and humanitarian intervention. The language of Wilsonian internationalism appeared to restore a sense of

America's historic mission. Ethical concerns, such as the human rights of others, seemed to provide a moral framework which could project a sphere of agreement and consensus and point beyond the cultural relativism and pessimism of 'postmodern' times. As Francesca Klug notes: 'the post-Cold War search for new ideals and common bonds in an era of failed ideologies appears to have contributed to a growing appreciation of human rights as a set of values' (Klug 2000:147). Joseph Nye devotes a major section of his recent book, *The Paradox of American Power*, to 'The Home Front' and argues that while the impact of the Culture Wars has not been so great as to 'inhibit our capacity to act collectively' there is, nevertheless, a problem of articulating a common interest:

> The problem of the home front is less the feared prospects of social and political decay or economic stagnation than developing and popularising a vision of how the United States should define its national interest in a global information age.    (Nye 2002:136)

It would seem that rather than a response to international pressures and global civil society mobilisation, this demand for a new 'national interest' or 'national ideals' has been generated by governing elites. In Britain, 'ethical' foreign policy was consciously seen as a key element in New Labour initiatives aimed at 'rebranding' Britain, creating a modern multi-cultural British identity (Brown 2001:16). Opinion studies have consistently demonstrated that the idea that there is public pressure for a policy shift towards more 'ethical' concerns has been exaggerated. For example, in the mid-1990s polls showed that only a minority of the American public backed human rights promotion as an important foreign policy goal, well behind stopping the flow of illegal drugs, protecting the jobs of American workers and preventing the spread of nuclear weapons.[4] This finding was illustrated by the fact that President Clinton had to explain where Kosovo was on the map, before attempting to promote military action in 1999, because there was so little public interest in the issue.

Perhaps the most important example of the British and US governments attempting to create an 'ethical' interventionist agenda is the case of Iraq. For the last ten years US and British political leaders have used Iraq as an international cause which they could use to raise their status at home and emphasise their commitment to a moral mission abroad. The British and UK publics had never been as enthusiastic as their governments in pursuing conflict with Saddam Hussein and the emphasis on Iraq in foreign policy initiatives had little to do with international lobbying or shifts in public opinion. For example, in July 2002 when George W. Bush and Tony Blair prepared the public for the military conquest of Iraq, polls showed that only a small, and declining, majority of American people were in favour (Tyson 2002). Opinion polls consistently demonstrated that the Western public tended to share a narrow view of foreign policy priorities, based on perceptions of personal interests, rather than the more ideological 'crusading' perspective often pushed by their government leaders (Schwarz 2000).

The attention to the articulation of a political mission, beyond the directionless of domestic politics, through foreign policy activism abroad, has been an important resource for the self-identity and internal coherence of British and US political elites. The ability to project or symbolise unifying 'values' has become a core leadership attribute. George W. Bush's shaky start to the US presidency was transformed by his speech to Congress in the wake of the World Trade Centre and Pentagon attacks, in which he staked out his claim to represent and protect America's ethical values against the terrorist 'heirs of all the murderous ideologies of the 20th century' (Bush 2001a). Tony Blair, similarly, was at his most presidential in the wake of the attacks, arguing that values were what distinguished the two sides of the coming conflict: 'We are democratic. They are not. We have respect for human life. They do not. We hold essentially liberal values. They do not.' (Blair 2001a)

The search for ethical or principled approaches emphasising the government's moral legitimacy has inexorably led to a domestic shift in priorities making international policy-making increasingly high profile in relation to other policy-areas. The emphasis on ethical foreign policy commitments enables Western governments to declare an unequivocal moral stance, which helps to mitigate awkward questions of government mission and political coherence in the domestic sphere. The contrast between the moral certainty possible in selected areas of foreign policy and the uncertainties of domestic policy-making was unintentionally highlighted when President George Bush congratulated Tony Blair on his willingness to take a stand over Afghanistan and Iraq: 'The thing I admire about this Prime Minister is that he doesn't need a poll or a focus group to convince him of the difference between right and wrong.' (UK 2002) Tony Blair, like Bush himself, of course relies heavily on polls and focus groups for every domestic initiative. It is only in the sphere of foreign policy that it appears that there are opportunities for Western leaders to project a self-image of purpose, mission and political clarity.

## Humanitarian intervention

In the aftermath of the Cold War the United States was the unchallenged world power with the preponderance of military might. Yet despite having unrivalled power, the US lacked an ideological framework to exercise its superiority. There was no grand project, no vision or policy framework to give the exercise of power meaning. It was in the context of this policy vacuum that the new doctrine of humanitarian intervention attempted to provide a new rationale, a new legitimacy for the exercise of US power.

In the international arena the new ideological framework initially promised success. The US was able to rewrite the laws of international relations opening up a new sphere for international policy activism. At the end of the Gulf War, UN Security Council resolution 688 on 5 April 1991 ruled that Iraqi government policies towards its civilian population were a threat to 'international peace and security' and therefore subject to legitimate international intervention (UN 1991). The interventions of the early 1990s in Iraq, Somalia and Bosnia extended the rights of major powers to project their authority and rolled back the gains of the UN Charter period. Driven by America's unchallenged power, the old Cold War framework of equal sovereignty and non-intervention was steadily undermined (see, for example, ICISS 2001b:79–128; Wheeler 2000). However, the US has found it difficult to shape a new national mission through humanitarian intervention for two reasons: firstly, it has failed to secure long-term international legitimacy and secondly, it has provided no broader positive vision or meaning that could give a sense of purpose to ruling elites. Rather than helping to overcome the Vietnam syndrome, attempts to project US power in the 1990s merely confirmed the corrosion of US confidence.

### International legitimacy

The concept of humanitarian intervention has not won long-term international legitimacy because it has failed to convince the majority of the world's governments, who fear that their sovereignty will be threatened, and has provoked resistance from European allies concerned that their international standing will be undermined by US unilateralism. The view that human rights could 'trump' sovereignty has been resisted by the majority of non-Western states, concerned about their own sovereign rights (Roth 1999). The war over Kosovo revealed that the UN Security Council was split, with Russia and China resisting, but more telling was the fact that the US and Britain were reluctant to take the issue to the UN General Assembly for fear that the necessary majority, under the 'Uniting for Peace' procedure, would not be forthcoming (UK 2000:§136).

While the US can build 'coalitions of the willing' in support of a particular intervention, the principle of humanitarian intervention itself has not won wider acceptance. There is no international consensus on any new international framework or amendment to the UN Charter restrictions on the use of force because both Western and non-Western states recognise that the blurring of domestic and international responsibilities could be fundamentally destabilising (see further Clapham 1999; Chandler 2002:174–8).

The problems with winning any broader legitimacy were drawn out in the International Commission on Intervention and State Sovereignty report, *The Responsibility to Protect*. The Commission explicitly recognised that it is unlikely for any collective international institution to sanction the use of force on humanitarian grounds without a consensus of support in the UN Security Council. They reasoned that the majority of smaller states would always be reluctant to sanction interference by the minority of larger powers (ICISS 2001a:54).

A more fundamental problem is that the US cannot tie in other Western states around this agenda in the long-term. Humanitarian intervention has been no substitute for the Cold War's political and ideological defence of Western security. The US's major European allies, the UK, Germany and France, have shown themselves to be increasingly reluctant to see the US sideline the UN Security Council and undermine the cooperative institutions which they have used to enhance their standing internationally.

The framework of humanitarian intervention openly threatens to sideline the United Nations as the authorising authority for military intervention and, through granting increased authority to ad-hoc 'coalitions of the willing', make the Security Council subordinate to US power (see, for example, UN 2000; Chandler 2001a). The European powers' concern to tie the US into multilateral institutions which preserve their positions of importance could be seen, for example, in resistance to the US opt-out from the International Criminal Court (ICC). The trans-Atlantic rows over the ICC were not based on the possibility of US services coming before the new court, the Europeans had already offered assurances that this would not be the case, but on the principle that American 'exceptionalism' could not be openly legitimised (FIL 2002).

## The vision thing

The problem with humanitarian intervention was that while the doctrine could serve to facilitate the exercise of US power, and to overcome the formal barriers posed by the existing framework of international politics and international law, it was unable to create any positive framework of legitimisation. Rather than resolving the domestic political malaise, foreign activism tended to export the problem to the international sphere. Coker argues that the reason for this is that the doctrine of humanitarianism offers no positive view of the future – there is no mission or political project that transcends the present. Humanitarian intervention is a doctrine of crisis management, which lacking any historical perspective becomes a slave of contingency, based on responding to emergency: 'And emergency does not constitute the first stage of a project of meaning: it represents its active negation.' (Coker 2001:157)

The doctrine of humanitarian intervention enabled the US to project its power internationally, but did not operate as a source of meaning. The prevention of conflict and the protection of victims of human rights abuses became an end in itself rather than part of a broader political or ideological project. Alain Badiou astutely noted that the new ethical agenda was a defensive one, concerned with maintaining the status quo, but more importantly, that at the heart of it was political incapacity. Humanitarian 'ethics designate[d] above all the incapacity, so typical of the contemporary world, to name and strive for a Good' (Badiou 2001:30). David Rieff highlighted the problem with taking the ideological vision out of international intervention and the projection of power:

> I think you can have just wars that don't have a humanitarian basis. One of the ways the conception of humanitarianism is being bent completely out of shape, losing its specific gravity to use another image, is that suddenly we talk about everything in humanitarian terms. My friend Ronnie Brauman at MSF France says if Auschwitz happened today they would call it a humanitarian emergency. We can have a just war without there being a humanitarian emergency. Indeed the opposite is true. In this sense the Left is surely correct. Wars tend to exacerbate humanitarian crises not improve them, that's the nature of war. So already it's a fantasy. (Rieff 2002b)

Rather than promote a positive political goal, a political challenge to abuses of human rights, Reiff bemoaned the non-political presentation of Western intervention as somehow 'ethical'. For Reiff, the rejection of a political understanding for ethical condemnation is a dangerous one (Reiff 2002a). The project of exercising power abroad through 'humanitarian intervention' is shot through with contradictions. As Rieff suggests, the project of 'ethical' foreign policy is a fallacy; it is impossible to develop a coherent political strategy based purely on prevention. No matter how many countries are intervened against, there can be no victory or lasting success. The logic of a consistent ethical foreign policy would be an untenable 'war without end' and the breakdown of the mechanisms holding together international society. To cite Coker:

> Victory is no longer an objective. Postmodern societies do not fight wars to secure a final peace; they use war to manage insecurity... Wars are no longer wars, they are police actions. For there is no 'peace', no world order, no imperial mission, only the endless prospect, to quote President Clinton, of 'a world in which the future will be threatened'.   (Coker 2001:163)

Rather than projecting power in a way which could reinstate a national vision, the predominant image of humanitarian intervention became one of weakness. The defining motifs were not ones of US strength and power – most manifest in the bombing of a major European capital, Belgrade – but weakness in failing to intervene in Rwanda and failing to act decisively in Bosnia until it was too late. The humanitarian framework made the aggressive assertion of US power appear content-less, without meaning and long-term justification. Even Kosovo, the leading example of intervention for moral values, is often seen as a failure, merely encouraging, or being powerless to stop, the 'reverse' ethnic cleansing of the Serb minority. The problems of the Balkans appeared to remain the same; all that had changed was the pecking order.

Without an ideological framework for the exercise of power, the use of military forces abroad contributed little to US self-confidence and produced no new sense of national unity. The most ardent advocates of humanitarian intervention, as symbolic of a new sense of Western political identity and moral vision, were caught in a bind. On the one hand they insisted that governments should be willing to sacrifice their own troops for a 'just' cause, on the other hand, they had no political framework to justify such a sacrifice. It was as if just acting in a morally committed manner could become a replacement for a grand mission. The key issue was the demonstration of social commitment and engagement rather than the exercise of power in itself.

Going to war was no longer enough to restore a sense of moral mission, the public had to be galvanised too. In Britain strident interventionists like Mary Kaldor argued that military action was not enough to give a sense of meaning to humanitarian intervention. Rather than just focus on bombs, the government needed to work on the 'home front' to convince the public on the question 'whether it is acceptable to sacrifice national lives for the sake of people far away' (Kaldor 1999a:130). David Rieff emphasised the need for the US government to involve the public in 'a truly democratic debate' about the 'kind of world the United States wants...and what it is willing to sacrifice...to achieve its goals' (Rieff 1999).

Rieff and others bemoaned 'the indifference with which the American and Western European public lethargically assented to the Kosovo war, always providing, that is, that there were no casualties on our side' (Rieff 2000). Perhaps the most trenchant criticism of the US government's failure to use humanitarian intervention to forge a new national vision came from Michael Ignatieff. The title to his book on Kosovo, *Virtual War*, highlights the problem (Ignatieff 2000). Unlike wars of the past, Ignatieff argues Kosovo failed to mobilise or cohere society and offer people 'a moment of ecstatic moral communion with fellow citizens' (Ignatieff 2000:186). The public were alienated and uninvolved:

> [Citizens of NATO countries] were mobilised, not as combatants but as spectators. The war was a spectacle: it aroused emotions in the intense but shallow way that sports do. The events were as remote from their essential concerns as a football game...commitment is intense but also shallow.   (Ignatieff 2000:3–4)

While the pro-war advocates wanted the moral mission abroad to have an impact at home, their moralisation of conflict illustrated just how deep the problems were. Even though there was little domestic opposition to the principle of military intervention, the impact of the Culture Wars, the lack of consensus around national values, weighed heavily in the domestic focus on military strategy, on the methods and practices of the intervening forces. A moral debate that started with the 'human wrongs' committed by the Milošević government was soon transformed into a critique of NATO strategy, the accidental or 'collateral' killing of civilians and the reluctance of the US government to commit ground troops, which it was held may have minimised the deaths of non-combatants.

The argument that US and British lives could not be treated as if they were more valuable than those of Bosnian, Albanian or Rwandan people demonstrated the difficulty of exorcising the ghost of Vietnam – of asserting a new national interest or identity through the humanitarian framework. Rather than winning wars, the moral mission of humanitarian intervention was self-defeating in its inevitable questioning of any strident use of power. As the International Commission on Intervention and State Sovereignty noted, traditional warfighting was no longer possible as 'democratic societies that are sensitive to human rights and the rule of law will not long tolerate the pervasive use of overwhelming military power' (ICISS 2001a:62). While the cause was popular, governments themselves achieved little moral authority. It was the humanitarian NGOs who gained legitimacy from the militarisation of humanitarianism rather than the military. The British Army could gain little credibility as the 'military wing of Oxfam' when military means were now seen as ethically suspect (Norton-Taylor 2000). After Kosovo, the concept of fighting war for purely humanitarian reasons was increasingly treated with scepticism by both governments and humanitarian organisations.[5] Rather than addressing the domestic malaise, through providing a framework for the coherent projection of power, the doctrine of humanitarian intervention proved only to have intensified it.

## The war on terror

It appeared as if the horrific events of 9/11 would rewrite the norms and practices of international society and provide the 'defining paradigm' missing from 'the global order' since the end of the Cold War (for example, Booth and Dunne 2002:ix). The doctrine of humanitarian intervention had exposed the US to accusations of double standards and given the moral high ground to aid agencies rather than military forces. In the wake of 9/11 the US government had the opportunity to regain the moral mantle. In a world of victim politics, the US could at last claim to be a victim itself. In the words of Martin Shaw, the US and Britain now had the 'moral capital' they needed to overcome the legacy of Empire and tackle the Culture Wars at home and abroad (Shaw 2001).

Initially Bush and Blair were upbeat about the possibilities for developing a new vision of the future. For the hawks in the US establishment, 9/11 provided the legitimacy to project US power in a more confident way and long term plans for war on Iraq were already considered on that day (Goldenburg and Borger 2003). US Vice President Dick Cheney and Secretary of Defense Donald Rumsfeld recognised from the beginning that the 'war against terrorism' was an opportunity to restore what America had lost in Vietnam. As Maureen Dowd noted in the *New York Times*:

> The administration isn't targeting Iraq because of 9/11. It's exploiting 9/11 to target Iraq. This new fight isn't logical – it's cultural. It is the latest chapter in the culture wars, the conservative dream of restoring America's sense of Manifest Destiny... Extirpating Saddam is about proving how tough we are to a world that thinks we got soft when that last helicopter left the roof of the American embassy in Saigon in 1975.   (Dowd 2002)

This confidence was most manifest in Tony Blair's triumphant speech to the Labour Party conference in October 2001:

> The starving, the wretched, the dispossessed, the ignorant, those living in want and squalor from the deserts of Northern Africa to the slums of Gaza, to the mountain ranges of Afghanistan: they too are our cause. This is a moment to seize. The kaleidoscope has been shaken. The pieces are in flux. Soon they will settle again. Before they do, let us re-order this world around us...'   (Blair 2001b)

While the US and British establishments talked a good 'war on terror', they found it much more difficult to fight one. The war in Afghanistan illustrated the problem. Because the 'war on terror' was driven largely by a desire to reap domestic rewards through a show of strength, there was a lack of political and military strategy on the ground. The aims of the war were not clear, and like the Kosovo war, appeared to shift with every new media deadline. Initially the aim was to capture bin Laden, then to remove the Taliban regime, but despite the fire power, the daisy-cutters and the clusterbombs there was little sense of achievement.

It soon appeared that 9/11 had not established a new paradigm for the projection of power. There was no problem in bringing US firepower to bear, but the 'war against terrorism' in Afghanistan provided little new context of meaning or purpose. The conflict was shaped by the doctrine of humanitarian intervention, with the dropping of food parcels along with missiles and an emphasis on the humanitarian and human rights cause. Again, the critics argued that a humanitarian war could not be fought from 35,000 feet and the sight of the most powerful military power on earth carpet bombing one of the poorest countries did little to reassert a sense of moral mission.

The biggest problem was that the war in Afghanistan was not framed in a context that linked it with any positive vision of the future. The 'war on terror', like 'humanitarian intervention', was a policing operation, not the beginning of a revived sense of purpose. The artificial nature of the project and the lack of commitment it could inspire meant that rather than asserting its power the US risked further being discredited. The use of local Afghan warlords to hunt down bin Laden in the mountains of Tora Bora, widely blamed for allowing him to escape, was a humiliating failure for the US. The lack of willingness to commit US troops in a situation where casualties were feared possible undermined the projection of US power and the US success in imposing 'regime change'.

In the aftermath of Tora Bora, the US government was even keener to shift the emphasis to Iraq and 'wipe the slate clean'. There has been little focus on post-war Afghanistan and the Western-sponsored Karzai government has been hamstrung by the US lack of willingness to enforce his rule outside of the capital Kabul. Policy reports contrast the 'light footprint' of international control in the state in comparison to the resources put into the more high-profile protectorates of Bosnia and Kosovo (Chesterman 2002:3). The victory/defeat for the US in Afghanistan appears emblematic of the failure of the 'war on terror'. Every attempt to use the international sphere to regain a sense of domestic mission seemed only to make the problems worse. In this sense, it would seem that whatever happens to post-war Iraq, the US government is unlikely to reap any long-term political gain.

During the Iraq war it appeared that the American establishment could not even convince itself of a sense of Manifest Destiny, let alone the rest of the world. As London *Times* columnist Mick Hume asserted: 'the fall-out from the Culture Wars is not only felt on campuses and in high cultural circles. The calling into question of America's traditional values has a corrosive effect on every institution including the US military.' (Hume 2002) Rick Perlstein noted that the opposition to the war on Iraq did not came mainly from the public but the establishment itself:

> ...the foreign policy establishment seems distinctly uneasy about war in Iraq. The military establishment is not necessarily any more enthusiastic; Gen. Anthony Zinni, President Bush's own sometime Mideast envoy, has spoken repeatedly against invasion and in favour of containment. The Central Intelligence Agency has let its coolness to the invasion idea become known.   (Perlstein 2002)

The messy war in Afghanistan and the divisions within the US establishment over Iraq illustrate the difficulties of policy-making in the absence of a political or ideological framework. While there may have been a consensus over taking some action against Iraq, there was no coherent vision shaping US policy in the region and therefore little long-term consideration given to the consequences of embarking on military action.[6] As the 'war on terror' continues, the lack of any clear sense of the future has meant that political leaders have inevitably lowered their aspirations. Compare, for example, Blair's aspiration to seize the opportunity to 'reorder the world' with his defensive justification for war on Iraq, voiced at Prime Minister's questions in January 2003 that 'the threat is real, and if we don't deal with it, our weakness will haunt future generations' (White and Borger 2003). The 'war on terror' had now become more of a holding operation than a noble mission.

Without a prior consensus on national purpose, or a strong 'idea of the state' (Buzan 1991) – a sense of what society stands for – foreign wars can do little to rejuvenate a collective sense of purpose. Rather, they have revealed increasing divisions within the British and US establishments and highlighted that today even professional soldiers are often reluctant to make sacrifices without a national vision which they can find a collective meaning in (Josar 2003). This 'postmodern' malaise, the contrast between the vast material and military power of the US and UK governments and their inability to internally generate a strong sense of political legitimacy and a shared framework of meaning, was most apparent in the US government's orders that US soldiers should not raise the Stars and Stripes as they swept though Iraq (Watt 2003; Grigg 2003) and in the British government's decision not to hold a 'Victory Parade' in the wake of the military success (White 2003; see also *New York Times* 2003).

Far from providing a sense of purpose, lacking in the domestic sphere, the 'war on terror' has heightened the domestic sense of uncertainty. With US and British society regularly disrupted by panics over the next potential terrorist 9/11 – which could include anything from hijacked planes being flown into nuclear plants to dirty bombs or releases of anthrax, botchulism, ricin, smallpox and other potential deadly toxins – governments increasingly appear unable to assert authority. Rather than creating a sense of mission, the 'war on terror' has fed society-wide views of vulnerability and powerlessness. It was this sense of vulnerability, rather than opposition to the Iraq war itself, which led to the Spanish Aznar government being defeated in the immediate aftermath of the 3/11 train bombings in Madrid (Tremlett 2004).

The inability to establish a political project which can cohere society at home has meant that the projection of power abroad can no longer be cast within a framework of national interest, with states setting a clear agenda. It seems that the 'war on terror' has cast marginal fundamentalist terror groups in the role of agenda setters in the same way as 'humanitarian intervention' gave an exaggerated importance to 'principled issue' NGOs. While it may appear that nation-states are losing their capacity to assert their national interests and that non-state actors are in the driver's seat, a closer look suggests that the level of appearances may well confuse cause with effect.

## Conclusion

The lack of focus of the 'war on terror' clearly highlights the problems of articulating a national interest in international or domestic politics, even for the most powerful state in the world. The projection of power internationally by the United States and its allies appears to have no more connection to 'narrowly defined' national interests than the domestic exercise of power by leading Western governments, which also appears to lack any clear political programme. At the empirical level, it would seem that the advocates of 'postmodern' values and a new liberal internationalism have a valid point which critics of Great Power interests behind international intervention would be churlish to ignore.

This chapter has suggested, however, that neither traditional realism nor idealist constructivism can fully grasp the rise of moral and ethical concerns today because the explanation for this shift away from the articulation of national interests cannot be found in the international sphere. Constructivist and liberal commentators argue that nation-states can no longer pursue national interests because of the pressures of global civil society, which has forced morality and cosmopolitan ethics on to the agenda. However, rather than focusing analysis from the 'outside/in', explaining Western government policy-making as a response to new international pressures from non-state actors, it seems highly likely that the projection of national interests in the international sphere has been undermined more by domestic than international change.

The failure of the US and European establishments to find a post-Cold War framework of meaning for the projection of power has made realist explanations based on national interests look outdated. Constructivist approaches, which focus on the role of ideas, attempt to provide an explanation for the lack of fit between the military and economic strength of major Western powers and their capacity to pursue national interests in the international sphere. However, rather than highlight a lack of domestic capacity to cohere a projection of power abroad, they assume the lack of fit is a product of non-state, global civic actors, in the international sphere, which have blunted national interests and reordered state identities through the articulation of global civic norms and 'principled-issues'. The following chapter draws out the consequences of this perspective.

# 4
# Morality and Power

## Introduction

The clearest clash between global morality and international or state-based international rules has been over humanitarian intervention and the international enforcement of human rights protections. For constructivist theorists of global civil society, the shift in the debate between the values of sovereignty and non-intervention and those of intervention and individual rights protection demonstrates the growing capacity of moral values to constrain the interests of power. A lead article in *Foreign Affairs* argues: 'Humanitarian intervention...is perhaps the most dramatic example of the new power of morality in international affairs.' (Gelb and Rosenthal 2003:6) As Mary Kaldor asserts:

> The changing international norms concerning humanitarian intervention can be considered an expression of an emerging global civil society. The changing norms do reflect a growing global consensus about the equality of human beings and the responsibility to prevent suffering... Moreover, this consensus, in turn, is the outcome of a global public debate on these issues.   (Kaldor 2001b:110)

Crucial for the constructivist perspective on the existence of actually existing global civil society is the belief that this 'global public debate' takes place not on the terms of power but that of morality. Kathryn Sikkink writes that activities of non-state actors have been able to 'transform', 'modify' and 'reshape' the meaning of sovereignty because sovereignty is a product of a set of 'shared' or 'intersubjective understandings about the legitimate scope of state authority' (Sikkink 1993:413, 441).

The debate over international humanitarian intervention and the protection of human rights is at the core of the constructivist thesis. As Jack Donnelly argues, this dialogue is a 'promising sign for the future' because it is a debate which takes 'place largely within a space delimited by a basic moral commitment' to the human rights cause (Donnelly 1999:99–100).

Since the end of the Cold War, debate over international peacekeeping has been dominated by the question of the so-called 'right of humanitarian intervention'. Advocates of the right of intervention, largely from Western states, have tended to uphold universal ethical claims that new international norms, prioritising individual rights to protection, herald a new era of global civic duty and that the realist framework of the Cold War period, when state security was viewed as paramount, has been superseded. As Martin Shaw writes:

> The crucial issue, then, is to face up to the necessity which enforcing these principles would impose to breach systematically the principles of sovereignty and non-intervention... The global society perspective, therefore, has an ideological significance which is ultimately opposed to that of international society.   (Shaw 1994a:134–5)

In an attempt to codify and win broader international legitimacy for the new interventionist norms of the international society perspective, the International Commission on Intervention and State Sovereignty released a two volume report *The Responsibility to Protect* in December 2001. In the light of this report and broader developments in international security in the wake of 9/11, this chapter suggests that rather than a moral shift away from the rights of sovereignty, the dominance of the constructivist thesis of the negotiated redefinition of sovereignty, in fact, reflects an increasingly hierarchical balance of power in the international sphere. Justifications for new interventionist norms as a framework for ethical foreign policy are as dependent on the shifting international balance of power as much as the earlier doctrine of sovereign equality and non-intervention.

This chapter firstly recaps the constructivist thesis and then analyses the argument forwarded in *The Responsibility to Protect* report which suggests that sovereignty is being redefined on the basis of shifting global normative values. The following sections consider how the constructivist framework of the Report shifts the focus of debate from rights to responsibilities in order to create the basis for productive dialogue, and suggests that this confuses rather than clarifies the major implications of this debate for sovereign rights and international law. The chapter concludes with a discussion on the relationship between morality and power in the current international context.

## The constructivist thesis

As considered in Chapter 2, the focus of constructivist empirical research is on the changing policy practices of non-Western states while the policy practices of Western states are often assumed to be a reflection of the demands of transnational actors operating in global civil society. This research emphasis is the key to the constructivist approach which sees the normative agenda as driven by global civil society actors, rather than states. There is much less attention given to the shifts in the policies of Western states or of international financial institutions under the assumption that these merely confirm the power and the importance of 'principled-issue' actors who had already 'identified, documented, and denounced human rights violations and had pressurised foreign governments to become involved' (Sikkink 1993:436). Western states are assumed a priori to act for normative reasons: 'We posit, first, that the transnational human rights networks – in conjunction with international regimes and organisations as well as Western powers – are crucial in the early phases...' (Risse and Sikkink 1999:33)

There is little accounting for where the influence lies in the 'conjunction' – without the support of 'Western powers' the transnational actors may have much less capacity to put 'repressive regimes on the international agenda' or for 'empowering and strengthening the initially weak domestic opposition' (Risse and Sikkink 1999:34). What needs to be explained is how these normative values operate in relation to Western state interests rather than merely the idealised impact of values and norms on subordinate and peripheral states. The question is never raised because it is assumed that 'Western powers' are working in conjunction with transnational human rights networks and therefore they are not guided by the interests of power.

Martin Shaw, for example, argues that in the promotion of ethical values there is a 'new, partial congruence between Western state interests and worldwide democratic movements' (Shaw 2000:261 n.3). He asserts that morality and right unite the global citizen activists with Western interventionists: 'Only for peoples threatened by violence, and those in civil society in the West who identify them, are the prevention of war and the conquering of misery overriding values.' (Shaw 2000:268) Western states have, in this thesis, established new social identities constructed through cooperation and shared value norms. Mary Kaldor provides supportive argumentation, suggesting that Robert Cooper's thesis of 'new imperialism' is closely linked to the global civil society perspective: 'Robert Cooper's postmodern states are what I would call multi-lateral states. They are close to what Ian Clark calls 'globalized' states and what Ulrich Beck calls 'cosmopolitan' or post-national states.' (Kaldor 2003:137) According to Kaldor:

> There is evidence to suggest a strong correlation between the degree of globalisation (the extent of interconnectedness of trade, capital, people and organisations), multilateralism (signing and ratifying treaties, respecting international rules, joining international organizations) and the density of global civil society (membership in INGOs, hosting parallel summits, tolerating strangers).   (Kaldor 2003:138)

She suggests that in the West there is a 'virtuous circle' in which each factor may reinforce the others and that 'global civil society itself contributes to interconnectedness and presses government in multilateral directions' (Kaldor 2003:138).

In the constructivist approach the debate over sovereignty between Western powers and international institutions and non-Western states is taken out of any social or economic framework of understanding and seen as the outcome of ideas. In the crudest frameworks this is presented as a struggle between backward ideas and progressive ideas. In Andrew Linklater's words the debate about moving towards internationalising individual rights takes place between 'progressive state structures' which 'deploy their powers to realise such objectives' and 'states which block these developments [which] are not as enlightened' (Linklater 1998:175).

There is a belief among constructivist thinkers that a new framework of global normative regulation is in the process of development, based on the confluence of progressive interests of transnational networks and leading Western states. For the advocates of the emergence of a global civil society, the fact that leading Western states have made moves towards challenging the primacy of state sovereignty 'poses a challenge to the neo-realist claim that states are bound to be functionally similar given the constraints within international anarchy' (Linklater 1998:177). As Thomas Risse and Stephen C. Ropp argue:

> The interests and preferences of actors involved in protecting or violating human rights cannot simply be treated as externally given by objective material or instrumental power interests. Rather, we argue

that conflicts over human rights almost always involve the social identities of actors.  (Risse and Ropp 1999:236)

Whereas Western states have assumed new 'social identities' and are no longer power-seeking actors but allegedly willing to limit sovereignty, non-Western states are often perceived as failing to adapt their 'social identities' to the new context. In which case, international pressure and external intervention on the basis of human rights promotion then appears to be the result of the work of 'principled-issue' transnational actors either directly, through lobbying and publicity, or indirectly, through their influence on Western states and international institutions.[1] The essence of the constructivist approach is that, through the guidance of transnational actors, a new set of international social norms has been created:

> International human rights norms have become constitutive for modern statehood; they increasingly define what it means to be a 'state' thereby placing growing limits on another constitutive element of modern statehood, 'national sovereignty'.  (Risse and Ropp 1999:236)

For constructivist theorists, the clash between the ethical practices responding to the demands of global civic actors, for example through humanitarian intervention, and the protections of sovereignty formally upheld under the UN Charter Framework, highlights the growing dominance of morality over the interests of power. This apparent shift was highlighted in 1999 with the conflict over Kosovo. The novel ethical nature of the Kosovo war was emphasised by Vaclav Havel, speaking in April 1999:

> But there is one thing no reasonable person can deny: this is probably the first war that has not been waged in the name of 'national interests', but rather in the name of principles and values. If one can say of any war that it is ethical, or that it is being waged for ethical reasons, then it is true of this war. Kosovo has no oil fields to be coveted; no member nation in the alliance has any territorial demands on Kosovo; Milošević does not threaten the territorial integrity of any member of the alliance. And yet the alliance is at war. It is fighting out of a concern for the fate of others. It is fighting because no decent person can stand by and watch the systematic, state-directed murder of other people. It cannot tolerate

such a thing. It cannot fail to provide assistance if it is within its power to do so.   (Cited in Falk 1999a:848)

Although the military intervention led by NATO lacked formal legal authority in the absence of a UN Security Council mandate, the advocates of intervention claimed that the intervention was humanitarian and thereby had a moral legitimacy and reflected the rise of new international norms, not accounted for in the UN Charter (IICK 2000).

The view of dialogue through global civil society challenges both the realist view, that war is an inevitable result of shifting balances of power in an anarchic world, and the pluralism of the English School approach, which emphasises the consensual status quo framework of the UN Charter, which accords equal rights of protection to states regardless of their domestic political framework. Global civil society theorists stress that international peace and individual rights are best advanced through cosmopolitan frameworks through which states representing global civic values and rejecting power-politics act in conjunction with non-state actors to take a leading responsibility for ensuring the interests of common humanity (see ICISS 2001b:129–38).

The central question posed by the constructivist thesis, and highlighted in international discussions of the right of humanitarian intervention, is that of matching moral authority with legal and political legitimacy. This question is particularly acute in today's circumstances, when the legal framework of international society still reflects Cold War state-based collective security concerns rather than the individual rights posited in the global civil society thesis. Since the end of the Cold War attempts to reform the international legal order have met with resistance. Opponents of intervention, mainly non-Western states, have been sceptical of the grounds for privileging a moral justification for interventionist practices and expressed concern that this shift could undermine their rights of sovereignty and possibly usher in a more coercive, Western-dominated, international order. Following the Kosovo intervention the problem of overcoming the North-South, or 'have' versus 'have-not', division over coercive 'humanitarian intervention' and establishing a framework which could generate an international consensus has come to the fore (ICISS 2001a:vii).

## The responsibility to protect

The demand for international 'unity' around the basic questions and issues involved in 'humanitarian intervention' was sharply highlighted by United National Secretary-General Kofi Annan at the UN General Assembly in 1999 and again in 2000. In response to this demand, at the UN Millennium Assembly in September 2000 the Canadian Prime Minister Jean Chrétien announced that an independent International Commission on Intervention and State Sovereignty (ICISS) would be established to address the moral, legal, operational and political questions involved in developing broader international support for a new framework legitimising 'humanitarian intervention' (ICISS 2001a:vii; see also 2001b:341).[2] The Commission's mandate was, in general terms, 'to build a broader understanding of the problem of reconciling intervention for human protection purposes and sovereignty' and, more specifically, 'to try to develop a global political consensus on how to move from polemics...towards action' (ICISS 2001a:2). The project involved consultation with governments, NGOs, academics and policy think tanks across the world and resulted in the publication in December 2001 of the final report *The Responsibility to Protect* along with a supplementary volume *Research, Bibliography, Background* with more detailed findings (ICISS 2001a; 2001b).

The Report argued that in order to build an international consensus for acts of 'humanitarian intervention', which may be legitimate in the eyes of Western powers but not formally sanctioned by the United Nations, the discussion needed to be refocused. Rather than posing debate in the confrontational terms of human rights 'trumping' sovereignty or 'the right of intervention' undermining 'the right of state sovereignty', intervention should instead be seen as compatible with a renegotiated and redefined concept of sovereignty. The Commission explicitly relied on a constructivist framework to suggest that rationalist or realist conceptions of the international sphere as one of competition and conflicting interests of power were no longer relevant today, and suggested that the redefinition of sovereignty as 'responsibility' was an ethical universal devoid of power implications:

> The notion of responsibility itself entails fundamental moral reasoning and challenges determinist theories of human behaviour and international relations theory. The behaviour of states is not predetermined by systemic or structural factors, and moral justifications are not merely after-the-fact justifications or simply irrelevant. (ICISS 2001b:129)

Rather than powerful states forcing the question of rewriting the rules of intervention, the Commission posed the shift as one of moral and ethical values which empowered individuals, noting that the 'compelling normative claim that all individuals have inalienable human rights has spread far and wide...as the ideas embodied in the [Universal] Declaration [of Human Rights] have become weapons that the powerless have mobilised against the powerful' (ICISS 2001b:134–5).

The Commission argued that their perspective was not based on power but morality. The 'responsibility to protect' implied a duty on the state to act as a 'moral agent' (ICISS 2001b:136). It should be highlighted that the moral action of states is crucial to the constructivist thesis as the demands of global civil society can only be enforced by state action.[3] States which fail to act in a morally responsible manner and abuse the human rights of their citizens are then held to necessitate intervention by other states which 'are indeed capable of acting as agents of common humanity' (ICISS 2001b:136).

## Compatibility with state sovereignty

Central to the Commission's report is the assertion that it is important that language does not become a barrier to carrying the debate forward. For this reason, 'past debates arguing for or against a "right to intervene" by one state on the territory of another state [are] outdated and unhelpful'. The Commission prefers 'to talk not of a "right to intervene" but of a "responsibility to protect"' (ICISS 2001a:11). The old language is held to be unhelpful for three reasons: firstly, it 'necessarily focuses attention on the claims, rights and prerogatives of the potentially intervening states' rather than the urgent needs of potential beneficiaries; secondly, 'the familiar language does effectively operate to trump sovereignty with intervention at the outset' setting up a conflict between the rights of intervention and the rights of sovereignty; finally, previous discussion of the 'right to intervene' focused on the less popular military aspects of the global normative framework rather than prior preventive efforts or post-conflict assistance (ICISS 2001a:16). These three concerns are considered below.

### Rights of intervening powers?

This was a key problem faced by the Commission which was keen to assert that 'what is at stake here is not making the world safe for big powers, or trampling over the sovereign rights of small ones' (ICISS 2001a:11). Rather than giving rights to the Great Powers, the change in terminology reflects 'a change in perspective, reversing the perceptions inherent in the traditional language' (ICISS 2001a:17). The 'responsibility to protect' was held to imply an 'evaluation of the issues from the point of view of those seeking or needing support' (ICISS 2001a:17). The spotlight was now on the victims of abuses, rather than their potential saviours in the West.

The Report stressed the 'value of shifting from an emphasis on rights to responsibilities, which focuses attention on concrete measures that states might take to operationalise a meaningful right to protection for affected populations' (ICISS 2001b:127). While the traditional terminology of 'rights' was removed from debate (both the rights of the intervening state and the rights of states intervened in), 'rights' were smuggled back in and given to the individuals who have the 'right to protection'. Despite the protestations of the Commission, the report overtly argues that individual human rights 'trump' the rights of sovereignty:

> Rather than accept the view that all states are legitimate...states should only qualify as legitimate if they meet certain basic standards of common humanity... The implication is plain. If by its actions and, indeed, crimes, a state destroys the lives and rights of its citizens, it forfeits temporarily its moral claim to be treated as legitimate... [T]his approach [has been called] 'sovereignty as responsibility'. In brief, the three traditional characteristics of a state... (territory, authority, and population) have been supplemented by a fourth, respect for human rights.   (ICISS 2001b:136)

The focus on the 'rights of protection' and the 'concrete measures that states might take to operationalise' this right, in effect puts the emphasis on the intervening powers in exactly the same way as the more confrontational assertion of a 'right of intervention'. The only difference is that where the UN Charter right of non-intervention put the burden of justification on the powers intervening, as we shall see below, the concept of 'sovereignty as responsibility' puts the burden of justification on the state intervened in to substantiate its 'moral claim to be treated as legitimate'.

## Supporting sovereignty?

Rather than delegitimising state sovereignty the Commission asserts that the 'primary responsibility' rests with the state concerned. In many cases this responsibility will be carried out with the active partnership of the international community, and only if the state is unwilling or unable to address the problem, or work in cooperation with the international community, would the international community assume direct responsibility. The Commission states that, viewed in these terms, 'the 'responsibility to protect' is more of a linking concept that bridges the divide between intervention and sovereignty; the language of the 'right or duty to intervene' is intrinsically more confrontational' (ICISS 2001a:17).

In avoiding 'confrontation' the Commission seeks to preserve the 'importance' of sovereignty by recasting the right to self-government, no longer as a 'right' but as a 'responsibility'. In this way the Commission seeks to downplay its judgement that 'sovereignty is not absolute but contingent' and can be 'temporarily suspended' (ICISS 2001b:11). Rather than the traditional view that sovereignty implies non-interference, the redefined concept of 'sovereignty as responsibility' implies the right of interference if 'the community of responsible states' decides this to be in the interests of protection. The background report spells out that 'sovereignty then means accountability to two separate constituencies: internally, to one's own population; and internationally, to the community of responsible states' (ICISS 2001b:11). This shift in 'accountability' clearly has major implications for sovereignty because a power which is 'accountable' to another, external, body clearly lacks sovereign authority (Jackson 1990:32). As the Commission co-chairs note, this shift changes 'the essence of sovereignty, from control to responsibility' (Evans and Sahnoun 2002:101). The Commission attempts to avoid discussion of this fundamental downgrading of the importance of sovereignty through 'shifting the terms of the debate'.

As Alex Bellamy notes, the constructivist framework of analysis enables this redefinition of sovereignty to take place, going beyond the sterile binary oppositions of human rights or sovereignty, intervention or non-intervention (2003:327–8; see also Dunne and Wheeler forthcoming). Christian Reus-Smit argues that the redefinition of the question has been vital to allow constructivist theorists to move beyond the strict legal concern with international rights which mired English School theorists in an 'unsustainable and increasingly unproductive debate between pluralists and solidarists' (Reus-Smit 2002:489). Redefining the terms of the debate bypassed the 'sticking point' of the traditional legal and political defences of sovereign rights which were no longer held to be shared global moral norms.

### Non-military focus?

International consultations demonstrated that the kind of intervention favoured by non-Western states was not military but economic. Many non-Western states wanted more attention paid to preventive assistance in terms of foreign aid and development assistance. Some state representatives argued that if Western powers were so concerned with people's rights to protection, that they were willing to go to war, why then couldn't they show the same concern when it came to providing assistance to address the social and economic problems which were perceived to be at the heart of most Third World conflict?[4] In recognition of the deep suspicion raised by the military focus of the ethical priorities taken up by major world powers, the Commission hoped that shifting the focus 'should help make the concept of [military] reaction itself more palatable' (Evans and Sahnoun 2002:101).

The concerns of non-Western states for non-military forms of assistance are understandable, but their conception of the relationship involved seemed rather different from the Commission's intentions. Rather than providing much needed assistance to enable states to tackle problems themselves it would appear that the Commission saw non-military assistance as part of the internationally-mandated responsibilities involved in securing the protection .of individual rights. Arguing the support of the UN Charter, the Report asserted that Article 55 'explicitly recognises that solutions to international economic, social, health and related problems; international, cultural and educational cooperation; and universal respect for human rights are all essential for "the creation of conditions of stability and well-being which are necessary for peaceful and friendly relations among nations".' In which case, according to the Commission, none of these questions can be seen as purely domestic, rather than international, concerns. 'The Charter thus provides the foundation for a comprehensive and long-term approach to conflict prevention based on an expanded concept of peace and security.' (ICISS 2001a:22)

This broader 'responsibility' is seen to provide 'conceptual, normative and operational linkages between assistance, intervention and reconstruction' (ICISS 2001a:17). In fact, the Commission argued that it is 'the fundamental thesis of this report that any coercive intervention for human protection purposes is but one element in a continuum of intervention' (ICISS 2001a:67). The concept of a 'continuum of intervention' inevitably blurs the line between the domestic and the international spheres. In arguing that the international community not only has 'a responsibility to react' but also has a 'responsibility to prevent' and a 'responsibility to rebuild' the Commission makes external intervention more legitimate and extends the rights of a 'continuum' of mechanisms of less and more coercive international interference. These range from imposed human rights monitoring and aid conditionality to the use of sanctions, arms embargoes, war crimes tribunals, preventive deployment of peacekeeping forces and the threat of force (ICISS 2001b:28).

The Commission advocated a focus on 'root cause prevention' as a guide to the additional 'responsibilities' of preventive and post-conflict intervention. This form of preventive intervention would institute comprehensive Western regulation under the threat of military intervention if non-Western states were 'unwilling or unable to cooperate'. The Commission highlighted four areas where preventive intervention would be legitimate; the political, economic, legal and military.

In the political field, the Report stated that the needs and deficiencies that the international community would be responsible for addressing 'might involve democratic institution and capacity building, constitutional power-sharing, power-alternating and redistribution arrangements; confidence building measures...; support for press freedom and the rule of law; the promotion of civil society; and other types of similar initiatives' (ICISS 2001a:23). In the economic field, 'root cause prevention may also mean tackling economic deprivation and the lack of economic opportunities' through development assistance and cooperation or encouraging economic and structural reform (ICISS 2001a:23). In the legal sphere, this might mean international assistance in legal reform, law enforcement, or enhancing protections for vulnerable groups. In the military sphere, international assistance might be necessary to train military forces, promote disarmament, prohibit land mines etc.

The Commission recognised that some states may be unwilling to accept internationally-endorsed preventive measures 'even of the softest and most supportive kind' because of a fear that any 'internationalisation' of the problem will 'start down the slippery slope to intervention' (ICISS 2001a:25). Their response was an illuminating one. Firstly, they suggested that international policy makers demonstrate 'sensitivity' and 'acknowledge frankly' the 'inherently coercive and intrusive' character of many preventive measures, and secondly, they warned that states which 'resist external efforts to help may well, in so doing, increase the risk of inducing increased external involvement, the application of more coercive measures, and in extreme cases, external military intervention' (ICISS 2001a:25).

There was a clear contradiction between the Commission's focus on a broad 'responsibility to protect' derived from the expanded concept of peace and security of the UN Charter and their assertion that their 'objective overall is not to change constitutional arrangements or undermine sovereignty, but to protect them' (ICISS 2001a:25). While the 'objective' may not be to undermine sovereign status, the broader 'responsibilities' assumed by the international community over a wide range of issues would fundamentally alter the relationship between non-Western states and international institutions. The Report cited one analyst who noted: 'All of this points toward an international change comparable to decolonisation, but operating in reverse gear, a counter-reformation of international trusteeship.' (ICISS 2001b:199)

## Summary

Shifting the focus away from the 'rights' of states to intervene has also acted to shift the focus away from the 'rights' of states to protect their sovereignty. The Commission cast the 'responsibility to protect' in a way that blurred any clear division between the domestic and the international.[5] Under the guise of shifting attention to the 'requirements of those who need help or seek assistance' the Commissions' report fundamentally challenged the rights of sovereignty while shoring up Western claims of a new 'right' or 'responsibility' to intervene.

## The implications for international law

In its consultations, the Commission found an 'overwhelming consensus' that the UN Security Council was the most appropriate body to deal with questions of military intervention. The Report stated:

> If international consensus is ever to be reached about when, where, how and by whom military intervention should happen, it is very clear that the central role of the Security Council will have to be at the heart of the consensus. The task is not to find alternatives to the Security Council as a source of authority, but to make the Security Council work much better than it has.   (ICISS 2001a:49)

The majority opinion of the world's states is that if there is to be any exception to Security Council authorisation there would have to be 'unequivocal and agreed criteria and safeguards' (ICISS 2001b:377). The Report stated that it was its task to meet these testing requirements: 'Our purpose is not to license aggression with fine words, or to provide strong states with new rationales for doubtful strategic designs, but to strengthen the order of states by providing clear guidelines to guide concerted international action' (ICISS 2001a:35). The Commission argued that 'the task is to define, with as much precision as possible, what these exceptional circumstances are, so as to maximise the chances of consensus being reached in any given case' (ICISS 2001a:131).

The Commission did not start from the UN Charter rules on whether intervention is permissible but theorised the legitimacy of intervention from the starting point of the 'protection' of the potential victim. This enabled the Commission to come up with a set of moral criteria for military intervention which were held to exist independently of international law or any particular political decision or consensus in the Security Council. The political reality that there is no possibility of international consensus on an acceptable amendment of the UN Charter to justify or legalise 'humanitarian intervention' has meant that the search for independent justification through the development of 'consistent, creditable and enforceable standards' has inevitably been a fruitless one. The Report's discussion of the possible criteria reveals that rather than clarifying the question, the end product can only be vague and ambiguous 'ethical checklists' which, rather than clearly defining, and limiting, 'exceptional cases', can easily be used to further erode the need for UN authorisation (ICISS 2001a:11; 2001b:360).

The Commission argued that six criteria must be satisfied for military intervention to be justified on the grounds of a 'responsibility to protect': just cause, right intention, right authority, last resort, proportional means and reasonable prospects (ICISS 2001a:32). While most governments might agree that intervention without UN Security Council authorisation can only be permissible if these criteria are met, there is little consensus on how these might be interpreted. The final three clearly rely on highly subjective judgements, particularly in the case of pre-emptive or preventive interventions. Below, the central concepts of just cause, right intention and legitimate authority are discussed.

## Just cause?

The Commission stated that 'large scale loss of life, actual or apprehended' and 'large scale ethnic cleansing, actual or apprehended' constituted the two broad sets of circumstances which could justify military intervention for human protection purposes. However, the Commission recognised that even here there was no clarity and no consensus. Where there was an attempt to reach some clarity, the effect was to stretch any definition rather than restrict it. The Commission stated that the definition of 'large scale loss of life' should have no minimum limit and therefore they would 'make no attempt to quantify "large scale"'. Despite the vagueness of the justification, the Commission confidently asserted that: 'What we do make clear, however, is that military action can be legitimate as an anticipatory measure in response to clear evidence of likely large scale killing.' (ICISS 2001a:33)

The support for anticipatory military intervention places a high, some would say impossible, premium on reliable evidence. The Commission argued that ideally this would be provided by 'a universally respected and impartial non-government source'. However, there was none to be found. The International Committee of the Red Cross was seen as an 'obvious candidate' but the Commission found that it was 'absolutely unwilling to take on any such role' (ICISS 2001a:34–5). The Commission concluded that 'it is difficult to conceive of any institutional solution to the problem of evidence, of a kind that would put the satisfaction of the "just cause" criterion absolutely beyond doubt' (ICISS 2001a:35).

### Right intention?

The Commission stated that the primary purpose must be 'to halt or avert human suffering'. Any use of military force 'that aims from the outset' to alter borders, to advance a particular combatant group's claims, to overthrow a regime or to occupy territory would therefore be seen to lack the right intention. Doubts would also be raised over any actions undertaken by individual states without international support. However, there were major caveats. Although not a 'primary purpose' the Commission argued that 'effective intervention may require a change of political regime' and the occupation of territory under new protectorates, temporary international administrations and trusteeships. Under the rubric of 'averting human suffering' it would appear that few actions can be excluded.

Furthermore, the Commission argued that *realpolitik* dictated that any prohibition on self-interests must be heavily restricted. Rather than being a negative factor which counted against the legitimacy of any intervention, the Report suggested that self-interest could be seen as positive: 'if risks and costs of intervention are high and interests are not involved, it is unlikely that states will enter the fray or stay the course. Those who advocated action to protect human rights must inevitably come to grips with the nature of political self-interest to achieve good ends.' (ICISS 2001b:140) Similarly, the Report argued that if an intervention was 'ethically sound' then 'it is hard to see why it would not remain so if conducted by a single state' even if this was a hegemonic power 'especially as these are among the few countries with the power to project military force beyond their borders' (ICISS 2001b:141;186).

### Right authority?

The Commission used the criticism of many non-Western states to argue that the Security Council was in need of reform and was undemocratic and unrepresentative (ICISS 2001a:51).[6] However, while the Commission found 'significant support' amongst non-Western states in favour of making the UN system more representative of world opinion when it comes to the controversial question of military intervention, the Report took a different approach (ICISS 2001a:53; 2001b:377). The Commission explicitly argued against making the final authority more democratic:

> An inhibiting consideration always is the fear that the tiger of intervention, once let loose, may turn on the rider: today's intervener could become the object of tomorrow's intervention. The numerical majority of any collective organisation, almost by definition, will be the smaller, less powerful states, suspicious of the motives of the most powerful in their midst, and reluctant to sanction interference by the powerful against fellow-weaklings.   (ICISS 2001a:54)

These concerns were fully brought out in the consultation sessions in Africa, India, the Middle East, China and Russia.[7] However, despite the Commission's professed concern to listen to non-Western voices and opinions, the Report rejected the consensus that where there is no consensus in the Security Council the General Assembly under the 'Uniting for Peace' provisions should have the authority.[8] The Commission argued: 'the practical difficulty in all this is to contemplate the unlikelihood, in any but [a] very exceptional case, of a two-thirds majority, as required under the Uniting for Peace procedure' (ICISS 2001b:53). Instead, the Commission favoured granting legitimacy to interventions by ad hoc coalitions or individual states acting without Security Council or General Assembly approval. Although its brief was to attempt to forge a consensus on this question, the Commission was forced to admit that such interventions 'do not – it would be an understatement to say – find wide favour' (ICISS

2001b:54). The Commission ostensibly abandoned its brief when confronted with the crucial question of authorisation, recognising that it was impossible to establish a consensus around a position which was only held by a minority of states:

> As a matter of political reality, it would be impossible to find consensus, in the Commission's view, around any set of proposals for military intervention which acknowledged the validity of any intervention not authorised by the Security Council or General Assembly.   (ICISS 2001b:54–5)

However the Commission argued that this 'political reality' cannot be allowed to undermine international idealism. The Report asserted that although the UN must make some concessions to political realism 'the organisation is also the repository of international idealism, and that sense is fundamental to its identity' (ICISS 2001b:52). This ideal, which gives the UN its moral legitimacy, must not be restricted by the selfish interests of the majority of states if 'unbridled nationalism and the raw interplay of power' are to 'be mediated and moderated in an international framework...dedicated to protecting peace and promoting welfare – of achieving a better life in a safer world, for all' (ICISS 2001b:52).

The Report affirmed that: 'It is a real question in these circumstances where lies the most harm: in the damage to international order if the Security Council is bypassed or in the damage to that order if human beings are slaughtered while the Security Council stands by.' (ICISS 2001b:55) The lack of consensus on intervention should not prevent action being taken on moral grounds, even if this meant undermining the institution of the UN. The supplementary volume clarified the 'moral consequences of too rigid an attachment to the non-intervention rule without Security Council imprimatur' and asserted that 'opposition by one or more of the permanent members', or, by implication, that of over a third of the General Assembly, should not prevent intervention as this would 'fly in the face of the moral impulses behind the sovereignty-as-responsibility doctrine' (ICISS 2001b:137).

## Summary

The Report highlighted two trends which made the UN central to the current uncertainty regarding the legitimacy of intervention. Firstly, the fact that the Security Council has steadily expanded the mandate of legitimate intervention by means of the redefinition of 'threats to international peace and security'. Secondly, the increasingly apparent lack of authority of the UN to enforce its mandate independently of the will of major powers.[9] This has led to ambiguous resolutions which have, in effect, given a free reign to the states which acted to enforce them:

> A series of ambiguous resolutions and conflicting interpretations have arisen over the extent and duration of the authority conferred by the Security Council. These were most notable in the operations against Iraq throughout the 1990s and in the Kosovo War in 1999. The weakening of the formal requirements may have undermined the substantive provisions of the Charter's collective security system and contributed to facilitating actions in advance of Council authorisation, or indeed without it.   (ICISS 2001b:120)

In this context, it appears that the shift towards intervention under the 'responsibility to protect' is as much a pragmatic response to changes in the balance of power internationally as it is a response based on concern for the world's victims. If the UN Security Council does not reach a consensus on intervention the Secretary-General has warned that 'there is a grave danger' that the Security Council will be bypassed, as over Kosovo (and later Iraq). The Commission argues that if the UN Security Council 'fails to discharge its responsibility' then it is 'unrealistic to expect that concerned states will rule out other means': 'If collective organisations will not authorise collective intervention against regimes that flout the most elementary norms of legitimate governmental behaviour, then the pressures for intervention by ad hoc coalitions or individual states will surely intensify.' (ICISS 2001a:55) As if predicting the future debates over Iraq, the Commission essentially recognised that there was little to stop the US and its allies from ignoring the UN Security Council and taking action against the sovereignty of non-Western states. In this context the Security Council 'veto' was not a veto at all and its use or threatened use would merely expose the fact that military intervention is dictated by 'might' rather than 'right'.

In arguing against the Security Council veto, the Commission focused on the dangers of the UN being sidelined by the major powers, but it gave little consideration of the problems this would lead to in terms of turning the UN into a rubber stamp for legitimising unilateral action by the US and its allies (either before or after intervention takes place). As Richard Falk and David Krieger argue:

> There are two main ways to ruin the UN: to ignore its relevance in war/peace situations, or to turn it into a rubber stamp for geopolitical

operations of dubious status under international law or the UN Charter. Before September 11, Bush pursued the former approach; since then – by calling on the UN to provide the world's remaining superpower with its blessings for an unwarranted war – the latter. (Falk and Krieger 2002)

It would appear that in seeking to ensure that the UN remains central to legitimising intervention, by giving UN legitimacy to any such intervention independently of the UN's political role in building an international consensus, the Commission runs the risk of discrediting the UN, rather than ensuring that it works 'better'.

## Post-9/11

The Commission was keen to assert the distinction between the 'responsibility to protect' and the 'war on terror'. However, it is increasingly apparent that the arguments developed by the Commission in support of the constructivist thesis appear to have been fully appropriated by the neo-conservative 'hawks' in the Washington establishment. Despite trying to distance the discussion around 'responsibility to protect' from the 'war on terror' the underlying concern with Great Power international regulation around preemption and prevention is clear. As the Report notes: 'Preventive strategies are appealing both from the point of view of a liberal humanitarian ethos and that of a *realpolitik*, national-security logic.' (ICISS 2001b:27)

It would appear that the advocates of the constructivist ethical case do not have a monopoly on the view that it is ideas that drive power rather than self-interest. George W. Bush has argued that moral universalism is a guide to state action in very similar words to those used in the Report:

Some worry that it is somehow undiplomatic or impolite to speak the language of right and wrong. I disagree. Different circumstances require different methods, but not different moralities. Moral truth is the same in every culture, in every time, and in every place. Targeting innocent civilians for murder is always and everywhere wrong. Brutality against women is always and everywhere wrong. There can be no neutrality between justice and cruelty, between the innocent and the guilty. We are in a conflict between good and evil, and America will call evil by its name. By confronting evil and lawless regimes, we do not create a problem, we reveal a problem. And we will lead the world in opposing it.   (Bush 2002b)

The concept which has most directly linked the 'war on terror' and the 'responsibility to protect' has been that of the danger posed by 'failed states'. For example, the British Foreign Secretary, Jack Straw, has argued that non-Western states could be assessed on a 'continuum of failure' based on preventive concerns similar to those expressed in the Commission's Report – relating to their capacity to provide security, effective governance and the rule of law and respect for human rights and economic growth, education and welfare. He argues that preventive intervention will often be necessary: 'rather than waiting for states to fail, we should aim to avoid state failure wherever possible... [P]revention is better than cure. It is easier, cheaper and less painful for all concerned.' (Straw 2002) The central theme of 'prevention', and the rejection of Cold War policies of containment for more interventionist policies, was also emphasised in the new US national security strategy, launched in September 2002, highlighting the new consensus around one of the central claims of the Commission's Report, the legitimacy of anticipatory strikes.[10] The shared theme of pre-emptive intervention demonstrates how easily the moral justification for intervention stands independently of, and inevitably undermines, the consensual framework of international law (see further Chandler 2002:185–90).

The lengthy public preparations for war against Iraq, although posed in the context of the 'war on terror' were also clearly shaped by the ongoing discussion around the imposition of global civic norms:

Firstly, the legitimacy of the UN Security Council was raised consistently, with US threats to take unilateral measures. George W. Bush consistently used the 'new perspective' and language of the Commission to demand that the United Nations met its' 'responsibilities' regarding Iraq. In his September 2002 address to the General Assembly, for example, Bush threatened that failure to support US action against Iraq, over the 'repression of its own people, including the systematic repression of minorities', in breach of Security Council resolutions, would make the United Nations 'irrelevant' (Bush 2002c).

Secondly, the military intervention was clearly posed in the terminology of the 'responsibility to protect' rather than traditional warfighting, as George Bush stated to the world's press in his 2003 New Year message at Fort Hood, in Texas, the largest military base in the US: 'Should we be forced to act...[US troops] will be fighting not to conquer anybody, but to liberate people.' (Cited in Borger 2003) The US threat to 'liberate' the people of Iraq raised inevitable questions about the accountability of the new post-imperial 'duty of care' implicit in the 'responsibility to protect' (ICISS 2001b:361). John Reid, the British Labour Party chairman, similarly emphasised that the UK government's fifth war in as many years was a product of the belief in international responsibilities as well as rights: 'We not only have rights to defend in the world, but we also have responsibilities to discharge; we are in a sense our brother's keeper globally.' (cited in Kampfner 2003)

## Legitimising power

Today, in purely pragmatic terms, it is far easier for Western powers to intervene abroad without risking a larger conflagration, whatever the mix of motivational reasons.[11] It would appear that the UN Charter restrictions on the use of force depended not only on the moral legitimacy of international law but also on the balance of power during the Cold War.[12] However, while there is little barrier to the assertion of US power around the world, as considered in Chapter 3, there is, as yet, no framework which can legitimise and give moral authority to new, more direct forms of Western regulation. The crisis of a legitimate framework would appear to be one dynamic driving the convergence of morality and power, whether expressed in the 'responsibility to protect' or the 'war on terror'. This crisis has provided the context in which the morally-based ideas of global civil society could move from being a marginal concern into the mainstream.

The less certainty there is regarding the international legal and political framework the more morality and ethics have come into play in an attempt to provide the lacking framework of legitimacy. It is no coincidence that the first modern moral war 'fought not for territory but for values', as UK Prime Minister Tony Blair described the war over Kosovo, was also fought without UN Security Council authorisation (Blair 1999). Rather than being condemned for its illegality, the Kosovo crisis was held by many leading Western government officials to have illustrated the growing importance of morality and ethics in international relations.[13] A clear example of the importance of moral or ethical legitimacy where the legal and political framework of the UN is disputed was provided by the 2003 Iraq conflict. Tony Blair, faced with the difficulty of winning the legal arguments, domestically and at the UN, increasingly emphasised the moral argument against leaving Saddam Hussein in power and the strength and honesty of his personal moral conviction.[14] The gap between what is considered to be 'morally legitimate' and what is permissible under international law would appear to reflect the transformation of the international balance of power; the world in 2004 is very different from that of 1945, when the UN Charter regime was established.

## Morality and power

Over recent years the legitimisation of intervention through claims of protecting new global norms has clashed with post-war UN Charter international law restrictions on interference in the internal affairs of sovereign nation-states. The 2000 report of the Independent International Commission on Kosovo acknowledged the gap between international law and the practice of leading Western states and suggested 'the need to close the gap between legality and legitimacy' (IICK 2000:10). However, rather than proposing to extend the formal reach of international law, the Commission sought to justify a new moral conception of 'legitimacy', one which differed from formal legality. They described their doctrinal proposal for humanitarian intervention as 'situated in a gray zone of ambiguity between an extension of international law and a proposal for an international moral consensus', concluding that 'this gray zone goes beyond strict ideas of *legality* to incorporate more flexible views of *legitimacy*' (IICK 2000:164).

That international commission was followed by the International Commission on Intervention and State Sovereignty, which held further discussions on the question throughout 2001.[15] These discussions, outlined above, have highlighted that even without any international consensus, formal legal equality between sovereign states is being fundamentally undermined by current 'developments' in international law. In a typical ICISS consultation panel, leading policy-advisor, Oxford professor Adam Roberts pointedly noted that it would be a mistake to 'focus mainly on general doctrinal matters' regarding rights under formal international law:

> The justification for a particular military action, if it is deemed to stand or fall by reference to the question of whether there is a general legal right of intervention, is likely to be in even more difficulty than it would be if legal considerations were balanced in a more *ad hoc* manner.   (Roberts 2001:2)

He recognised that in the current international context, where 'there is no chance of getting general agreement among states about the types

of circumstances in which intervention may be justified', it was necessary to counterpose 'powerful legal and moral considerations' (Roberts
2001:3; 13). The attempt to resolve the clash between the partial
demands of Western powers and the universal form of law means that
the advocates of new global norms, allegedly legitimised by global civic
actors, assert the need for new, more flexible legal forms:

> It may be for the best that the question of a right of humanitarian
> intervention, despite its undoubted importance...remains shrouded
> in legal ambiguity. While there is no chance of a so-called right of
> humanitarian intervention being agreed by a significant number of
> states...answers to the question of whether in a particular instance
> humanitarian intervention is viewed as legal or illegal are likely to
> depend not just on the circumstances of the case...but also the per-
> spectives and interests of the states and individuals addressing the
> matter: in other words, they are not likely to be uniform.   (Roberts
> 2001:13–14)

Whether a military intervention is 'legal' is increasingly held to be a
matter of 'the perspectives and interests' of those involved. This viewpoint, implicitly adopted by the International Commission, is an open
argument for law-making by an elite group of Western powers sitting
in judgement over their own actions.

The constructivist theorists allege that this 'ethical' framework can
lead to a more equal society, as any state can be pressurised by global
civic actors and Western states, once support for new moral or ethical
norms are established. However, it is the larger and more powerful
states which will have the resources and opportunities to intervene
against allegedly recalcitrant states, whereas weaker states will be
unable to take on interventionist duties on behalf of 'global citizens'.
The Independent International Commission on Kosovo, for example,
stated that 'not only is the interventionary claim important, but also
the question of political will, perseverance, and capabilities' (IICK
2000:169). The question of will and capacity are commonly highlighted as crucial to the legitimacy of military intervention. As
Ramesh Thakur, vice rector of the United Nations University in
Tokyo, argues, if there is no normative consensus on intervention
there has to be 'realistic assessments of our capacity to coerce recalcitrant players' (Thakur 2001:43). This approach sets up the scenario
where intervention is the prerogative of the powerful against the
weak.

This flexible and multi-layered framework, where the strict hierarchies of international law are absent, and there are no established frameworks of accountability in decision-making, undermines the UN Charter protections for non-Western states. The realities of unequal power relations mean that the more flexible decision-making is, and the less fixed international law, the easier it is for more powerful states to dictate the international agenda. International regulation, which is no longer based on sovereign equality, means excluded states will no longer have the opportunity to have a say in or consent to international regulation, abolishing the universal equality of international law (Chandler 2000b).

The restrictions of formal equality in the international sphere and of non-intervention in the affairs of weaker states will have disappeared but no other constitutional framework will have replaced it. This does not mean that we will have international anarchy, but it does indicate a return to the days of 'might equals right' where the only limits on the capacity of major states to exert their influence internationally will be their ability to enforce their wishes. Smaller and weaker states were always under the influence of larger powers. The difference today is that it is increasingly difficult to call on international law as a formal barrier to direct intervention and domination.

The close relationship between power and morality is not a contradictory one. *The Responsibility to Protect* demonstrates that while morality can work in the service of power the opposite relationship cannot apply. It may well be that: 'A settled principle of ethical reasoning is that "ought implies can".' (ICISS 2001b:150) However, the Commission recognised that when it came to international relations 'it would be foolish to ignore the reality' (ICISS 2001b:150). For example, even if all the Commission's criteria for intervention were met, military intervention against any of the five permanent members of the Security Council or other major powers would not be justifiable on prudential grounds (ICISS 2001b:143). Nevertheless, 'the reality that interventions may not be mounted in every case where there is justification for doing so, is no reason for them not to be mounted in any case' (ICISS 2001a:37). It may appear that this adaptation to the reality of power politics by the Commission is not an insurmountable problem for the claim of emerging new global civic norms. It is clear that waging war against major powers for human protection purposes could easily result in triggering a larger conflict and even greater loss of life.

However, the Commission seeks both to have its cake and to eat it. If states can only be guaranteed to act morally through their

'accountability' to international society and the threat of intervention, there can be no guarantee that major powers, immune to
'accountability' through such coercion, will not abuse their powers
(ICISS 2001b:136). As Andrew Linklater notes:

> Debates about whether this commitment allows the strong to inter-
> vene in societies where certain practices contravene this [human
> rights] principle inevitably arise at this point, but this is not the
> primary issue. Ensuring that the most powerful groups in inter-
> national society honour this cosmopolitan principle in their own
> relations with the weak is a prior ethical consideration.   (Linklater
> 1998:103)

Those who argue the constructivist case that non-state actors have
been successful in morally redefining the meaning of sovereignty can
only bypass the problem of power through translating the question
into one of ethics. There has to have been a 'prior ethical consideration', a starting assumption, that the most powerful states are also the
most ethical in order for power to be seen to be enforcing ethics (rather
than the other way around).

If there can be no guarantee of the 'morality' of the actions of major
powers it makes little sense to celebrate the dismantling of the UN
Charter restrictions on the use of force as a victory for moral dialogue
led by civic actors. The assumption that major powers, tasked with
intervening as 'good international citizens', will act with higher moral
legitimacy than powers which lack military and economic resources,
relies on morality directly correlating with power, i.e., 'right equalling
might'. The constructivist assumption that in the post-Cold War world
'right equals might' is little different from the realist doctrine that
'might equals right'. As the International Commission itself notes
'changing the language of the debate...does not of course change the
substantive issues' (ICISS 2001b:12).

## Conclusion

The problems with the constructivist assumption of the growing coa-
lescence of the demands of morality and power have only been sharply
posed with the replacement of the Clinton administration with that of
George W. Bush, particularly with the Bush doctrines of unilateral
intervention and pre-emptive action. David Clark, former UK Foreign
Office special adviser, wrote in the *Guardian* of the problems the liberal

internationalists have in defending the constructivist thesis (Clark 2003). The morality of the intervention thesis depended on US power being seen as a force for good in the world rather than as a projection of power and self-interest:

> As long as US power remains in the hands of the Republican right, it will be impossible to build a consensus on the left behind the idea that it can be a power for good. Those who continue to insist that it can, risk discrediting the concept of humanitarian intervention...the problem is this: the interventionists who supported the Iraq war want those of us who didn't to believe that George Bush is a "useful idiot" in the realisation of Blair's humanitarian global vision. We can only see truth in the opposite conclusion. (Clark 2003)

Clark argues that, with neo-conservatives in power in the US, it is difficult to believe in the liberal constructivist thesis that power is serving morality, rather than the realist thesis that morality is serving power. Mary Kaldor claims that George Bush's 'war on terror' is 'profoundly inimical to global civil society' and is 'an attempt to re-impose international relations', i.e., the logic of a state framework. For Kaldor, America is the 'last nation-state' (Kaldor forthcoming). She implicitly argues that while the rest of the world would be in favour of new global civic norms, one state is ruining the party by emphasising the importance of power. However, this critique is not a critique of idealist interpretations of the influence of actually existing global civil society; it is a critique of America. American power appears to be the only barrier to the realisation of the idealist vision of a fairer, more ethical, world where power relations have no place.

Unfortunately, it is unlikely that the 'problem of America' will entirely undermine the consensus of support for idealist constructivist approaches to the international sphere. Morality may be the last refuge of the powerful, because it can provide legitimacy to actions which undermine the constraints of the rule of law and sovereign political equality. However, more importantly, power is also the last refuge of the idealists.

In today's context, where there are few apparent political alternatives, it seems that moral change depends on the powerful, rather than the struggles of the powerless. Ironically, the strength of the constructivist consensus, on the moral action of major state powers, reflects the lack of an actually existing global society capable of independently setting the international agenda. Despite arguing that their moral schemas to extend the notion of global civil society are reflected in actually existing international relations, constructivist theorists of global civil society are inevitably forced to appeal to the powerful to implement and impose them. This is highlighted in the critical analyses of Hopgood (2000), Baker (2002b), Chandler (2000b; 2002) and others.

As considered in the chapters above, attempts to empirically substantiate the existence of an actually existing global civil society have always tended to exaggerate the influence of non-state actors. In Chapter 8 it will be suggested that this is because even the empiricist approaches to global civil society are overly influenced by the normative concerns which underpin their work. These concerns suggest that the current difficulties faced by liberal constructivist theorists will do little to undermine the consensus behind their approach. In fact, as will be discussed in Part II, it is the normative project of global civil society which drives the idealist constructivist re-representation of power relations.

# Part II
# The Normative Project

# 5
# The Communicative Realm

•

## Introduction

Constructivist approaches focus on empirical analysis and attempt to straddle the two worlds of rationalist international relations theory and normative non-rational communicative approaches. As argued in the foregoing chapters this approach has some useful descriptive insights but offers little in the way of understanding the interplay between morality and power in international relations.

Where the descriptive or empirical project of actually existing global civil society struggles to apply an idealist top-coat to the international order, the normative project of global civil society has no difficulty in accepting that we live in an international world shaped by power inequalities. Rather than communicative relations overlaying those of power and inequality, normative approaches argue that an alternative moral force which can challenge and restrain the amoral world of international relations can only develop in isolation or separation from the world of states and power politics.

The normative nature of global civil society theorising is rooted in its rejection of the instrumental interests of the international sphere of state-orientated *realpolitik* and the primacy given to alternative transnational forms of engagement, based on communicative rationality. Where realism argues that morality acts in the service of power, and constructivist approaches argue that power increasingly acts in the service of moral ideals, the normative project of global civil society counterposes the worlds of morality and power, separating them into two distinct spheres.

Global civil society as a normative project avoids some of the empirical and analytical problems associated with the work of the constructivist theorists. Mary Kaldor argues that, in this respect, the concept of global or transnational civil society 'is less a descriptive or analytical term and more a political project' (Kaldor 1999b:195). It is a political project in the sense that its advocates seek to assert universal values and global concerns in the international sphere, in a direct political challenge to the particular, or instrumental, interests pursued by states either individually or through international organisations. These universal values are held to be established through a communicative, rather than an instrumental, approach; in the global dialogue and global interaction of civil society actors.

This chapter outlines the nature of the normative project and the basis on which global civil society is held to establish an alternative political approach, based on the communicative realm of 'global space', freed from the territorial exclusions of state-based politics. It particularly focuses on the importance of Jürgen Habermas' work, which is drawn on to establish a set of communicative values and global norms, which form the basis of the normative critique of present international practices. The concluding sections outline the limitations of this political project, highlighting the gap between the universal norms established by the theorists of global civil society and the agency of global civic actors. It will be suggested that this gap, between normative values and subjective agency, questions the claims made for these approaches. As will be drawn out further in the following chapters, this concern applies both to global civil society approaches which attempt to build their alternative political project starting from 'bottom-up' radical activism and those which start from the need for 'top-down' global governance.

## The normative political project

The normative attraction of global civil society appears to be the development of an alternative way of doing politics. This is heralded as the birth of a new type of politics and political discourse, one which is not based on states and rejects the formal political competition for power based on instrumental rationality.

Leading normative theorists of global civil society, John Keane and Mary Kaldor, argue that the normative aspects of the global civil society project are more important than the empirical reality. Keane argues that global civil society has an 'elusive, idealtypisch quality': 'the concept of global civil society is infinitely "purer" and much more abstract than the form and content of actually existing global civil society' (Keane 2003:7–8):

> For purposes of descriptive interpretation...it is best to use the concept carefully as an ideal-type – as an intentionally produced mental construct or 'cognitive type'... When the term global civil society is used in this way, as an ideal-type, it properly refers to a dynamic non-governmental system of interconnected socio-economic institutions that straddle the whole earth...with the deliberate aim of drawing the world together in different ways. These non-governmental institutions and actors tend to pluralise power and to problematise violence; consequently their peaceful or 'civil' effects are felt everywhere.   (Keane 2003:8)

Mary Kaldor admits that the normative aspirations she has for global civil society differ from the 'real' or 'actually existing civil society' (the subject of constructivist theorising):

> This definition of civil society is both an aspiration and a description of a partial and emergent reality. It presupposes that the moral autonomy of individuals does not imply selfish behaviour and it encompasses the potential for human beings to develop institutions that express universally agreed norms based on actual discursive practice... 'Real' civil society or 'actually existing' civil society is a realm bombarded by images and influences, perpetually 'colonized' both by political salesmanship and consumerist pressures...the space for deliberation and discussion is constantly subject to invasion.   (Kaldor 2003:46)

Kaldor's definitional starting point, the 'moral autonomy' of those engaged in a discursive sphere, where non-instrumental 'good-tempered' conversation takes place, is explicitly based on a normative desire rather than empirical grounding. It is important to emphasise that, for the normative theorists of global civil society, the subject at the centre of the theoretical study, i.e., what is 'defined' as global civil society, is a set of varying 'ideal' normatively-derived characteristics, rather than anything solely derived from the 'real' or 'actually existing' object of study (as is the case with constructivist approaches considered in Part I).

### 'Global space'

The key point about the normative project of global civil society is the construction of a new global space for politics which is institutionally separate from the political frameworks of both the state and the inter-national, or inter-state, system. The idea of global civil society as a dis-tinct 'space' is crucial to the theoretical assertions regarding its moral distinctiveness.

To describe this new 'space', often normative theorists use the abstract notion of 'globality', which posits the idea of a non-state, non-territorial space. Jan Aart Scholte argues:

> ...globality refers to a particular kind of social space – namely, a realm that substantially transcends the confines of territorial place, territorial distance, and territorial borders. Whereas territorial spaces are mapped in terms of longitude, latitude, and altitude, global rela-tions transpire in the world as a single place, as one more or less seamless realm. Globality in this sense has a 'transworld' or 'trans-border' quality.   (Scholte 2002:286)

This new 'kind of social space' is alleged to carry within it certain implicit values, values which oppose those of older 'territorial' spaces. For Scholte, globalisation has not just undermined the power of states but also 'loosened some important cultural and psychological under-pinnings of sovereign statehood' with some people giving 'superterrito-rial values', for example, those of human rights or environmental concerns, a higher priority than the territorial interests of sovereignty (Scholte 2002:288). This global space is often seen to be occupied by non-governmental actors interacting independently of government. As Ronnie Lipschutz argues:

> What exactly is encompassed by the concept of global civil society? To find it, we have to look for political spaces other than those bounded by the parameters of the nation-state system. The spatial boundaries of global civil society are different, because its autonomy from the constructed boundaries of the state system also allows for the construction of new political spaces.   (Lipschutz 1992:393)

This separate global space is defined not by geographical or spatial limits but by ideological ones, by adherence to global values rather than the particularisms of place:

> Surrounded by global symbols and global events, current genera-tions think of the planet as home far more than their forbears did...

We no longer live in a territorial*ist* society. Rather, territorial spaces now coexist and interrelate with global spaces.  (Scholte 2002:286)

For the advocates of global civil society, changes in the media have been of central importance in the emergence of global civil society or 'the consciousness of a global community' (Kaldor 2003:104; see also Shaw 1996). Analysts assert that whereas the 'imagined community' of nations was created by technological developments, for example, the printing press (Anderson 1991), new information technology, which can make people aware of events on the other side of the earth at the same time as they actually happen, has radically transformed people's consciousness from the national to the global level. Gearóid Ó Tuathail argues: 'Global space becomes political space. Being there live is everything. The local is instantly global, the distance immediately closes. Place-specific struggles become global televisual experiences'. (Cited in Kaldor 2003:104) Keane similarly describes the creation of globality as a result of a change in consciousness; today, global civil society is 'the image of ourselves' as involved in a political project 'carried out on a global scale' (Keane 2003:1):

> Of great importance is the fact that these cross-border patterns have the power to stimulate awareness among the world's inhabitants that mutual understanding of different ways of life is a practical necessity, that we are being drawn into the first genuinely bottom-up transnational order, a global civil society, in which millions of people come to realise, in effect, that they are incarnations of world-wide webs of interdependence...  (Keane 2003:17)

The transformation of consciousness is key to the normative global civil society argument. This is because the creation of a global space is at the same time, explicitly or implicitly, a normative space. As Kaldor states, 'the emergence of a common global consciousness' puts an 'emphasis on human agency' (Kaldor 2003:112). This is drawn out further by Martin Shaw:

> By global, we mean not just transformed concepts of time and space but the new social meaning that these have involved. I propose that we understand this as the development of a *common consciousness of human society on a world scale*. We mean an increasing awareness of the totality of human social relations as the largest constitutive framework of all relations. We mean that society is increasingly

constituted primarily by this inclusive framework – rather than by distinct tribes, nations or religious communities although all of these remain in increasingly complex and overlapping ways within global society.   (Shaw 2000:11–12)

For Shaw, it is the growing complexity of experienced life, under the processes of globalisation, which has impacted on human conscious-ness, undermining 'particularist' perspectives:

Fractures in human society...appear less determinate... Tensions reappear in novel terms, which are increasingly relativized by the greater consciousness of the global human whole... there is a power-ful new impetus behind those who demonstrate the mutuality of all these human viewpoints. Thus partiality is exposed, and particular-ist visions are forced to address commonality.   (Shaw 2000:26)

As Yoshikazu Sakamoto asserts, it is 'the creation of a global perspec-tive and values in the depths of people's hearts and minds, [which is] establishing the idea of a global civil society.' (Sakamoto 1991:122) Similarly, for Keane, peoples' awareness of global interconnectedness lays the basis of the normative space of global civil society. The com-plexity of the global means that: 'For its participants...this society nur-tures a culture of self-awareness about the hybridity and complexity of the world... They are more or less reflexively aware of its *contingency*.' (Keane 2003:15–16) Keane suggests that the number of 'globally aware' people will grow and with this the strength of the global norms of global civil society:

While most others have not (yet) thought over the matter, or don't much care, or are too cynical or self-preoccupied to open their eyes and ears, the aggregate numbers of those who are globally aware are weighty enough to spread awareness that global civil society exists; that it is a force to be reckoned with...   (Keane 2003:16)

### From global space to global agency

Despite the stress on human agency by normative global civil society theorists, the starting point of a separate 'global space' appears to rely as much on the subject-less agency of globalisation as that of many mainstream international relations approaches. The mere fact of being global often appears to be a positive and progressive feature. In this way, almost by definitional fiat, global civil society assumes a moral importance through being distinct from the world of states. Paul Ghils, for example, argues, this makes 'civil society and its transnational networks of associations...the *universum* which competing nations have never succeeded in creating' (Ghils 1992:429). Martin Shaw asserts that the 'idea of the global' in itself has a 'positive meaning' (Shaw 2000:7). He expands:

> The global is the largest and most inclusive spatial framework of social relations – and, interplanetary exploration apart, the maximum possible framework. Its development represents the partial overcoming of the major divisions of the world – cultural as well as territorial. Precisely for these reasons, globality includes both the spatially and non-spatially defined differentiations of the world.   (Shaw 2000:71)

The space or 'spatial framework' of the global is held to be a progressive space because it is the most inclusive, a space which is shared by every diverse identity. The discovery of the 'global' is hailed by Shaw as marking a revolution in social theorising, enabling theorists to overcome the 'methodological nationalism' of the past (Shaw 2000:71; see also Anheier et al 2001b:1–19; Beck 2002).

John Keane gives a clear view of the vastness of this global civil society 'space':

> It comprises individuals, households, profit-seeking businesses, not-for-profit non-governmental organisations, coalitions, social movements and linguistic communities and cultural identities. It feeds upon the work of media celebrities and past or present public personalities... It includes charities, think-tanks, prominent intellectuals...campaigning and lobby groups, citizens' protests...small and large corporate firms, independent media, Internet groups and websites, employers' federations, trade unions, international commissions, parallel summits and sporting organisations. It comprises bodies like Amnesty International, Sony, Falun Gong, Christian Aid, al Jazeera, the Catholic Relief Services, the Indigenous peoples Bio-Diversity Network, FIFA, Transparency International, Sufi networks like Qadiriyya and Naqshabandiyya, the International Red Cross, the Global Coral Reef Monitoring Network, the Ford Foundation, Shack/Slum Dwellers International, Women Living Under Muslim Laws, News Corporation International, OpenDemocracy.net and unnamed circles of Buddhist monks.   (Keane 2003:8–9)

For Keane, the actual membership of global civil society appears to be literally every non-government group or association. But what is the point of this apparently inexhaustible list? Keane explains:

> Considered together, these institutions and actors constitute a vast, interconnected and multi-layered non-governmental space that comprises many hundreds of thousands of more-or-less self-directing ways of life. All of these forms of life have at least one thing in common: across vast geographic distances and despite barriers of time, they *deliberately* organise themselves and conduct their cross-border social activities, business and politics outside the boundaries of governmental structures.   (emphasis added) (Keane 2003:9)

The point of the list is that these groups and associations have organised themselves in such a way so that they are not part of government structures. In fact they are 'self-directing'; they are independent of and external to government. So far there is little that is earth-shattering in the observation that spheres of economic and social life exist outside the formal institutions and structures of government. What is unusual is that these non-government groups and associations are held to be part of a normative political project. The political nature of this is highlighted in two ways.

Firstly, by the otherwise senseless addition of the word 'deliberately'. This implies that the social and economic activities described are forms of conscious political activity, i.e., deliberately chosen forms of organisation and implicit rejections of the sphere of government. The mere existence of social and economic non-government activity is held to be, in-and-of-itself, a form of politics. Here we have a complete inversion of the political or the extension of the political to social and economic everyday life, which is held to have a new political importance.

The second, and key, highlighting feature of the political nature of the everyday existence of individuals, households, firms and voluntary associations is the use of the small word 'space'. The word 'space' links these actors together so that 'these institutions and actors constitute a vast, interconnected and multi-layered non-governmental space'. Rather than just activities taking place outside formal institutions of government, these activities are 'interconnected' through taking place in one vast 'space'.

Thus global 'space' has been transformed into global agency and acquires political qualities. For Ken Booth, the 'space' outside the state system is described by analogy: 'The [metaphor for the] international system which is now developing...is of an egg-box containing the shells of sovereignty; but alongside it a global community omelette is cooking.' (Booth 1991:542) What was once just a figurative 'space' now becomes a conscious political and moral collective, a 'community'.

Keane attempts to give analytical coherence to the argument that a 'political' space is created. This is done negatively. The global civil society 'space' is not, as some critics allege, 'used as a residual or dustbin category that describes everything and nothing...all those parts of life that are *not* the state' (Keane 2003:9). Keane argues that the normative ideal of global civil society, '*when carefully defined*, is not some simple-minded alter ego of the "the State"... The truth is that in a descriptive sense global civil society is only one special set of "non-state" institutions.' (emphasis added) (Keane 2003:10)

Keane would exclude, for example, hunting and gathering societies and tribal orders, insofar as they have survived under modern conditions, as well as mafias and mafia-dominated structures which rely on kinship bonds. Mary Kaldor defines global civil society differently to Keane, as she generally excludes market-orientated actors; however, this makes surprisingly little theoretical difference. She also argues that the concept of global civil society 'space' has theoretical depth and is not merely an ad hoc descriptive list of non-government actors:

> Civil society thus consists of groups, individuals and institutions which are independent of the state and of state boundaries, but which are, at the same time, preoccupied with public affairs... Defined in this way, civil society does not encompass all groups or associations independent of the state. It does not include groups which advocate violence. It does not include self-organised groups and associations which campaign for exclusivist communitarian concepts. Nor does it include self-interested private associations like those of criminals or capitalists. A bank or a corporation is only part of civil society to the extent that it views itself, as many do, as a public organisation with a responsibility to society that takes precedence over profit-making.   (Kaldor 1999b:210)

Membership of global civil society, according to Kaldor, is dependent on moral outlook rather than any political, sociological or economic categorisation. This lack of categorisation gives global civil society its flexible quality. It is very much in the eye of the beholder. Keane argues that:

> Global civil society is the most complex in the history of the human species. It comprises a multitude of different parts, which are connected in a multitude of different ways...a special form of unbounded society marked by constant feedback among its many components.   (Keane 2003:17)

Everything is changed with the imagination of global civil society, yet at the same time nothing is changed: 'In this way, the three little words "global civil society" potentially enable millions of people to *socialise* definitions of our global order – even to *imagine* its positive reconstruction'. (Keane 2003:140)

### 'Global Values'?

The political space and political agency of global civil society begins to take shape as a mental construct. For Keane, global civil society 'is also a form of *society*' (Keane 2003:10). It is a 'form' of society, albeit a 'paradoxical' one:

> It refers to a vast, sprawling non-governmental constellation of many institutionalised structures, associations and networks within which individual and group actors are interrelated and functionally interdependent. As a society of societies, it is 'bigger' and 'weightier' than any individual actor or organisation or combined sum of its thousands of constituent parts – most of whom, paradoxically, neither 'know' each other nor have any chance of ever meeting each other face-to-face.   (Keane 2003:11)

Keane also argues that global civil society is a society with its own dynamics, rules and norms:

> Like all societies in the strict sense, it has a marked life or momentum or power of its own. Its institutions and rules have a definite durability, in that at least some of them can and do persist through long cycles of time... [Global civil society] actors are enmeshed within codes of unwritten and written rules...[which] obliges them to refrain from certain actions, as well as to observe certain norms, for instance those that define what counts as civility.   (Keane 2003:12)

Similarly for Lipschutz, the actors networking in global civil society 'are all united, more or less, by common norms or codes of behaviour that have emerged in reaction to the legal and other socially constructed fictions of the nation-state system' (Lipschutz 1992:398). These norms and values, which are shared by actors of global civil society but not by state actors, are alleged to have communicative, non-exclusivist, universalist ethics at their heart. Daniel Deudney calls this 'earth nationalism' and Alberto Melucci, 'the planetarization of international relations' (cited in Lipschutz 1992:399, see further Deudney 1993; Melucci 1989). For Keane, the key defining norm is that of civility, 'respect for others expressed as politeness towards and acceptance of strangers' (Keane 2003:12).

The normative project of global civil society is based on the communicative norms imputed to this normatively constructed global civil society. John Keane describes the shared norms in more detail:

> ...global civil society is marked by a strong and overriding tendency to...marginalize or avoid the use of violence... Its actors do not especially like mortars or tanks or nuclear weapons. They have an allergic – sometimes disgusted – reaction to images of gunmen firing rockets, or to supersonic fighter planes, or to tanks crashing mercilessly into people or buildings. The actors of global civil society, in their own and varied ways, admire the peaceful... Thanks to such shared norms, the participants within this society are prone to exercise physical restraint, to mix non-violently with others, 'foreigners' and 'strangers' included.   (Keane 2003:13–14)

For radicals Michael Hardt and Antonio Negri, the shared norms of the 'virtual' global civic space are shaped by a desire to be rid of the particularistic values used to oppress, exclude and divide the 'multitude', the universal people united in struggle against domination:

> The virtuality of world space constitutes the first determination of the movements of the multitude...[which] must achieve a global citizenship. The multitude's resistance to bondage – the struggle against the slavery of belonging to a nation, an identity, and a people, and thus the desertion from sovereignty and the limits it places on subjectivity – is entirely positive.   (Hardt and Negri 2001:361–2)

Similarly, for Kaldor, it is non-exclusivist values which lie at the heart of global civil society, constituting it as a normative political project:

> ...in the post-Cold War period, the fundamental political cleavage, which could define the way in which we view contemporary society and the way in which we address a whole range of problems, is likely to be less the traditional left/right divide but rather the division between those who stand for internationalist, Europeanist, democratic values, including human rights, and those who remain wedded to national or exclusivist thinking. The terms 'civil society' or 'civic values' have become forms of political shorthand that characterise the first group.   (Kaldor 1999b:195)

Keane argues that global civil society has a central role to play in the construction of 'a new theory of ethics beyond borders' (Keane 2003:196). It can do this because the definition of global civil society is a negative one. Not merely anti-state and in opposition to territorially-bound politics, but also against the ideological foundationalism alleged to be behind this perspective. Global civil society is therefore 'a condition of the possibility of multiple moralities – in other words, as a universe of freedom from a singular Universal Ethic' (Keane 2003:196).

## The communicative project

The normative project is based on building and extending the separate space of autonomy from the political sphere, winning back ground claimed by the amorality and instrumental rationality of both the state and the market. The unifying factor here is not the politics of the actors but their morality, which, as Kaldor notes, highlights 'the idea of civil society as an independent ethical realm' (Kaldor 1999b:200).

The normative project of global civil society is based on perfection while the constructivist empirical project is apparently doomed to compromise. Where the constructivist project is imperilled by the empirical inequalities and power relations of real international society, global civil society is the space of purity. This is because the defining principles of the normative project of global civil society are derived from universal norms rather than real life actors. John Keane defines this global 'society' as 'marked by a proclivity towards non-violence and respect for the principles of compromise, mutual respect, even power-sharing among different ways of life' (Keane 2003:14). In case the detailed norms imposed upon the ideal-type, rather than the actually existing reality, seem arbitrarily plucked out of the air, Keane explains the purpose of the normative project:

> The implication is clear: global civil society is not just any old collection of ways of life that have nothing in common but their non-identification with governing institutions. *Factually speaking*, this society encourages compromise and mutual respect. (emphasis added) (Keane 2003:14)

The pluralist and non-instrumentalist ethic of global civil society supports 'justice and freedom for all' ethically rather than politically. Global civil society is less a campaigning policy-changing realm which challenges or makes demands on states (as it is for constructivist theorists considered in Chapter 2) than a realm of discussion and debate where within this realm injustice and unfreedom are excluded through definitional fiat.

'Factually speaking' the ideal-type abstraction of global civil society very much resembles the radical alternative to instrumental politics forwarded by Jürgen Habermas. He argues that civil society:

> ...comprises those non-governmental and non-economic connections and voluntary associations, organisations, and movements...more or less spontaneously emergent...that institutionalises problem-solving discourses of general interest... These 'discursive designs' have an egalitarian, open form of organisation that mirrors essential features of the kind of communication around which they crystallise and to which they lend continuity and permanence. (Cited in Kaldor 2003:21–22)

Following Habermas' views on communicative action a new type of progressive and radical politics is premised:

> ...by a deliberative procedure which is realized through the reality of public discord and debate that is experienced in civil society. Civil society is a way of countering what Habermas calls the 'colonisation' of the 'life-world' both by capitalism and by communism...a form of enlightenment, in which individuals can 'live in truth' (Havel) or, in other words, act according to reasoned morality and not the dictates of the totalitarian state. (Kaldor 2003:27)

Global civil society is understood as an arena for the creation of regimes of tolerance, civility and pluralism and its advocates assume that activism within civil society will promote these values globally. Mary Kaldor argues that what is important about the concept of global civil society is the fact that:

> ...at a transnational level [there] is the existence of a global public sphere – a global space where *non-instrumental communication* can take place, inhabited by transnational advocacy networks like Greenpeace or Amnesty International, global social movements... international media...[and] new global 'civic religions' like human rights and environmentalism.   (Kaldor 2003:8)

For many global civil society analysts, the concept captures an ideal space in which values and norms emerge through negotiation and dialogue, rather than through the reproduction of power relationships through the formal political process. At the heart is the idea that this is a new type of politics without instrumentality and competing interests. Mary Kaldor asserts that the importance of global civil society lies in the fact that what takes place: '...is not just [political] bargaining but the existence of a public conversation, a "good-tempered" conversation. It involves reason and sentiment and not just the conflict of interests and passions.' (Kaldor 2003:45)

In this reading, the importance of global civic activism, of the myriad of social, economic and political exchanges in the non-government sphere, is not in the politics which they espouse or their particular (and particularist) causes. Their importance is, as Keane notes, established by the fact that activism in the global space becomes more than the sum of 'good causes' put together or their collective weight at lobbies of WTO summits or those of other international institutions (as analysts of actually existing global civil society would argue). As Keane asserts:

> These movements are marked by a cross-border mentality... Their participants...do not see their concerns as confined within a strictly bounded community or locality... For them the world is one world. So they nurture their identities and publicise their concerns in 'translocalities', as if they were global citizens.   (Keane 2003:61–2)

The activities of the disparate groups, individuals and associations collectively shape and create global civil society as a 'space' and as a normative political project. In fact, as a 'project of projects' (Walzer, cited in Keane 2003:19). This normative 'project of projects', which contains within it everything associated with non-territorially bounded, non-government normative aspirations, is world politics in the fullest sense of 'a *worldly* politics that cultivates the need for transnational mobility of viewpoint and action in support of justice and freedom for all of the earth's inhabitants' (Keane 2003:139).

Keane argues that global civil society is both a 'space' which celebrates plurality and difference and an 'ethical idea that is universally applicable' (Keane 2003:201–2). In his view 'the *universalisable* Ethic of global civil society' is derived from an idealised interpretation of 'actually existing global civil society':

> Global civil society is...to be interpreted as an implied logical and institutional precondition of the survival and flourishing of a genuine plurality of different ideals and forms of life. The precondition is anchored within the actually existing global civil society, whose functioning relies upon the more or less unuttered inference that it is a space of many ideals and ways of life, and that civil society for that reason is a good thing. It is as if global civil society, requires each of its participants or potential members to sign a contract: to acknowledge and to respect the principle of global civil society as a universal ethical principle that guarantees respect for their moral differences.   (Keane 2003:202)

The framework of Habermasian communicative dialogue is then the gel that secures the reproduction of the pluralist values of the global civil society project and which posits the existence of a space for morally-guided, non-instrumental dialogue outside the sphere of government and formally institutionalised political processes.

## The strength of the normative thesis

Not only does the normative focus avoid some of the empirical problems which undermine the constructivist thesis, the attraction of the normative approach is also in the freedom it provides the individual theorist. The concept provides a blank slate because once the emphasis shifts from an empirical to a normative one, the thesis cannot be empirically measured and disputed, proved or disproved. Some global civil society advocates argue that they reject empirical measurement on the grounds that global civil society is growing so fast that the concept lags behind its 'subject on the run, striding unevenly in many different directions' (Keane 2003:8). Others argue that the term is necessarily imprecise and 'fuzzy' because of its youth and therefore: 'Any measurement of global civil society will be simpler and less perfect that the richness, variety, and complexity of the concept it tries to measure.' (Anheier, 2001:224)

This of course is where the normative project parts company with the constructivist thesis, considered in the first part of this book. Helmut Anheier argues that: 'Defining global civil society as a sociosphere goes beyond the notions of network or infrastructure. As Kaldor [2003] and Shaw [2000] suggest, global civil society includes aspects of civility and value dispositions.' (Anheier, 2001:226) This somewhat underestimates the problem, as all the numbers and measures in the world cannot capture what, he notes, is an 'essentially normative concept'. Global civil society as an ideal 'communicative space' cannot be measured by either an analysis of networks and structures or some measure of 'civility and value dispositions' in the real world.

The normative rather than empirical focus enables normative theorists to implicitly, rather than explicitly, link their analysis to claims about the developments in the international sphere. This enables them to side-step critiques based on their political claims. The most widely articulated critique is that their abstract schema ignores power relations. It is not difficult to find commentators asserting that the normative division between the realm of government instrumentality and the non-governmental communicative realm is also a literal one, for example, Cincinnati law professor Gordon Christenson argues in *Human Rights Quarterly*:

> The international society of nation-states operates in the public sphere of balance of power and interests, explained by international relations theory. World civil society operates within the voluntary sphere of cultural values and shared well-being in a dimension beyond political boundaries and dominion. (Christenson 1997:731–2)

However, for leading global civil society theorists, especially commentators like John Keane and Mary Kaldor, the normative and empirical distinction is never consistently articulated, leaving them open to similar criticism (see Hutchings forthcoming). Neera Chandhoke, argues that although there may be some heuristic value in making the distinction between the sphere of state instrumentalism and global civic communicative association:

> What *is* problematic is the assumption that appears to underlie theorising in this mode, namely, that these domains of collective

existence do not influence each other, or that they do not affect each other, or indeed that they do not constitute in the sense of shaping each other... To put it plainly, the separation of collective human existence into mutually exclusive spheres of thought and action elides the way in which each of these domains is constructed by power, which spilling over arbitrary boundaries underpins the whole.   (Chandhoke 2002:35; see also 2001)

Chandhoke argues that those who assert that global civil society operates in a distinct social space, either separate from the state (White 1994:379; Taylor 1991:171; Honneth 1993:19) or as an independent 'third realm' differentiated from both the state and market (Cohen and Arato 1992:18), falsely provide 'a picture of global civil society that seems to be supremely uncontaminated by either the power of states or that of markets (Chandhoke 2002:36).

The critique that global civil society does not constitute a separate and 'pure' space from power inequalities is one that clarifies that the normative concept should not be confused with actually existing global civil society. However, while drawing attention to the issue of power is central to the critique of those international relations theorists who posit the existence of 'actually existing global civil society' it is not adequate as a critique of global civil society as a normative project. Normative commentators can accept the empirical critique and would suggest that the reality should then be challenged to meet the normative demands.

There are two other critiques, engaging with the normative project itself, which have more potency. The first also emphasises the importance of power relations, but is focused on the utopian nature of the normative theorising rather than on existing relations of power per se. The critique strikes at the heart of the legitimacy of this type of critical theorising, by suggesting that there are no indications of immanent possibilities for power relations to be overcome in this manner. Here the focus is on the claims made on behalf of the Habermasian communicative community. Stephen Hopgood highlights that the operation of communicative ethics depends on a number of strict conditions which demonstrate the highly abstract nature of normative theorising (Hopgood 2000:9; see further Habermas 1990). Linklater lays out the procedures Habermas defines as 'essential to authentic dialogue':

These include the convention that no person or moral position can be excluded from dialogue in advance, and the realisation that authentic dialogue requires a particular moral psychology. True dialogue...only exists when human beings accept that there is no a priori certainty about who will learn from whom and when all are willing to engage in a process of reciprocal critique as a result. Cooperation in dialogue requires that agents are prepared to question their own truth claims... What guides participants is a commitment to be moved simply by the force of the better argument.    (Linklater 1998:92)

Hopgood argues that a critique of this abstract schema for its complete lack of relationship to the world as it is now, and for the fact that its starting assumption of other-regarding equality proceeds by denying the existence of the very problems it purports to solve, would be 'obvious and utterly facile, and easy to make' (Hopgood 2000:10). The communicative community alleged to be the basis of global civil society values and its democratising potential is so far removed from any existing reality that it initially appears strange that Habermas' work is so central to these projects.

However, the gap between the assumptions and reality is willingly acknowledged by normative theorists. Cosmopolitan theorist David Held, for example, asserts that the 'reframing' of the market system to ensure social equity and accountability may raise 'enormous political, diplomatic and technical difficulties' but that this is a challenge that 'cannot be avoided' if cosmopolitan principles are to prevail (Held 2002:318–9). The empirical world is clearly taken very lightly in these schemas. Hopgood suggests that the lack of attention to real relations and the focus on communicative rationality is necessary to 'ground' the moral claims which Linklater and others seek to make and insightfully notes that the moral claims would appear to come first and the framework of justification second (Hopgood 2000:10).

The second critique is related less to power relations and more to the implicit relationship between the normative project and 'actually existing global civil society'. It suggests that the idealised view of global civil society relies on claims about global civic actors which have little connection to reality. As Keane states, quoted above, global civil society is paradoxical in that most of its members 'paradoxically, neither "know" each other nor have any chance of ever meeting each other face-to-face' (Keane 2003:11). This rather underestimates the fictional nature of the normative project. The lack of real space and shared values which were the source of the Habermasian ideal would indicate that the implicit link between the normative ideal and international developments is a forced and illegitimate one.

Völker Heins notes that the analogy of Ken Booth's of the 'empty shells' of sovereignty and the 'omelette' of the global community, cited earlier (Booth 1991:542), is based on two unfounded assumptions: firstly, that there is a convergence of worldviews among global civic actors; and secondly, the existence of a 'globalizing civil society de-coupled from the imperatives and constraints of state sovereignty' (Heins 2000:38). There is no social engagement linking diverse differ-ent groups across a global political space of global civil society. In which case, the normative project of global civil society falls down in so far as it implicitly derives its norms from an observable 'actually existing' global civil society.

The strength of the normative thesis is that it intimates a relation-ship to reality without openly relying on it for its validity. The lack of relationship between the theory and the reality then allows the theo-rists to impose their own set of views or set of normative demands. The importance of the concept of global civil society for normative theo-rists is that it provides a blank slate on which any normative schema can be written. The fact that the normative theorists derive their definitions of global civil society from their own norms and aspirations explains why the descriptive part of the normative project varies widely (as noted above, Keane, for example, includes the private sector, while Kaldor does not). The empirical information, such as the cam-paign descriptions, the lists of NGOs, or the values surveys, which purport to describe the all inclusive 'project of projects', are merely a backdrop to the normative claims, which have already been ascribed from the outset.

In the case of communicative approaches to global civil society it is worthwhile restating the obvious fact that there is no literal 'global space' where arguments are freely exchanged on a non-instrumentalist basis. There is no literal 'global civil society' with its norms and values and rules and regulations. There are disparate non-governmental spheres of activity but the interconnections and the shared pluralist norms exist only in the subjective projections of the beholder. As Keane notes actually existing global civil society is, of course, 'marked by the absence of widely held "common values"' (Keane 2003:142). As Heins empirically details, there is no evidence of a 'structural conver-gence of the worldviews, addresses and ultimate goals of activists who keep crossing borders without however merging into a globalized civil society' (Heins 2000).

As noted in Part I, the irony is that if a global civil society really existed, if there was a real communicative discussion by real actors, then normative theorists would not be able to impose their assertions of common norms and values. The fictional character of the global communicative space is essential for the normative appeal of the concept. As has already been highlighted, normative theorists can define the parameters of global civil society very differently, what they all agree on is that their definitions lead to the establishment of a set of normative values which can be supported by their theoretical analysis. In a circular methodology, normative values are the starting point rather than derived from any empirical study (Hopgood 2000; Chandler 2001c). This is why any empirical analysis is usually a secondary concern in normative works; the focus tends to be on the values held to stem from the global civic 'space'.

## The conservative limits of the communicative project

At first sight it may appear that the circular argument of the normative global civil society theorists is one that is easily dismissed. It will be suggested here, that the success of the Habermasian normative vision of communicative moral engagement has little to do with the strength of the theoretical argument. Global civil society is not defined by what links actors together, but by an imputed moral perspective which seeks to go beyond the political sphere of instrumental self-interest. This moral perspective constitutes the normative project and also explains the appeal of this radical desire to overcome the perceived limitations of the political sphere. The normative project is not merely a moral one; it is explicitly also a political project. However, it is a political project which seeks to contest the legitimacy and purpose of the political sphere itself. Rather than merely operating in the sphere of morality, separate to the sphere of politics, the non-state, non-political, communicative dialogue of global civil society attempts to assert itself over and against the political sphere by privileging universal values against the self-interests which form the basis of competition within the political process.

The normative project of global civil society seeks to de-emphasise the importance of the political sphere in favour of an asserted framework of universal norms and values, held to be derived from global communicative reasoning. This is achieved through deriving universal moral norms from the individual moral autonomy of global civic actors, freed from the political sphere of self-interest and held to be operating in a new 'global space'. These universal norms are derived from the abstract individual, the 'unencumbered self' freed from any social, economic or political context, in very similar terms to those used by John Rawls in establishing a normative framework in his *Theory of Justice* (1999). Whereas Rawls' framework was advocated as a philosopher's 'thought experiment', global civil society theorists assert that theirs is derived from a political commitment to the norms and values held to be emerging from global civil society.

The problem with this approach is that the universal values, privileged above the political sphere, are abstractly grounded and asserted purely in ideal terms. The normative project seeks to transform the political not by engaging with politics but by bypassing the political sphere. The 'unencumbered self' of Rawls or Habermas is posited as entirely autonomous, not just removed from preconceived self-interests but also removed from any collective framework which could mediate between the interests of the individual and those of society as a whole (see Sandel 1998). Rather than constructing shared norms through reasoned argument and consensus-building in the political process, these norms are ideally imposed from outside this process. The lack of any mediating framework, between the asserted 'moral autonomy' of actors in global civil society and the global norms allegedly derived from them, makes global civil society theorisation innately conservative in character. Because these asserted universal norms are ideally derived, and purely abstract, any genuine autonomy, or the assertion of self-interests through the political process, can only be seen as negative and threatening. Far from offering a transformative vision, the normative project is a fixed and static one, which sees political autonomy in negative rather than positive terms. This point is drawn out below through a brief initial consideration of the abstract, pre-social, 'autonomous' individual and the abstract universal norms which form both sides of the fixed communicative equation.

### Individual autonomy

Following Theodor Adorno, Habermas rejected 'instrumental reason' as fundamentally flawed, precisely because it was deliberately willed activity aimed towards a definite goal. Rather than political ends being important, the central concern for Habermas was the means, the process itself. In the place of collective engagement in politics, orientated around ends or political goals, which Habermas (writing in the shadow of fascism and Stalinism) viewed to be problematic, the key to social progress was held to be 'communicative action' and intersubjective understanding. Curbing the dangers of democratic politics or collective autonomy also meant curbing individual subjectivity or instrumental 'practical reason'. As Habermas states: 'Communicative reason differs from practical reason first and foremost in that it is no longer ascribed to the individual actor or to a macrosubject at the level of the state or the whole of society.' (Habermas 1997:3) There is no room here for the political subject; the communicative sphere is shaped by morally autonomous subjects engaged in dialogue based on communicative reason, not competing political interests. Mary Kaldor rightly argues that global civil society is no substitute for representative democracy. In fact, she makes the claim that it is of a qualitatively different nature:

> Global civil society cannot claim to 'represent' the people in the way that formally elected states can and do. But *the issue is less one of representation than of deliberation.* Parliamentary democracy was always about deliberation. The idea was not to mandate members of parliament but rather to vote for individuals who could be trusted to debate and deliberate issues in an honest way in the public interest. That idea has been undermined in a national context for a variety of reasons, including media sloganizing and party discipline. (Kaldor 2003:140–141)

Of course, parliamentary democracy was never intended to be a matter of pure deliberation but the negotiation of interests, represented by elected delegates. For Kaldor, it would appear that rather than establishing a collective project of changing society it is the autonomy of the individual that is of primary importance:

> What participation of global civil society does is to provide an alternative vehicle for deliberation, for introducing normative concerns, for raising the interests of the individual and not just the state... [T]he fact that global civil society is in principle open to all individuals offers the possibility of participation and deliberation at global levels... [T]he concept offers a platform for much wider engagement. It provides a method for reclaiming autonomy on particular issues. It is an opening that needs to be seized if ordinary people are to try to influence the events that affect their lives. (Kaldor 2003:141)

The moral autonomy of the participant in the communicative community is posited in distinction to their political autonomy. Political subjectivity at an individual or collective level would bring in particular interests constituted prior to membership of the communicative community. The autonomy of the global civil society actor is dependent on their autonomy from the political sphere. In effect, this theorises the end of competitive politics, and its replacement by a pluralist framework where participation in dialogue is more important than any specific viewpoint. According to James Heartfield:

> Habermas is saying that the thing we should value is not our free will, but the way that the clash of many wills prevents any one will from taking precedence. He means that the rules we all observe to get along are more important than what any one of us wants.   (Heartfield 2002:78)

The rejection of purposive action, or what is pejoratively termed 'instrumental rationality', makes political engagement problematic and puts less emphasis on the conscious action of political subjects.

The communicative concept of global civil society depends on the rejection of formal political activity. The defining aspect of global civil society activism is the rejection of representation and state-level politics. This is what separates 'new' social movements from 'old' movements such as trade unions and political parties. Global civic actors are only held to truly 'represent' the people as long as they are attempting to open up the boundaries of discourse and extending moral communicative norms.

The normative project of global civil society is an idealist one; it exists, literally, in the realm of ideas rather than practice. The ideals of the Habermasian communicative realm challenge formal political power but can never constitute it. What the normative advocates of global civil society celebrate in the 'anti-globalisation' protests at Seattle and subsequently is the fact that there is no collective 'anti-globalisation movement'. As John Keane approvingly notes:

> There is in fact a wide variety of such movements, whose activists specialise in publicising their experiences and applying their campaigning skills in particular policy areas as diverse as sexual politics, trade rules, religiosity, corporate power, post-war reconstruction, clean water, education and human rights. The targets of these movements are equally variable: they take aim at a whole spectrum of opponents and potential allies, from local institutions that have global effects to global institutions that have local effects. The spectrum of political loyalties within these movements is also very

broad, ranging from deep-green ecologists to Christian pacifists, social democrats, Muslim activists, Buddhist meditators and anarcho-syndicalists...they do not speak in one voice, with one point of view.   (Keane 2003:59–60)

The problem of agency goes deep to the heart of the normative 'project of projects'. Despite protestations to the contrary (Keane 2003:10; Anheier et al 2001a; Glasius et al 2002) global civil society cannot have a transformatory dynamic; it cannot have any collective agency, because this would constitute a consensus bringing dialogue to an end (see Linklater 1998:123). This approach is similarly expressed in Hardt and Negri's ambiguous support for political movements which challenge the constitution of power and assert the rights of autonomy and self-organisation, for example, black separatists or the Palestinian Intifada:

> ...these ambiguous progressive functions of the concept of sovereign nation exist primarily...when the nation remains merely a dream. As soon as the nation begins to form as a sovereign state, its progressive functions all but vanish... With national 'liberation' and the construction of the nation-state, all of the oppressive functions of modern sovereignty inevitably blossom in full force.   (Hardt and Negri 2001:109)

As soon as global civic groups take power they immediately lose their attraction, as Solidarity and other East Europeans were to discover, this celebration of anti-politics could only happen as long as these movements were restricted to opposition. As Heartfield notes:

> Movements that aimed simply to open up dialogue, like the civic groups of Eastern Europe were good, but those that aimed to exercise power, like the Peronists were bad. Lech Walesa's doughty shipyard workers were worthy of...patronage when they were breaking up the old order, only to see it withdrawn when they dared to try to rule themselves.   (Heartfield 2002:79)

The individual freed from the constraints of the political is a passive and constrained object rather than an active subject of change. The work of sociologists like Anthony Giddens is central here to the perspective of individual empowerment, or 'self-reflexivity' and the concomitant rejection of the political (Giddens 1992, 1994). Normative cosmopolitan democracy theorists, such as David Held, have used Giddens' analysis to theorise a post-liberal democratic constitution of relations between the individual and society. As Anthony McGrew rightly argues (1997:250) Held's model of cosmopolitan democracy is not underpinned by the classical liberal tradition of the self-interested individual but instead refers to:

> ...a structural principle of self-determination where the 'self' is part of the collectivity or 'majority' enabled and constrained by the rules and procedures of democratic life... Hence, this form of autonomy can be referred to as 'democratic autonomy' – an entitlement to autonomy within the constraints of community. (Held 1995:156)

The individual freed from the collective sphere of political equality has an 'autonomy' which is constraining rather than liberating. This is highlighted in the work of John Ruggie who has explored alternatives to territorially-based rights and duties (Ruggie 1993:149–150). One alternative is that of 'primitive government', where systems of rule were based on kinship relations, territory was occupied by kinship groups but crucially did not define the rights of group members. Another area of relevance may be that of nomadic property rights, where, for example, as for Mongol tribes, pastoral land would be easily exhausted making territorial rights less important than 'the sovereign importance of movement'. For Ruggie, a third possibility is that of 'nonexclusive territorial rule, such as the 'patchwork of overlapping and incomplete rights of government' as found in medieval Europe. The progressive possibilities of a 'new Medievalism' have been high-lighted by several advocates of global civil society initiatives, and of the various historical analogies would probably seem the most fruitful (see for example, Linklater 1998:193–5; see also Falk 2000b). Ruggie highlights that the:

> ...medieval system of rule was structured by a nonexclusive form of territoriality, in which authority was both personalized and parcelized within and across territorial formations... The medieval ruling class was mobile in a manner not dreamed of since, able to assume governance from one end of the continent to the other without hesitation or difficulty because 'public territories formed a continuum with private estates'. (Ruggie 1993:150)

Ironically, the social fixity of medieval and pre-modern social categories, where economic, political and legal entitlements were private grants rather than public rights is seen by today's normative global civil society theorists as, in fact, demonstrating the 'looseness' of the social bond and limitations on the state's 'capacity to trap human beings in bounded spaces' (Linklater 1998:133–4). The celebration of the political 'freedoms' of pre-modern society belies the claims to progress and 'emancipation' made by these critical theorists. What every form of non-territorial system of rights had in common was the lack of any separation of the private and public spheres. There was no political sphere above and beyond the personal membership of the kinship group, tribe or feudal estate.

While rule and regulation can exist without territorial boundaries, the political sphere of formal political equality, which depends on the institutionalisation of rights regardless of personal distinctions, cannot. This is highlighted by Linklater, who celebrates the overlapping jurisdictions and multiple loyalties of feudalism, compared to the 'totalising project' of the nation-state which is based on the allegedly 'hegemonic proposition' that 'all citizens should possess exactly the same legal and political rights' (Linklater 1998:29, 44). If equal legal and political rights are seen to be 'oppressive' then it is clear that 'emancipatory' theories of global civil society are based on a diametrically opposing conception of the political to that, at least, formally upheld under the liberal democratic framework.

Ironically, the attempt to 'free' politics from states and fixed territorial boundaries instead frees the individual from the formal political sphere. This celebration of the 'autonomy' of the individual is a celebration of the breaking of the individual from the social claims of political ties beyond the particular.

## Universal norms

Rather than derive moral values from abstract universals such as natural law or relativise values denying a universal morality, normative global civil society theorists seek to ground universal values without foundational truths. This is the attraction of Habermas' work. For Andrew Linklater, communicative rationality is a framework for preserving moral universals after the discrediting of ideas of natural law through historical frameworks of understanding. More specifically, historical thinking discredited the idea of moral universals as the product of power. Habermas' theory posits the possibility of an open-ended universal morality achieved through the dialogue of other-regarding equals. A Habermasian communication community based on dialogue and consent rather than dominion and force, is held to rescue universal morality from power and to provide an 'impartial moral standpoint' (Linklater 1998:8–9; Held 2002:311).

Habermasian theory provides legitimacy for certain moral claims made on behalf of universal morality. The concept of the Habermasian 'universal communication community' enables the grounding of 'a thin conception of universality which defends the ideal that every human being has an equal right to participate in a dialogue to determine the principles of inclusion and exclusion which govern global politics' (Linklater 1998:107). Hopgood critiques the methodology but does not fully expand on the importance of the content of the Habermasian discourse. It is not merely an attempt to 'ground' moral claims, this could be done in a number of alternative ways (for example, through positing the moral primacy of the interests of the victims, the environment or social and economic equality).

The reason Habermas' communicative community is central to critical theorists of global civil society is that it attempts to ground regulatory political institutions in the non-political language of morality and 'space' rather than in the legal and political equality of liberal democratic institutions. For Linklater, Keane and others, global civil society can have no goal beyond its own regulatory existence. The communicative community does not regard dialogic discourse as 'a vehicle for reconciling value-differences but defend[s] it as the medium through which greater human variety can be discovered and explored' (Linklater 1998:41).

Instead of the unification of the universal and the particular through a political process, the political 'end points' are given in the normative rules of communicative dialogue. Richard Falk's imperative sums up the regulatory assertion behind the language of autonomy: 'global civil society must be both respectful of and celebratory toward cultural diversity, and mindful of human solidarity and planetary unity in the struggles against cruelty, violence, exploitation, and environmental decay' (Falk 1995:3). The communicative norms of global civil society promise 'autonomy from' but never 'autonomy to'. The irony is that rather than assert individual autonomy against the state, the emphasis of the communicative realm is designed to assert normative rules of social regulation. As Linklater states: 'Discourse ethics sets out procedures to be followed... It does not offer putative solutions to substantive moral debates, envisage historical end points or circulate political blueprints.' (Linklater 1998:92)

Linklater notes that, under the Habermasian framework: 'The emphasis shifts away from universalisable conceptions of the good life to the procedural universals which need to be in place before true dialogue can be said to exist in any social encounter.' (Linklater 1998:41) Despite the focus on expanding possibilities and overcoming the boundaries of the political, the 'emphasis' is one of normative regulation.

The communicative framework, in which values and dialogue matter more than interests, votes or power, is essential to the normative concept of global civil society. In reality, it is these normative rules, held to be derived from communicative ethics, which are asserted against the state rather than the 'voices' of the excluded. When normative theorists assert that the growth of global civil society can 'act as a check or constraint on the power of the state' it appears that they actually mean the procedures or norms they advocate for should act as a constraint on political power (Kaldor 1999b:200). It is the restrictive norms which are important, not the power of the civic actors per se. Global civil society advocates privilege frameworks of pre-determined rules and norm-governed behaviour which can only constrain human agency rather than liberate it.

This is the reason why advocates of communicative ethics worry little about the problem of agency. Their focus is the normative framework which global civil society is held to both reflect and to establish. As Falk asserts: 'humane governance is the principal project of emergent global civil society', for Linklater, using similar language: 'its function is to promote the goal of the universal communication community' (Falk 1995:46; Linklater 1998:212). The details of agency are really neither here nor there: 'Whether or not ecofeminism or some as yet unimagined coalition of societal and spiritual energies is the agency of transformation, the outcome must be a democratic and benevolent form of geogovernance.' (Falk 1995:45) Whatever the agency the ideal outcome is already established; it is the one that meets the normative theorist's starting definition of global civil society.

## Conclusion

The limitation of the normative communicative project is that, despite claims to the contrary, it is not a project of social and political change. The normative project of global civil society is a circular one; there is no goal outside of the project itself. This means that it is ill-suited to the task of reconstituting a new type of politics. Politics is about aspirations for the future and the contestation of ideas rather than the acceptance of difference and humility. The struggle for space and civilised conversation would appear to be a rejection of political contestation rather than a progressive alternative.

The values of global civil society, imputed by ostensibly radical commentators, are entirely negative. There is no positive aspiration to engage in social and political life. Habermasian communicative discourse strips its participants of their particular aims and interests, making the process of communication an end in its self. This is the negation of an alternative political project, because the 'project of projects' is itself the rejection of any political project. As Joseph Raz notes, the morality thus engendered is a stunted and restrictive one which celebrates:

> ...only those principles which restrict the individual's pursuit of his personal goals and his advancement of his self interest. It is not 'the art of life', i.e., the precepts instructing people how to live and what makes for a successful, meaningful, and worthwhile life. (Raz 1984:186)

Rather than encourage political engagement, Raz argues that a life devoted to respecting the rights of others would be one of 'total servitude' (Raz 1984:198). In the Habermasian space of global civil society the values and norms which are celebrated are not political perspectives or views but rather non-instrumentalism and the rejection of the political in exchange for the 'live and let live' of the political pluralism of the global ethic. As Keane asserts: 'Its morals are humble morals'. (Keane 2003:197) Its politics, as we have seen, are even more humble.

The non-political ethic of global civil society is both start and end point of a circular argument. It was the ethic of global civil society that made it more than a 'residual or dustbin category' and constituted global civil society as an 'ideal' 'space' or 'society'. Then, tautologically, the constitution of this space or society was held to reveal a global ethic of pluralism. The pluralist ethic is derived from the ethical ideal of global civil society and the ethical ideal of global civil society is derived from the pluralist ethic. To put it another way, the definition of global civil society as associational activity outside the formal political sphere of government results in an ethic which rejects the contestation of the formal political sphere in favour of the promise of 'unbounded space' and cosmopolitan humility.

The next two chapters will draw out further the conservative consequences of the normative project of global civil society. Both the
radical, postmodern approach, of building global civil society from the
bottom-up, and the liberal cosmopolitan approach, of imposing global
norms from the top-down, depend on breaking the mediating links
between the individual and the social. For cosmopolitan theorists this
facilitates new forms of less accountable regulative authority or global
governance (see further, Chapter 7). For the radical 'globalisation from
below' theorists, considered in the next chapter, the rejection of the
mediating role of politics makes individual action immediately global
in character and casts the rejection of collective political engagement
in a positive moral light.

# 6
# Radical Resistance 'From Below'

## Introduction

Whereas the morality of global civil society was seen to lie in political ends in the constructivist approach and in the separate sphere of communicative ethics in the Habermasian approach. The radical approach of constructing global society 'from below' derives the morality of global civil society from the methods and organisation of its members, from their refusal to participate in territorial state-based politics. The social movement approach sees global civil society as morally progressive in so far as its demands do not 'seek to replace one form of power with another' and instead have the 'objective of "whittling down" the capacity of concentrated centres of power' (Stammers 1999:1006). As Richard Falk and Andrew Strauss argue:

> Individuals and groups, and their numerous transnational associations, rising up from and challenging the confines of territorial states, are promoting 'globalization from below', and have begun to coalesce into what is now recognized as being a rudimentary 'global civil society'.   (Falk and Strauss 2003:209–10)

As considered in the previous chapter, the communicative realm of global civil society separates moral engagement from the formal political sphere. Radical global civil society theorists share this perspective but tend to focus less on theorising global civil society as a totality and more on the highlighting of new forms of informal political activism, activism which is held to reconnect politics and morality. In this sense global civil society is more narrowly defined on the basis of political activism and political advocacy, rather than purely non-governmental

141

interactions. Mario Pianta, for example, defines global civil society as 'a sphere of international relationships among heterogeneous actors who share civil values and concern for global issues, communication and meanings, advocacy actions, and self-organization experiments' (Pianta 2003:237).

Advocates of this global civil society approach suggest that the radical movements, attempting to institute 'globalisation from below', bring politics and morality together by expanding the sphere of moral concern and by developing political strategies which avoid and bypass the constraints of state-based politics. Falk argues that: 'If there is to be a more benign world order enacting a transformed politics of non-violence and social justice, it will be brought about by struggles mounted from below based on the activities of popular movements and various coalitions.' (Falk 1995:18) Whereas state-based political action is held to reinforce frameworks and hierarchies of exclusion, new social movements from below are seen to herald new forms of emancipatory political action, which seek to recognise and include diversity and build new forms of global 'counter-hegemonic' politics.

In this perspective, states are no longer perceived to be the focus for political organisation and political demands. Unlike the empirical project of global civil society, which involves (Western) states in the moral sphere of international relations, the normative theorists, informed by critical, postmodern and cosmopolitan approaches, argue that nation-states are a barrier to emancipatory political practice. Rather than capturing state power, the normative goal of global civil society is to constitute alternatives to the enclosed space of territorial politics. As Nikhil Aziz explains:

> Broadly speaking, the new transnational social movements' concerns with eliminating political, economic, and social inequalities are the same as the goals of past socialist and communist movements. However, the new movements seek non-violent as opposed to violent revolution; and they generally abjure power in the sense of control of the state, seeking instead political alternatives to the state itself.   (Aziz 1995:14)

Advocates of global civic activism assert that the state-level focus of old movements limited their progressive potential:

> ....it was through the state that 'old' movements were 'tamed'. This was true both of workers' movements, which became left political

parties and trade unions, and anti-colonial struggles, which were transformed into new ruling parties.   (Kaldor 2003:86)

For example, Hardt and Negri write that sovereignty is a 'poisoned gift', where ostensible revolutionaries 'get bogged down in "realism"', resulting in 'the opposite of the nationalist dream of an autonomous, self-centered development' as new structures of domestic and international domination become established (Hardt and Negri 2001:133). Their critique of national sovereignty is essentially a critique of the liberal democratic process:

> The entire logical chain of representation might be summarized like this: the people representing the multitude, the nation representing the people, and the state representing the nation. Each link is an attempt to hold in suspension the crisis of modernity. Representation in each case means a further step of abstraction and control.   (Hardt and Negri 2001:134)

The alternative to formal representation, held to legitimise and strengthen state hierarchies, is global civic action, which empowers individuals. For Hardt and Negri, global civil society activism challenges the politics of representation:

> ...the global People is represented more clearly and directly not by governmental bodies but by a variety of organizations that are at least relatively independent of nation-states and capital... The newest and perhaps most important forces in the global civil society...NGOs [are] synonymous with 'people's organizations' because the People's interest is defined in distinction from state interests... They go further than that. What they really represent is the vital force that underlies the People, and thus they transform politics into a question of generic life, life in all its generality.   (Hardt and Negri 2001:311–14)

Global civil society advocates are convinced that political activity at the level of the state is inherently repressive. Peace and democracy at a national level are held to be maintained by exclusion and war. According to Andrew Linklater, global civil society seeks to challenge the 'totalising project' of the state which is based on 'accentuat[ing] the differences between citizens and aliens in order to meet the challenges of inter-state war' (Linklater 1998:6). For Mary Kaldor, the relationship is inversed, following Carl Schmitt, she suggests democracy and progress could only be pursued at a domestic level if there was an external enemy which ensured that the process of political debate was followed within narrow confines which did not threaten the state (Kaldor 2003:36). Either way, there is an intimate link between state-based politics and war and conflict. This perspective shares much with postmodern international relations theories, which assert that war, ethnic cleansing and genocide, are not exceptional policy choices for nation-states but rather an essential part of their make-up (for example, Campbell 1998b).

In order not to legitimise state-based systems of exclusion and conflict, global civil society theorists put an emphasis on autonomy and self-organisation rather than formal collective political mechanisms, such as political parties. In much of the literature it is argued that this anti-state approach has its origins in the East European and Latin American experience, where political activists first put the emphasis:

> ...on withdrawal from the state. They talked about creating islands of civic engagement...[and] also used terms like 'anti-politics', 'living in truth' – the notion of refusing the lies of the regime or 'parallel polis' – the idea of creating their own Aristotelian community based on the 'good' i.e., moral life.   (Kaldor forthcoming)

The rejection of state-based approaches links a large variety of different campaigns and projects which span from the 1980s civic 'oppositionists' in Eastern Europe to the Seattle protests and the anti-globalisation and anti-capitalism movements of today. This chapter seeks to examine the claims made on behalf of the radical normative project of global civil society 'from below' and suggests that, rather than bringing politics and morality together, by expanding the sphere of inclusivity, global civic activism tends to undermine community connections. This is because the political morality which is advocated has aspects which can be deeply corrosive of social engagement and prone to elitist rather than inclusive consequences. Once it is argued that the individual should have no higher political allegiance beyond their own moral conscience there is a danger of the rejection of collective political engagement and its replacement by elite advocacy and personal solipsism. The following sections consider why these approaches argue that the state no longer constitutes the key site of political power and highlight that their radical hostility to the state often reflects an elitist rejection of mass politics, representation and democratic legitimacy.

## The strong state?

The post-1989 genesis of global civil society is often rooted in the development of the concept in East European and Latin American opposition movements and groupings operating in the context of authoritarian state regulation. As Mary Kaldor argues:

> As the term emerged in Eastern Europe and Latin America, the emphasis was on self-organization and civic autonomy in reaction to the vast increase in the reach of the modern state, and on the creation of independent spaces, in which individuals can act according to their consciences in the face of the powerful influences from the state on culture and ideology. (Kaldor 2003:21)

In the 1990s, it was not just under the circumstances of authoritarian state regulation that the opening up of 'independent spaces' was held to be necessary. As Kaldor notes: 'This concept was taken up by Western radicals who saw civil society as a check both on the power and arbitrariness of the contemporary state and on the power of unbridled capitalism.' (Kaldor 2003:21) Kaldor sees global civil society as intimately connected to recent concerns 'about personal autonomy, self-organization [and] private space', initially raised by oppositionists in Eastern Europe as 'a way of getting round the totalitarian militaristic state' (Kaldor 2003:4):

> The rediscovery of the term 'civil society' and related terms such as 'anti-politics' or 'power of the powerless' seemed to offer a discourse within which to frame parallel concerns about the ability to control the circumstances in which individuals live, about the substantive empowerment of citizens.   (Kaldor 2003:4)

However, the argument that it is the strength of the contemporary Western state and the 'power of unbridled capitalism' which has led to a focus on empowerment through 'anti-politics' is open to challenge. The strength of the state, or the power of the market, has not inevitably led to the new politics of individualised and private responses rather than collective resistance. There are other factors at work drawing global civil society theorists to the experience of East

European dissidents; one factor is their similar experience of social isolation:

> After 1968, the main form of opposition was the individual dissident. The dissidents saw themselves not as precursors of a political movement but as individuals who wanted to retain their personal integrity. Dissidence was about the dignity of the individual as much as about politics. It was about the possibility of honest interaction even at a private and personal level, about being able to read, think and discuss freely.   (Kaldor 2003:53)

Kaldor expands, outlining the aspirations of leading dissident intellectuals, such as Adam Michnik in Poland, credited with rediscovering the concept of civil society:

> Michnik argues that the task of the opposition was not to seize power but to change the relationship between state and society. Through self-organization, it was possible to create autonomous spaces in society... [H]e used [the term civil society] in a new way...the emphasis was on self-organization, autonomy, solidarity and non-violence.   (Kaldor 2003:55)

While the term 'civil society' was used in Poland, perhaps more explanatory is the similar concept, developed elsewhere in Central Europe, *Anti-Politics*, the title of a book by Hungarian dissident George Konrad (1984) and also popularised by Vaclav Havel in Czechoslovakia (Kaldor 2003:55). For Kaldor, 'anti-politics is the ethos of civil society' (Kaldor 2003:57). The dissident movement was one of political refusal rather than political participation:

> The realm of 'anti-politics' or the parallel polis was one where the individual would refuse such [political] collaboration... In all these discussions, the role of the individual and the importance of personal links, something that was central to individual dissidence, were considered primary, overriding claims to political authority... [A]nti-politics...was a new type of politics because it was not about the capture of state power; it was the politics of those who don't want to be politicians and don't want to share power.   (Kaldor 2003:56)

For leading normative global civil society theorists, the political tactic of 'refusal' is not described primarily as a tactical reflection of the weakness and social isolation of East European intellectuals. Rather it is promoted as revealing a higher moral virtue – the rejection of the instrumental political contestation of ideas for a focus on ethics and self-expression:

> ...concepts like civil society (Michnik), anti-politics (Havel and Konrad), and 'living in truth' (Havel)...were fundamentally about the need for self-organised groups and institutions outside the state and for political parties able to act and speak honestly without concern for the capture of power...   (Kaldor 1999:200)

According to Kaldor, the politics of refusal was a sign of strength rather than weakness, in fact this approach of the East European dissidents is credited with bringing down the Soviet regimes in Central Europe: 'The spread of these [dissident] groups, however small, began to undermine the sustainability of the regimes, which depended on total control – small autonomous spaces were multiplying.' (Kaldor 2003:59) The attraction of global civil society would appear to be the capacity to achieve political ends without actually doing traditional 'politics'. For Martin Shaw, the 'revolutions' of 1989 were a success precisely because they placed the 'emphasis on avoiding direct confrontation over state power' and instead relied on 'essentially Gandhian moral propaganda and passive resistance, and a general embrace of non-violence' (Shaw 2000:66).

The individual moral rejection of the political was held to be more inclusive than political engagement through formal representative parties, leading advocates to argue the virtues of the 'non-party political process' (Kaldor 2003:85). This rejection of political engagement has enabled global civil society activists to assert that they represent the disengaged and marginalised; Kaldor cites Rajni Kothari:

> ...this is a whole new space. It is a different space, which is essentially a non-party space. Its role is to deepen the democratic process in response to the state that has not only ditched the poor and the oppressed but has turned oppressive and violent. It is to highlight dimensions that were not hitherto considered political and make them part of the political process.   (Kaldor 2003:85)

It is crucial to note that the concept of global civil society became increasingly popular when what was promoted as a liberal protest, against the lack of democracy in Eastern Europe, was implicitly transformed into a post-liberal critique of the limitations of democracy. This was not difficult as the East European intellectuals were no supporters of mass politics; 'anti-politics' was, in fact, a reflection of their disillusionment with the masses. Their 'refusal' was more about engagement with mass society than any reluctance to deal with the bureaucratic regimes themselves. Kaldor acknowledges the impulse behind East European intellectual dissent: 'They described themselves not as a movement but as a civic initiative, a "small island in a sea of apathy".' (Kaldor 2003:56)

It is this disillusionment with the people, rather than the dissidents' hostility to the state per se, which is highlighted by Kaldor's application of Konrad's 'anti-politics' and Havel's ideas of 'post-totalitarianism' to Western democratic life. She quotes Havel:

> It would appear that the traditional parliamentary democracies can offer no fundamental opposition to the automatism of techno-logical civilisation and the industrial-consumer society, for they, too, are being dragged helplessly along. People are manipulated in ways that are infinitely more subtle and refined than the brutal methods used in post-totalitarian societies... In a democracy, human beings may enjoy many personal freedoms...[but] they too are ultimately victims of the same automatism, and are incapable of defending their concerns about their own identity or preventing their superficialisation... (Kaldor 2003:57)

It becomes clear that it is not the critique of the strong state, under East European or Latin American authoritarianism, which has enabled the concept to appeal to radical Western advocates of global civil society, but rather the condemnation of mass politics. According to Richard Falk:

> The modern media-shaped political life threatens individuals with a new type of postmodern serfdom, in which elections, political campaigns, and political parties provide rituals without substance, a politics of sound bytes and manipulative images, reducing the citizen to a mechanical object to be controlled, rather than being the legitimating source of legitimate authority. (Falk 1995:253)

Ronnie Lipschutz similarly argues that mass politics cannot lead to emancipatory progress because 'in a sense, even societies in the West have been "colonized" by their states' (Lipschutz 1992:392). William Connolly writes that Western mass politics are a form of 'imprisonment' because progressive demands can be derailed by national chauvinist sentiments:

> Today the territorial/security state forms the space of democratic liberation and imprisonment. It liberates because it organises democratic accountability through electoral institutions. It imprisons because it confines and conceals democratic energies flowing over and through its dikes. The confinement of democracy to the territorial state...consolidates and exacerbates pressures to exclusive nationality... The state too often and too easily translates democratic energies into national chauvinist sentiments. (Connolly 1991:476)

Beneath the surface of postmodern radicalism, which condemns the state as the site of power and control, stands a more conservative thesis on the limits of democracy. Darrow Schecter also asserts that the state-based political realm is one of domination rather than liberation: 'the source of the political legitimacy of the state is the will of the people; but where does the legitimacy of the will of the people come from – the state?' (Schecter 2000:123) For postmodern and critical theorists, the fiction of the social contract is required to hide the fact that the coercive power of the state created the political sphere not the freely-willed demos (Foucault 2003:98–99; Connolly 1991:465–6; Pogge 1994:198). State-based democracy is, by definition, held to be based on hierarchies of power, exclusion and division. Ricardo Blaug, for example, argues that engaging in the formal political framework of states only increases the legitimacy of political hierarchies by channelling 'the utopian energies of the lifeworld' into legalistic arguments about rights on terms set by the state (Blaug 1999:121).

Representation is seen as a mechanism of domination over civil society, whereby political identities and interests are imposed from above. For Gideon Baker: 'a discursive-institutional division between representatives and represented actually constitutes subjects as citizens' (Baker 2003:10). Instead, Baker argues for the freedom of 'self-legislation' and 'doing politics for ourselves rather than on behalf of others', allowing identities to remain fluid and avoiding the 'game of power' (Baker 2003). He argues that, given their 'permanent domination of the political', states 'cannot be legitimate' and that new social movements can be, 'but only for as long as they resist incorporation' into the statist framework of law and rights (Baker 2002b:942). The radical 'bottom-up' approach of global civil society rejects any attempt to reconstitute traditional understandings of the political, which are territorially tied, even the 'post-national' frameworks of cosmopolitan democracy (Baker 2002b; Hutchings 2000, Jabri 2000).

## Radical 'autonomy'

The disillusionment with mass politics, highlighted in the 1980s in Central Europe and in the 1990s and beyond in the West, can be understood better in relation to the first movements to put issues and values before power, the 'new social movements', generally considered to be the offspring of the 1968 student protests (Kaldor 2003:84). The 'new' social movements were defined in opposition to the 'old' social movements of trade unions and Communist Party politics. Rather than engaging in formal politics, monopolised by the 'old' left, these groups stressed their radical opposition to traditional political engagement. As James Heartfield notes:

> The new generation of radicals did not, as a rule, challenge the official leadership of the trade unions, but side-stepped the organ- ised working class altogether, to find new constituencies and fields of activism. Taking the path of least resistance, these radicals took their struggle elsewhere.   (Heartfield 2002:142)

The radical struggle was shaped by a rejection of the conservative poli- tics of the organised left. Particularly in France, where the left (includ- ing the Communist Party) supported the war in Algeria, discrediting its claim of representing universal interests (Heartfield 2002:120). How- ever, rather than dispute the claims of the old left to represent a collec- tive political subject, the new left rejected the existence of collective political interests per se. This resulted, by default, in either a reduction of emancipatory claims to the 'self-realisation' of the individual (expressed, for example, in the women's movement and the *movement autogestionnaire* in France or the *Alternativbewegung* in Germany) or in the search for subaltern subjects on the margins of society (Wagner 2002). Instead of the construction of new collectivities, radical con- sciousness was dominated by a critical approach to organisation, a 'hermeneutics of suspicion', which derided mass politics and inevitably reduced political aspirations (Wagner 2002).

   The critique of, and political distancing from, organised labour, on the grounds of the rejection of any collective political subject, went hand-in-hand with a critique of mass politics and liberal democracy, which similarly implied a collective political subject, i.e., the electorate.

Leading theorists of the 'new left' Ernesto Laclau and Chantal Mouffe, argued that democratic struggles were not necessarily popular struggles, to be legitimated through the formal equality of the ballot-box (Laclau and Mouffe 2001). They denied the central importance of state-based politics of democratic representation, arguing that there was no one ontologically privileged political space (Laclau and Mouffe 2001; see also Jessop 1990). For these theorists of 'radical democracy', democratic struggles (for example, the feminist or anti-racist struggles) took place in a 'plurality of political spaces' shaped by their own, relatively autonomous 'ensemble of practices and discourses' (Laclau and Mouffe 2001:132). There was no longer one 'political space'; the key demands were therefore not for equal political rights of participation but for the recognition of difference and 'autonomy' (Laclau and Mouffe 2001:184).

For the advocates of new social movements, the state is perceived as a site of subordination, as part and parcel of the oppressive system of capitalist exploitation and bureaucratic domination. For this reason, it is argued, global civil society activists must remain autonomous of the institutionalised political system. The centrality of autonomy to the definition and nature of new social movements makes them implicitly anti-state, not so much because of their subjective political views but because of their organisational practices. As Kaldor notes:

> Whereas the 'old' movements aimed at persuading states to act and in the process helped to strengthen them, the 'new' movements are much more concerned about individual autonomy, about resisting the state's intrusion into everyday life. Claus Offe has argued that the 'new' movements represent a demand for radical democracy. 'Among the principal innovations of the new movements, in contrast with the workers' movement, are a critical ideology in relation to modernism and progress; decentralised and participatory organisational structures; defence of interpersonal solidarity against the great bureaucracies; and the reclamation of autonomous spaces rather than material advantages.'     (Kaldor 2003:84–85)

Global civic action, whether through NGOs or new social movements, is held to expand politics beyond the artificial construction of the formal political sphere (see also Walker 1994; Baker 2002b). As Hardt and Negri claim:

> Today the militant cannot even pretend to be a representative, even of the fundamental needs of the exploited. Revolutionary

political militancy today, on the contrary, must rediscover what has always been its proper form: *not representational but constituent activity.*   (Hardt and Negri 2001:413)

The radical approach sees the bearers of a new globalised democracy as social organisations which reject formal political processes and work at the sub-political level. For Alberto Melucci, new social movements exist outside of the traditional civil society-state nexus, submerged in everyday life. It is the 'alternative' politics which attracts civil society theorists to the formally non-political sphere (Arato and Cohen 1992; Seligman 1992:11–17). These new social movements are no longer concerned primarily with citizenship, rather than focus on political community, 'they have created meanings and definitions of identity' which contrast with traditional political boundaries (Melucci 1988:247). Melucci argues that traditional measurements of efficacy or success miss the point: 'This is because conflict takes place principally on symbolic ground... The mere existence of a symbolic challenge is in itself a method of unmasking the dominant codes, a different way of perceiving and naming the world.' (Melucci 1988:248)

Melucci highlights the choices thrown up by new social movements and their ambiguous relationship to the political:

A new political space is designed beyond the traditional distinction between state and 'civil society': an intermediate *public space*, whose function is not to institutionalise the movements or to transform them into parties, but to make society hear their messages...while the movements maintain their autonomy.   (Melucci 1985:815)

This ambiguity is the key to global civil society, understood as a space whereby moral movements can make their claims but also maintain their difference and specificity. They become 'visible' but are not institutionalised, that is they do not have to make claims to legitimacy based on public electoral or financial support (see Martin 2003). This, in Melucci's words, is the 'democracy of everyday life', where legitimacy and recognition stem from 'mere existence' rather than the power of argument or representation (Melucci 1988:259).

The focus on the everyday and the marginal has led to a growing appreciation of non-state networks least linked into political institutions and a celebration of the 'everyday' survival strategies of the Southern poor, which are held to 'reposition the locus of power' and 'transform the nature of power'. From this perspective, isolation and the reliance on contacts within 'local communities result in a de-centralized strength, rooted in the autonomy of the national and local process' (Patel, Bolnick and Mitlin 2001:244). Unlike the formal polit-ical struggle for representation, the struggle of global civil society 'from below' is for autonomy, held to be a self-constituting goal or end-point.

The radical self-constitution of the political subject avoids the medi-ating link of the political process. Political legitimacy is no longer derived from the political process of building support in society but rather from recognition of the movement's social isolation. This is a logical consequence of the new left's rejection of any legitimate collec-tive political subject. As Laclau and Mouffe assert in their summation of the essence of 'radical democracy':

> Pluralism is *radical* only to the extent that each term of this plurality of identities finds within itself the principle of its own validity... And this radical pluralism is *democratic* to the extent that the auto-constitutivity of each one of its terms is the result of displacements of the egalitarian imaginary. Hence, the project for a radical and plural democracy, *in a primary sense*, is nothing other than the strug-gle for a maximum autonomization of spheres on the basis of the generalization of the equivalential-egalitarian logic. (Laclau and Mouffe 2001:167)

In plain language – the claim is not for equality but for autonomy; for recognition on the basis of self-constituted difference rather than col-lective or shared support.

## Globalising the resistance

Not only do radical civil society theorists argue that the state is too strong, they also argue that it is too weak. The multiplicity of transna-tional actors and power of international institutions is held to make the state no longer capable of defending or articulating the interests of its citizens. For Kaldor:

> The role of global civil society in a system of global governance is not a substitute for democracy at a national level, but rather should be viewed as a supplement in an era when classical democracy is weakened in the context of globalisation. (Kaldor 2003:13)

The shift away from a focus on the state is often taken for granted in the global civil society literature. Jan Aart Scholte, for example, argues that globalisation has made the old international system of sovereign states 'impracticable', giving greater power to global economic institutions and that, as a consequence of this, 'citizens will understandably and rightly seek to engage more and more with these institutions' (Scholte 2001:103; see also Rosenau 1992). Kaldor asserts:

> The salient feature of globalisation is the rapidity of technological and social change. The modern state, in its twentieth-century form, is too top heavy, slow and rigid to find ways of adapting to the myriad of unintended consequences of change. Civil society, a combination of different movements, NGOs and networks, is a way of expressing the reflexivity of the contemporary world.   (Kaldor 2003:108)

Scholte suggests that the reason for the rise of global civil society is in response to the 'democratic deficits in prevailing patterns of globalization' (Scholte 2002:285). Globalisation is held to explain the need for global civic activism and to create the possibility for its success. Rather than being so strong that it oppresses democratic forces, the state is too weak to be a vehicle for democratisation:

> In the context of globalisation, democracy in a substantive sense, is undermined, however perfect the formal institutions, simply because so many important decisions that affect people's lives are no longer taken at the level of the state... [A] framework of global governance and an active global civil society at least offers some openings for participation at other levels.   (Kaldor 2003:110)

Many radical commentators see power as increasingly exercised on a global rather than national level, in which case, global civil society activism is seen as a vital 'counter-hegemonic' project of change (Cox 1983, 1999; Colas 2002). There is a strange *schadenfreude* or optimism about these views of state weakness and the possibility of new global protest movements setting the agenda. For Martin Shaw:

> ...the global revolution portends (if it has not yet achieved) a decisive movement beyond [the old] structure of world politics... [T]he fundamental state relations of the new era are no longer national and international in the historic sense. There is a unification of core

world state institutions, so that the political structure of social relations on a world scale has fundamentally changed. (Shaw 2000:17)

Even less radical commentators are happy to pay lip-service to the immanent possibilities of global civic movements, David Held, for example arguing: 'The struggle over the accountability of the global economic order has become increasingly intense. Violence in Seattle, Prague, Genoa and elsewhere has marked a new level of conflict about globalisation, democracy and social justice.' (Held 2002:305)

Rather than emphasise the problematic nature of increasingly unaccountable forms of power, that would inevitably flow from the alleged decline of representative government institutions, radical theorists tend to accentuate the positive. As one critic notes, these alleged changes are seen as 'an exciting and revolutionary phenomenon that demands a new democratic project' (Evans 2001). A radical optimism about the future of global civil society tends to be predicated on the strength of global governance mechanisms which are held to be beyond the constraints of nation-states.

One does not have to be a died-in-the wool cynic to consider the possibility that for many isolated radical commentators, marginalised by the electoral political process, the end of formal politics cannot come soon enough. It would seem to be their disillusionment with the domestic political process which is the dynamic behind numerous interpretations of the new powerlessness of the nation-state. The assertions about the unconstrained power of global governance give these radical normative ethical schemas, which seek to bypass democratic politics, a less defeatist (or elitist) legitimacy.

For example, John Keane today places a key emphasis on the intermeshing mechanisms of global governance in his work on 'cosmocracy'. Logically and chronologically Keane's theory of cosmocracy came after his long-standing interest in civil society, rather than his emphasis on global civil society flowing from an understanding or opposition to global governance. He explains why 'cosmocracy' or global governance is central:

The theory of cosmocracy anyway implies that our world is not principally composed of sovereign states; that the peaceful integration of political structures into governmental hybrid forms is a precondition of a global civil society; and that political order therefore can be restored in a variety of ways, not simply by chasing after the will-o'-the-wisp ideal of state integrity.   (Keane 2003:160, n.59)

It would appear that for the radical theorists of global civil society, 'my enemy's enemy is my friend'. In other words, the desire to undermine the legitimacy of state-based politics leads to an exaggeration of the importance of global governance mechanisms which are held to be independent of the control of nation-states; but which are allegedly open to pressure from autonomous global civic actors, operating outside the state-based framework.

For most global civil society theorists this apparent contradiction, between the two arguments that question political activity at the level of the nation-state, that of the state being too strong and too weak, is hardly considered. One commentator, who does flag this up, Rob Walker, argues that there is not necessarily a contradiction because the state may be increasing in strength measured in terms of its capacity to coerce civil society, and at the same time be weakened in relation to the global structures of economic and social power (Walker 1993:170). The problem is that, even if this was the case, the weakness of civil society vis-à-vis the state does little to support the idea that civil society operating globally could have any more success than at a national level, or that global civil society could hold global structures to account more effectively than powerful states.

### New global agency?

The radical proponents of globalisation 'from below' seek to discover a new source of political agency to replace those of the past. As Hardt and Negri note: 'The proletariat is not what it used to be' – the task is, therefore, to discover new forms of global agency (Hardt and Negri 2001:53). Martin Shaw argues that the progressive movement of global politics is one of 'conscious human agency' but that while 'there is no single guiding force, such as a revolutionary party...there are many actors whose conscious interactions shape the new era' (Shaw 2000:18). This is a 'global revolution' with a difference, there is no collective conscious agency but rather a new pluralist 'agency' which 'involves a radical redefinition of the idea of revolution' (Shaw 2000:18).

For Hardt and Negri, the plural source of global agency is to be found in disparate forms of resistance 'from below' from the 1992 Los Angeles riots, to the Palestinian Intifada and the uprising in Chiapas. These are local struggles with little in common and little that could be generalisable. This local character and isolation from any broader political movement, is described by Hardt and Negri as 'incommunicability': 'This paradox of incommunicability makes it extremely difficult to grasp and express the new power posed by the struggles that have emerged.' (Hardt and Negri 2001:54) Because these struggles are isolated and marginal, and express no broader political aspirations, they do not at first sight appear to be particularly powerful. However, for Hardt and Negri, a focus on their purely local and immediate character, for this reason, would be a mistake. They are also seen to have a universal character, in that they challenge facets of global capitalist domination. For example, the Los Angeles rioters are held to challenge racial and hierarchical forms of 'post-Fordist' social control, the Chiapas rebels to challenge the regional construction of world markets, etc. The key point is that: 'Perhaps precisely because all these struggles are incommunicable and thus blocked from travelling horizontally in the form of a cycle, they are forced instead to leap vertically and touch immediately on the global level.' (Hardt and Negri 2001:56)

It would appear that the decline of traditional international social movements, capable of generating mass support, has led radical theorists to see a new importance in increasingly disparate and isolated struggles. As Hardt and Negri illustrate:

> We ought to be able to recognize that this is not the appearance of a new cycle of internationalist struggles, but rather the emergence of a new quality of social movements. We ought to be able to recognize, in other words, the fundamentally new characteristics these struggles all present, despite their radical diversity. First, each struggle, though firmly rooted in local conditions, leaps immediately to the global level and attacks the imperial constitution in its generality. Second, all the struggles destroy the traditional distinction between economic and political struggles. The struggles are at once economic, political, and cultural – and hence they are biopolitical struggles, struggles over the form of life. They are constituent struggles, creating new public spaces and new forms of community. (Hardt and Negri 2001:56)

Until the Seattle protests of 1999, the most noted example of global civil society globalisation 'from below' was the Zapatistas, whose use of the internet to promote their struggle over land rights was picked up by Western academics, who turned the limited success of the Chiapas rising into a revolutionary 'postmodern social movement' (Burbach

1996; Debray 1996; Esteva 1999; Esteva and Prakash 1998). The Zapatistas' message was held to transcend the local. Charismatic leader, and former university lecturer, Subcomandante Marcos has promoted the movement as embodying the essence of global civil society. In response to the question 'who is he?' the reply was given:

> Marcos is gay in San Francisco, a black person in South Africa, Asian in Europe, a Jew in Germany...a feminist in a political party. In other words, Marcos is a human being in this world. Marcos is every untolerated, oppressed, exploited minority that is beginning to speak and every majority must shut up and listen.    (Cited in Giles and Stokke 2000).

Rather than political leadership the Zapatistas argue they offer a mirror reflecting the struggles of others (Klein 2002:210–12). Instead of a political or ideological struggle for a political programme, the Zapatista movement claims to seek support within the diverse heterogeneous movements of global civil society (Holloway 1998:180). The message is that subaltern subjects should celebrate difference rather than seek integration on the terms of power. Gideon Baker, for example, cites Marcos on the need to operate not on the state's terms but on those of global civil society, 'underground' and 'subterranean', rather than taking up formal avenues where they would be 'admitted only as losers' (Baker 2002b:941).

The EZLN (Zapatista Army of National Liberation) at its founding congress decreed it would not take part in elections or even allow its members to join political parties and the rejection of all ambition to hold political office became a condition of membership (Cunninghame and Corona 1998:16). Despite the geographic distance, the Zapatistas have a very similar approach to that of the East European 'anti-politics' intellectuals of the 1980s, accepting their weakness vis-à-vis the state and, instead of challenging governing power, following the less ambitious project of creating 'autonomous counter-publics' and thereby demonstrating the exclusionary practices of the Mexican state (Baker 2002a:140). As Naomi Klein notes: 'Marcos is convinced that these free spaces, born of reclaimed land, communal agriculture, resistance to privatisation, will eventually create counter-powers to the state simply by existing as alternatives' (Klein 2002:220). Baker highlights that what really makes the Zapatista struggle part of global civil society is not just the rejection of engagement with state-level politics but the declaration that their struggle is a global one, against transnational capitalism and neo-liberalism or just 'Power' – a conceptual shorthand for capitalism and its enforcers at a global and national level (Baker 2002a:142–3; see also Vidal 2003).

This rhetoric of global resistance coexists with a remarkable failure of the struggle to achieve any relief from abject poverty for the indigenous villagers of the area. Ten years after the Zapatistas' twelve day rebellion, which began on New Year's Day 1994, the Zapatista's demands are still ignored by the government of President Vicente Fox. The EZLN argue that their failure to deliver resources is a secondary question since they 'know their "dignity" is worth more than any government development project' (Tuckman 2003).

This contrast between the claims made for global civic actors and the reality of their marginalisation was clear in the alternative anti-globalisation conference held at the same time as the World Trade Organisation talks at Cancun in September 2003. Meeting in a bad-minton court in central Cancun, overhung with pictures of Che Guevara and Emiliano Zapata, WTO protesters could allege they represented 100 million peasant farmers – who would have been there but couldn't afford to come – while radical Western publishers launched their new books to an audience of Western spokesmen and women who talked-up the event. For example, Peter Rossett, from US think tank Food First, argued that the Cancun meeting demonstrated the strength of new social movements: 'These movements are growing fast, everywhere. For the first time you have global alliances forming...' (Cited in Vidal 2003). Barry Coates, of the World Development Movement, concurred: 'What we are seeing is the emergence of mass movements from across the spectrum of the developing world.' (Cited Vidal 2003) Even at this event, the highlight was a message of international support from Zapatista leaders, their first international message for four years (Marcos 2003; Vidal 2003).

Whether we would need the self-appointed spokespeople of Food First, the World Development Movement or the countless other think tanks and NGOs which advocate for the 'millions of dispossessed' if there was really the emergence of any type of mass movement is a mute point. It seems that, from anarchist squatters in Italy to the Landless Peasant's Movement in Brazil, the smaller and more marginal the struggle the more pregnant with possibility it is and the more it transgresses traditional political boundaries, whether conceptual or spatial. One might wonder whether there is an inverse relationship between the amount of progressive 'new characteristics' these struggles have and their strength and influence. A sceptical observer would no doubt suggest that the more marginal an opposition movement is, the more academic commentators can invest it with their own ideas and aspirations, and then these normative claims can be used by any institution or individual to promote their own importance and moral legitimacy.

If this is the case, it seems possible that if global civil society did not exist it would have had to have been invented. As Rob Walker notes, liberal and radical commentators have drawn 'heavily on the notion of a global civil society, not least so as to avoid falling back on some pre-political or even anti-political claim about an existing ethics of world politics' (Walker 1994:674).

## The narrowing sphere of political community

In Chapter 3 the international dynamic towards ethical foreign policies, and foreign intervention more generally, was seen to lie in the domestic political malaise and search for defining values and legitimacy. However, the search by Western governments for new ways of 'doing politics', in the absence of the collective social bonds which shaped and cohered state-based political projects, is a fairly recent phenomena. The search for an international identity to make up for domestic failings was, until the end of the Cold War, essentially a problem for those groups most reliant on a collective political identity, those on the political left.

While the 'new left' emphasises the moral distinctiveness of new social movements engaged in 'globalization from below' they are also keen to stress the 'global' nature of these 'movements'. The claims put forward for global civil society as a new way of doing politics appear to overcome the isolation of the left in their own societies – or put another way – their inability to engage with people, now seen to be only arbitrarily connected by the territorial (rather than political) ties of the nation. John Keane argues that this view of new social movements as the 'world proletariat in civvies', while comforting for the left, is highly misleading (Keane 2003:65). In contrast, Richard Falk describes this process in glowing terms of:

> ...transnational solidarities, whether between women, lawyers, environmentalists, human rights activists, or other varieties of 'citizen pilgrim' associated with globalisation from below... [who have] already transferred their loyalties to the invisible political community of their hopes and dreams, one which could exist in future

time but is nowhere currently embodied in the life-world of the planet. (Falk 1995:212)

The interconnectedness which is celebrated is, in fact, the flip-side of a lack of connection domestically: 'Air travel and the Internet create new horizontal communities of people, who perhaps have more in common, than with those who live close by.' (Kaldor 2003:111–112) What these 'citizen pilgrims' have in common is their isolation from and rejection of their own political communities. The transfer of loyalties to an 'invisible political community' is merely a radical re-representation of their rejection of a real and all too visible political community – the electorate.

In fact, the global movement for emancipation 'from below' could be read as a product of the end of any genuine transnational struggle. When radical theorists celebrate 'the early 1990s' as 'the time when civic transnationalism really came of age' (Falk and Strauss 2003:211), they betray a certain lack of historical imagination. Alejandro Colás in *International Civil Society* (2002) makes the point that the idea that transnational politics has recently emerged demonstrates a lack of historical awareness on the part of the advocates of 'globalization from below'.

In the nineteenth and twentieth centuries the main political currents, whether they were conservatives, communists, anarchists, socialists, pacifists, feminists or even nationalists were in fact internationally- as much as nationally-orientated. For example, the People's International League, a cross-European association of nationalists, was established by Mazzini in 1847, the International Working Men's Association or First International was formed in 1864, and the International Congress of Women was established in 1888 (Colás 2002:55–57). Rather than being new or on the rise, transnational political activism is in a parlous state today. The transnational social movements of modernity had the independence of aim and capacity to effect meaningful political change at both domestic and international levels without either relying on states to act on their behalf or, at the other extreme, avoiding any engagement with formal politics for fear of losing their 'autonomy'.

The fiction of global civil society as a normative project has its roots in the politics of the left, whose lack of support within their own societies was historically softened by the illusion of being part of an international movement. While their own groups may have been marginal to domestic politics adherents took heart in messages of 'solidarity'

from similarly marginal groups in other parts of the world and exaggerated tales of success of the New Zealand or Swiss 'section'. This international fiction was initially the mainstay of the 'old left' dependent on
the Communist International or international trade union federations.
However, the post-'68 'new left' soon followed the trend as peace, environmental and women's groups sought legitimacy more in their international connections than their capacity to win a domestic audience.

The transformations in Eastern Europe in 1989 leant new life to
this narcissistic form of internationalism. Isolated dissident groups in
Eastern Europe, whose oppositional politics was influenced by the new
left's rejection of mass politics and claims for 'recognition', found themselves to be the short-term beneficiaries of the collapsing Soviet systems
and the bureaucracy's search for a negotiated regime change. A new
'East-West' dialogue between Central and East European dissidents and
the West European peace movement gave an international legitimacy to
both sets of participants which were marginal in their own states.

Mary Kaldor's own experience of active involvement in the waning
European peace movements in the 1980s was an instructive one.
Perceiving themselves as isolated due to being 'unpatriotic' and 'pro-
Soviet', the European Nuclear Disarmament (END) group took their
critics' rejection literally when they said 'Why not demonstrate in
Moscow?' (Kaldor 2003:48):

> Hundreds of activists travelled to Eastern Europe and identified local
> groups, individuals, town councils and churches, with whom they
> could talk and exchange ideas. I have before me as I write a leaflet
> published by END called 'Go East': 'Forget smoke-filled rooms, this
> political organisation is asking you to take a holiday – in Eastern
> Europe.'   (Kaldor 2003:64)

The new strategy of 'Going East' was hardly a sign of political
dynamism, but rather of giving up on winning the arguments at home.
In the same way, today liberal and radical commentators are drawn to
the international realm, not because it is a sphere of political struggle
but, precisely because it appears to be an easier option where there is
less accountability and little pressure for representational legitimacy.

It would seem that the dynamic towards the creation of global civil
society is one of domestic marginalisation and the attempt to avoid the
pressures and accountability of national politics rather than the attraction of the international sphere per se. As Kaldor states: 'almost all
social movements and NGOs...have some kind of transnational rela-

tions. Precisely because these groups inhabit a political space outside formal national politics (parties and elections).' (Kaldor 2003:82) Claire Fox, writing about the burgeoning international activities of British local authorities, ranging from multiple twinning, to capacity-building partnerships as far a field as Indonesia, Vietnam and Kosovo, notes that it seems that easy-sounding solutions to problems elsewhere are more attractive than engaging with domestic difficulties. For her, it appears that 'New Internationalism is in danger or becoming a con-trick, a worthy sounding escape-route from the angst and insecurity of running and representing local areas' (Fox 2003).

Rather than be exposed through a formal struggle to win the argument with people in a genuine debate, isolated activists are drawn to the forums of international financial and inter-state institutions where there is no democratic discussion and they have no formal rights or responsibilities. Protesting outside meetings of the WTO or the G8 does not involve winning any arguments. At worst it is a technique of avoidance and at best a matter of courtier politics and elite lobbying, shortcutting any attempt to win popular representative support.

## Courtier politics

The attempt to give elite lobbying a moral legitimacy leads to the exploitation of marginal struggles in the non-Western world, where people are least likely to complain about Western advocates claiming to represent them and guide their struggle. Mary Kaldor echoes Keck and Sikkink approvingly in the use of the 'boomerang effect' to describe the way civil society groups could 'bypass the state' through appealing to transnational networks, international institutions and foreign governments (Kaldor 2003:5). Kaldor describes the relationship as 'a kind of two-way street':

> [which links Southern] groups and individuals who directly represent victims, whether it be the victims of human rights violations, poverty or environmental degradation, with the so-called Northern solidarity 'outsiders'. The former provide testimony, stories and information about their situation and they confer legitimacy on those who campaign on their behalf. The latter provide access to global institutions, funders or global media as well as 'interpretations' more suited to the global context. (Kaldor 2003:95)

The popularity of 'global civil society' for Western radicals would seem to be a reflection of the problems of East European oppositionist figures in the 1980s – the weakness of their own domestic position. While East European activists justified their 'anti-politics' on the basis of the state's domination of the political sphere, the Western radicals argue that theirs is based on the state's lack of relevance to policy-making. Instead, they have talked-up the importance of international institutional gatherings which previously attracted little interest. Pianta arguing, for example, that 'the new power of summits of states and inter-governmental organisations' needed to be confronted through the invention of parallel summits (Pianta 2003:238). In the face of an inability to make an impact at home, the transnational activists have sought to latch on to the ready-made agenda of international institutions. It is increasingly apparent that these radical movements are shaped and cohered by external agendas, by the timetable of meetings of the G7, WTO or the UN, more than by any collective drive of their own.

Ironically, rather than bringing pressure to bear on institutions, it is these institutions, particularly the UN, which have been largely responsible for creating a global activist network, providing an agenda of forums which could act as a cohering focus for the establishment of a 'loose coalition of groups and individuals worldwide' (Bunch 2001:217–21). Rather than being seen as a threat to the powers that be, in the international establishment, the 'new' social movements are more often than not seen as making a positive contribution. For example, following the G8 summit in Genoa in 2001 global institutions responded by welcoming the dialogue. The IMF and the World Bank invited lobby groups including Global Exchange, Jobs with Justice, 50 Years is Enough and Essential Action to engage in public debate. Guy Verhofstadt, Prime Minister of Belgium and President of the European Union at the time, wrote an open letter to the anti-globalisation movement, published in major national newspapers around the world, and collected the responses. The French Prime Minister, Lionel Jospin, welcomed 'the emergence of a citizen's movement at the planetary level' (Kaldor 2003:103).

As highlighted by George W. Bush's relationship with U2 rock star Bono, governments and international institutions can only gain from their association with radical advocates (Vidal 2002; Carroll 2003). The reason for the positive approach of the establishment lies in the fact that the relationship of advocacy implies a mutual interest rather than any radical opposition (see Heartfield forthcoming). The power of the advocate depends more on their access to governing elites than any authority gained independently through representation. This lack of representational accountability (at any level) leaves control in the hands of the powerful, while offering the appearance of 'openness', 'transparency' and 'accountability'. Under these circumstances, the more 'radical' global civic actors become the more the doors of inter-state forums have been opened to them (see Heins forthcoming).

Despite the claims of many critical theorists, there are few indications that operating outside the formal political sphere of electoral representation facilitates a radical challenge to political power and existing hierarchies of control. Compared to 'political' social movements of the past, new social movements based on advocacy pose much less of a threat to the status quo. However, for Kaldor:

> [the advocacy movement] represents, in some respects, a revival of the great anti-capitalist movements of the late nineteenth and early twentieth centuries. At the World Social Forum in Porto Alegre in 2002, the activists defined themselves as a 'global movement for social justice and solidarity'. (Kaldor 2003:101)

The activists may have declared themselves to constitute a 'global movement' but it could be argued that what is distinctive about global civic activism is precisely the individual character of global civic activism rather than the collective mass character of the 'great anti-capitalist movements' of the last two centuries. According to Grugel:

> Recent anti-globalisation movements include: the Jubilee 2000 campaign against third world debt; mass protest against the policies and strictures imposed by the IMF, the symbol of global regulation; street protests at European Union summits; and local protests against the onward march of globalising capitalism, such as that encapsulated within the Chiapas rebellion in Mexico... At the same time, social organisations, many with roots as far back as the 1960s and 1970s, based around issues of justice, human rights and ecology and composed of globally active NGOs, continue to present alternative visions of globalisation from below. These organisations privilege lobbying at the global level over national strategies of mobilisation. As a result, even the voices of communities geographically isolated from, and economically unimportant to, the core of the global economy and decision-making can now be heard in the decision-making centres of the global political economy. (2003:276)

The anti-globalisation movement brings together disparate groups and organisations which choose to prioritise global lobbying and advocacy politics over the struggle for democratic legitimacy at the national level. The rejection of the mass politics of liberal democracy is radically re-represented as the claim to be operating on a higher moral level, that of making common cause with the most marginalised social groups least influential to the workings of the global economy. Moral advocates who take up the (selective) demands of (selective) marginal groups, and provide '"interpretations" more suited to the global context', can then lobby for their political ends without the trouble of democratic legitimacy.

The advantage of the politics of moral advocacy is that individuals can engage in politics without having to win electoral accountability. As Slavoj Zizek notes, this limited interactivity is based on 'interpassivity', the virtuous activity of a minority being presupposed by the passivity of others, who are spoken for (Zizek 2003; see also Mendel 2003). Rather than expand the horizon of democratic politics, this is a form of politics which is neither 'democratic' nor 'inclusive' (see Lipschutz forthcoming). It is focused around the 'freedoms' of the individual advocate who engages in courtly politics and elite lobbying.

This highly individualised approach is reflected in the work of Mary Kaldor, who argues: 'I develop my own definition of civil society as the medium through which social contracts or bargains between the *individual* and centres of political and economic power are negotiated, discussed and mediated.' (Kaldor 2003:12) Where, in the past, the 'social contract' was made through collective and egalitarian political engagement, for Kaldor, civil society takes the place of collective politics and facilitates an individual 'negotiation' with centres of power. The normative project of global civil society ends up rejecting democratic accountability for the courtier politics of elite advocacy.

### Living in truth

In the same way as the courtier politics of elite advocates makes the personal act a political one, through bypassing the mediation of a collective political process, there has also been a startling emergence of a new type of individuated civic activism, one which engages in politics through private moral acts. The old peace movement slogan 'Think globally, act locally' has been reversed by global civil society activists to read 'Think locally, act globally' or even to 'Think locally *and* globally; act locally *and* globally together' (Clark 2001:18; Gaventa 2001:276). However, the actions, whether local or global or both, are those which prioritise the moral quality of the individual over any collective project. Ann Mische highlights that this is a 'type of civic participation in which human subjectivity is not sacrificed to politics' (Mische 1993:245). This is a form of politics which privileges the individual subject above the collective one. The 'anti-politics' or 'living in truth' of East European intellectual oppositionists, such as Havel, is the model of today's political activism which seeks to blur the distinction between the private and the public life of an individual:

> ...the aim is not to maintain two mutually opposed realms, but rather to understand the one as a 'holding area' of the self, from which the self must necessarily emerge to act publicly within the other. In Havel's view, it is the recovery of the 'hidden sphere' of subjectivity that provides the basis for the 'independent life of society'. (Mische 1993:245)

Gideon Baker suggests that personal morality should be the basis of the public resistance to power. This blurring of the private and the public is central to the liberatory promise of post-political activism: 'This holds out the hope of both personal and political autonomy, in short, of self-rule.' (Baker 2002a:149)

23-year-old Caoimhe Butterly is a leading example of the new breed of transnational political activists. Brought up in a culture of liberation theology and with her father working around the world as an economic advisor to the UN, she worked in soup kitchens in New York, in Guatemala and with the Zapatista communities in Mexico before working in pre-war Iraq with an activist group opposing sanctions and then moving to Palestine working in Jenin camp. Interviewed in the *Guardian*, after being shot by Israeli troops, she was asked if she planned to leave. Her reply was 'I'm going nowhere. I am staying until this occupation ends. I have the right to be here, a responsibility to be here. So does anyone who knows what is going on here.' (Barlow 2002)

This is a very different form of political activism from the solidarity work of trade unionist and political activists in the past. Rather than engaging in political debate and discussion with colleagues and workmates or raising concerns in election campaigns, the new breed of postmodern activist is more concerned to act as a moral individual than to engage in collective political action. The rights which are claimed are those of individual engagement with other people's struggles rather than any specific political claims of the Palestinians or of others.

Caiomhe argues she has a duty to be in Palestine, to bear witness and to negotiate with Israeli forces on behalf of Palestinian victims, and, implicitly, that any morally-aware person has a similar duty. The self-centredness of this type of moral politics is highlighted in the title of leftist British comedian Jeremy Hardy's film of his experience in the region: *Jeremy Hardy versus the Israeli Army* (see also Hardy 2003).

Ken Nichols O'Keefe, leading the volunteer mission of peace activists acting as human shields during the 2003 Iraq war, spells out the transnational ethos. According to O'Keefe 'we the "citizens" are responsible for the actions of "our" governments...we are collectively guilty for what we allow to be done in our name' (O'Keefe 2002). For this reason O'Keefe has renounced his US citizenship and would 'invite everybody to join me in declaring themselves not citizens of nations but world citizens prepared to act in solidarity with the most wretched on our planet and to join us' (O'Keefe 2002). Along with Caiomhe, O'Keefe is implicitly critical of those who do not take up the invitation to put morality first. O'Keefe would 'rather die in defense of justice and peace than "prosper" in complicity with mass murder and war' (O'Keefe 2002).

It would appear that the motivation of the global civic activists acting as human shields and witnesses in Iraq and the West Bank has less to do with the politics of the conflicts and more to do with their own personal need to make a moral statement. Ronald Forthofer, from the Episcopal Church in Longmont, Colorado, a human shield in Beit Jalla on the West Bank, stated: 'We believe that we who are protected in America should experience and live in the same way that Palestinians are living in the suffering.' (Hazboun 2001) Kate Edwards, a community worker from Manchester, explained why she joined the International Solidarity Movement in the occupied territories: 'I wanted to challenge myself to see if I could cope working in a place like this. I have good friends and a comfortable life. I wanted to do something for those who were not as fortunate as me.' (Beaumont and Wainwright 2002) But rather than donate to the Red Cross or another professionally trained organisation, Kate felt the need to put her own life at risk, suffering severe internal injuries from bullet wounds in Bethlehem, after refusing to follow Israeli troop orders to halt. A similar individual mission has driven young British Muslims to volunteer as suicide bombers in conflicts abroad. As Josie Appleton notes:

> This is less a case of militants finding common cause in Palestinians' fight for their land and livelihood, than of finding themselves – of finding their own individual identity and mission... In this context,

the nihilistic tactic of suicide bombing seems to allow these young Western militants to fight their own war. Unlike fighting in an army over a sustained period of time, suicide bombing is an individual act that requires no engagement with the conflict itself. It is *my* act, the sacrifice of *my* life – it allows suicide bombers to construct in their heads the mission that they are making the sacrifice for.   (Appleton 2003)

In the not so recent past it was religious leaders and moral authority figures who 'intervened' in other people's struggles in the hope of bringing a peaceful resolution by bearing witness to the suffering and attempting to help. Today, the collapse of a broader political or moral framework has led to individuals claiming their own moral right of 'intervention' without any legitimacy derived from a collective authority.

## Conclusion

The celebration of global civil society 'from the bottom up' would appear to be less about global change than the attempt to justify the avoidance of accountability to any collective source of political community or elected authority. The focus on the shared interests with those 'excluded', or the global community of radical activists, is a way of legitimising the avoidance of connection with those still 'trapped inside' – the electorate. William Connolly highlights this:

Cross-national, non-state democratic movements...contest the cultural assumption of alignment between a citizen's commitment to democracy and her commitments to the priorities of a particular state... To the extent that such movements unfold...a fundamental imperative of the late-modern time becomes more clear to more people: today a decent democrat must sometimes be disloyal to the state that seeks to own her morally and politically; she must do so in the name of allegiances to a global condition that transcends the confines of any state. As things stand now, corporate elites, financial institutions, criminal networks, communication media and intelligence agencies exercise considerable independence in this regard. Only democratic citizens remain locked behind the bars of the state in the late-modern time.   (Connolly 1991:479)

The corrosive essence of the 'anti-politics' of global civil society is that it legitimates a highly individual political morality as one that can be advocated in the name of a spurious 'global allegiance'. As Kaldor states:

> Advocates of transnational civil society share with the eighteenth-century theorists of civil society the notion of a public morality based on individual conscience. This is indeed the reason for retaining the term. The difference is that the ethical arena, the realm of public morality, is greatly extended. It is a plea for cosmopolitan rights that takes us well beyond the [Kantian] right to hospitality. (Kaldor 1999b:211)

The problem is that the area of 'public morality' is not extended through this moral claim on behalf of 'individual conscience'; instead the political is reduced to the personal and no claim on behalf of a collective community is sustainable. Rather than address the 'global wrongs' of the world, the normative project of global civil society is a retreat into 'individual conscience'. As Ellen Meiskins Wood notes, the focus on identity and difference differs greatly from the early view of interest group politics in that it rejects 'an inclusive political totality – like the "political system", the nation, or the body of citizens' and instead insists on the primacy and 'irreducibility of fragmentation and "difference"' (Wood 1995:260).

The struggle for individual moral and political autonomy, the claim for the recognition of separate 'political spaces' and for the 'incommunicability' of political causes, demonstrates the limits of the radical claims for the normative project of global civil society 'from below'. The rejection of the formal political sphere, as a way of mediating between the individual and the social, leaves political struggles isolated from any shared framework of meaning or from any formal processes of democratic accountability. The consequences of this will be considered further in the following chapter, where it will be suggested that rather than constituting a challenge to unaccountable frameworks of global governance, the struggle for 'autonomy' from below is, in fact, the ideological counterpart of the struggle for 'autonomy' for unelected and unaccountable forms of governance 'from above'.

# 7
# The Cosmopolitan Paradox

## Introduction

Cosmopolitan normative global civil society theorists envisage a process of expanding cosmopolitan democracy and global governance, in which for the first time there is the possibility of global issues being addressed on the basis of new forms of democracy, derived from the universal rights of global citizens expressed largely through global civic actors. They suggest that, rather than focus attention on the territorially-limited rights of the citizen at the level of the nation-state, more emphasis should be placed on new methods of citizen engagement and representation outside the bounds of national political mechanisms of accountability. This chapter raises problems with extending the concept of rights beyond the bounds of the sovereign state, without a mechanism of making these new rights accountable to their subject. It is highlighted that the emerging gap, between holders of cosmopolitan rights and those with duties, tends to create dependency rather than to empower. This indicates that, while the new rights remain tenuous, there is a danger that the cosmopolitan framework can legitimise the abrogation of the existing rights of democracy and self-government preserved in the UN Charter framework.

This chapter addresses the question of how to assess the trend towards increasing prominence for advocacy rights of global civic actors in the international sphere and for the restricted interpretation of traditional rights of sovereign independence and self-government. Over the last decade, many leading international relations theorists have developed a cosmopolitan perspective, which sees current trends as benign or potentially positive.[1] Leading cosmopolitan theorists seek to challenge the inter-state framework of the UN Charter period, established in the aftermath of the Second World War, which prioritised the principles of sovereign equality and of non-intervention. They argue that these principles need to be replaced by new ones based on a higher level of public accountability, which make the individual rights of members of global civil society the primary focus. As noted in the previous chapters, the growing political importance of the international sphere is often promoted as a result of globalisation and the declining importance of the nation-state. For many advocates of cosmopolitan rights, 'we are moving ineluctably towards a global epoch characterised by post-territoriality'. In which case: 'Creating democratic structures beyond the nation-state is therefore seen as a far more urgent requirement than simply strengthening democratic procedures within states.' (Grugel 2003:273)

Rather than the rights of states being the founding principle of international society, it should be the rights of global citizens, given voice through global civil society. Today, a new consensus is forming that 'there is a pressing need to rethink the concept and practice of sovereignty' (Camilleri and Falk, 1992). Andrea Bianchi argues that the values and principles governing international law are under challenge:

> The two opposite poles of the spectrum are evident. On the one hand, there stands the principle of sovereignty with its many corollaries...on the other, the notion that fundamental human rights should be respected. While the first principle is the most obvious expression and ultimate guarantee of a horizontally-organized community of equal and independent states, the second view represents the emergence of values and interests...which deeply [cut] across traditional precepts of state sovereignty and non-interference in the internal affairs of other states. (Bianchi 1999:260)

Geoffrey Robertson QC, a leading advocate of individual rights and author of *Crimes Against Humanity: the Struggle for Global Justice*, argues:

> Customary international law is in the human rights field anachronistic, to the extent that it is an emanation of agreements between sovereign states. ...[M]illions of ordinary men and women...do not talk about *jus cogens* and *erga omnes*: they believe in the simple language of the Universal Declaration, and they are not bound by Article 2(7) of the UN Charter to avert their eyes from repression in foreign countries... These citizens, of global society rather than the nation-state, cannot understand why human rights rules should not rule. (Robertson 1999:82)

Cosmopolitan normative theorists argue that democracy and accountability can no longer be equated with sovereignty and non-intervention: 'democracy must transcend the borders of single states and assert itself on a global level' (Archibugi 2000:144). Cosmopolitans allege that without this the dominant relations of power and inequality will be perpetuated. For Richard Falk, Western states 'do not even purport to represent the great majority of women and men on the planet. Moreover such states represent only the dominant class, gender, and race within their own territorial space.' (Falk 1995:50) To meet the needs of cosmopolitan or global citizens it is necessary to extend democracy beyond the nation-state. Andrew Linklater states that:

> Transcending state sovereignty which remains the constitutive principle of modern political life is understood as essential to promoting narratives of increasing cosmopolitanism. Expanding the realm of dialogic commitments is regarded as necessitating measures to reduce or eradicate the asymmetries of power and wealth which exist within sovereign states and in the global economic and political system.   (Linklater 1998:109; see also 192)

David Beetham asserts that in a world of nation-states 'the *demos* that is democracy's subject has come to be defined almost exclusively in national terms, and the scope of democratic rights has been limited to the bounds of the nation-state' (Beetham 1999:137). He argues that in the same way that democracy was extended from the level of the town to that of the state in the eighteenth century it should, in the twenty-first century, be extended from the nation to humankind as a whole. Similarly, Jan Aart Scholte suggests that globalisation has generated the 'growth of cosmopolitan bonds, where people identify the demos in terms of humanity as a whole', while conventional 'mechanisms of democracy tend to define "the people" only in territorial-state-nation terms' (Scholte 2002:290).

The rationale behind calls for a new and more expansive institutionalisation of democracy is held to be the impact of globalising processes, which have created a 'democratic deficit' at the national level. As Anthony McGrew notes:

> ...democratic thinkers, from J. S. Mill to Robert Dahl, have assumed a direct symmetry between the institutions of representative democracy and the political community which they serve...but this presumes a direct correspondence between rulers and ruled, a correspondence

which is disrupted by the existence of global and regional networks of power.   (McGrew 1997:237)

Daniele Archibugi and David Held assert that decisions made democratically by citizens of one state or region can no longer be considered to be truly democratic if they affect the rights of 'non-citizens', i.e., those outside that community, without those people having a say. Held argues that, for example, villagers in sub-Saharan Africa, who live at the margins of some of the central power structures and hierarchies of the global order, are profoundly affected by the policies made in these inter-state forums (Held 1998:14). Archibugi stresses that the inequalities of global power relations mean that decisions democratically restricted to the nation-state cannot be considered democratic from a cosmopolitan perspective:

> ...few decisions made in one state are autonomous from those made in others. A decision on the interest rate in Germany has significant consequences for employment in Greece, Portugal and Italy. A state's decision to use nuclear energy has environmental consequences for the citizens of neighbouring countries. Immigration policies in the European Union have a significant impact on the economic development of Mediterranean Africa. All this happens without the affected citizens having a say in the matter.   (Archibugi 1998:204)

Cosmopolitans highlight that, for democracy to exist in a globalised world, it is necessary to have the consent of the entire community which will be affected by a particular decision. To this end, new political constituencies need to be created to address these questions. These constituencies may be smaller or larger than the nation-state, depending on the issue at stake. For David Held, in a cosmopolitan democratic system:

> People can enjoy membership in the diverse communities which significantly affect them and, accordingly, access to a variety of forms of political participation. Citizenship would be extended, in principle, to membership in all cross-cutting political communities, from the local to the global.   (Held 1995:272)

Linklater suggests that: 'Images of community which envisage the transfer of power and authority to new centres of decision-making inside and outside national boundaries promise to preserve the strengths and cancel the weakness of orthodox conceptions of citizen-ship.' (Linklater 1998:217) The roots of cosmopolitan democracy in Habermasian discourse ethics (discussed in Chapter 5) are clear (see also Falk's emphasis on a 'Habermasian ethos', 1995:150). As Linklater states:

> As the most sophisticated test of legitimacy, discourse ethics endorses a system of justification which stresses answerability to all human beings who stand to be affected by any action rather than accountability to the narrower circle of those with whom moral agents are linked by special ties and shared dispositions.   (Linklater 1998:92)

In order to address this moral and democratic deficit, cosmopolitans propose replacing the territorially-bounded political community of the state as the subject of international decision-making by new flexible frameworks based on the rights of the global citizen, freed from territo-rial restrictions. To quote Daniele Archibugi:

> If some global questions are to be handled according to democra-tic criteria, there must be political representation for citizens in global affairs, independently and autonomously of their political representation in domestic affairs. The unit should be the indi-vidual, although the mechanisms for participation and repre-sentation may vary according to the nature and scope of the issues discussed.   (Archibugi 1998:212)

Cosmopolitans argue that there is still an important role for the state and for representative democracy, but that these institutions cannot have the final say in decision-making. In certain circumstances, where this is not democratic enough, it must be possible for sovereignty to be overridden by institutions which are 'autonomous and independent' and whose legitimacy is derived from the universal rights of the global citizen, unconstrained by the nation-state framework. In this way, it is held, cosmopolitan democracy can 'capture the central problem of pol-itics which is how to create communities which do not subject aliens and subaltern domestic groups to the tyranny of unjust exclusion' (Linklater 1998:219). Ken Booth claims that:

> In 1948, with the Universal Declaration of Human Rights, the indi-vidual was potentially brought back to the centre. A building block

was constructed for the possible development of a cosmopolitan democracy in a world of post-sovereign states... This is the hope of progressively leaving behind the politics of the concentration camp – the ultimate sovereign space – for a cosmopolitan democracy aimed at reinventing global human being – being human globally – based on the politics of the-I-that-is-an-other, and badged with common humanity. (Booth 1999:65–66)

This limitation on state-based mechanisms of democracy and accountability, and on states as the subjects of international law, relies on the possibility of a 'higher law' derived from the individual global citizens as new, and prior, subjects of international relations. It is at this point that the theoretical underpinnings of the cosmopolitan project appear fragile. The citizen-subject of international decision-making appears overburdened with both theoretical and practical problems. The following section raises some theoretical questions about the essence of the cosmopolitan perspective: the extension of democracy beyond states and the development of the global citizen as a subject of international law. Further sections will develop the theoretical and practical implications of the cosmopolitan framework for questions of state sovereignty and the relationship between states and international institutions.

## Cosmopolitan democracy?

Cosmopolitan theorists accept that there is no global state or global federation or institutional framework and also argue that, if there were, it would be a bad thing. They are clear that the establishment of democratic institutions on a global level would meet the opposition of nation-states and that, even if this could be brought into existence, it would involve such a high level of homogenisation, through social, economic and cultural regulation, that it could only be imposed through war and repression (Falk 1995:6; CGG 1995:xvi; Kaldor 1999a:148; Held 1995:230). In which case, there can be no cosmopolitan framework of formal political rights, which enable individual citizens to be represented as political equals (see also Canovan 2001:212). The promise of the cosmopolitan framework is that citizens and aliens can participate equally in decision-making (Linklater 1998:202–3). However, the global citizen cannot have the same sorts of rights as the citizen of a nation-state and creating equality between citizens and non-citizens clearly involves redefining the rights of both. The formal rights of the global citizen are a thorny issue for cosmopolitan theorists and for many the question falls 'outside the scope' of their immediate concerns (Kaldor 1999a:148). Archibugi states: 'World citizenship does not necessarily have to assume all the demands of national citizenship. The real problem is to identify the areas in which citizens should have rights and duties as inhabitants of the world rather than of secular states.' (Archibugi 1998:216)

The rights of the global citizen are certainly 'less demanding'. For cosmopolitan theorists, the new institutions, through which the cosmopolitan citizen can exercise their rights, must exist independently of states and their governments. Theorists, who develop the implications of this approach, go further to add that national political parties, which are orientated around national questions rather than global ones, also cannot be vehicles for cosmopolitan citizenship as they are incapable of representing individuals on global issues (Archibugi 2000:146). For this reason the global citizen can only be represented through the framework of global civil society, which it is argued can forward non-statist concerns and hold governments to account, through transnational campaigning and media pressure (Beetham 1999:142).

There are several difficulties with this perspective. Firstly, there is little agreement on the extent to which global civil society groups and campaigns can influence government policy-making and thereby create a new mechanism of political 'accountability' (Scholte 2002; Forsythe 2000:169; Charnovitz 1997). Secondly, and most importantly, even if global civil society groups did wield influence over policy-makers, this may not necessarily enhance the level of democratic accountability (Scholte 2002; Baker 2002b; Kenny 2003). Global civil society operates in close relationship to the sphere of formal politics but, by definition, global civil society organisations – whether they are community groups, single issue pressure groups, NGOs, grassroots campaigns, charities, media organisations, research groups, or non-government-funded policy advisers – operate outside the political sphere of institutionalised democratic equality and accountability. Global civil society groups play a legitimate and often crucial role in policy-making but, as Michael Edwards notes, it is vital to 'differentiate between the views of special interest groups (however well intentioned) and formal representation from below' (Edwards 1999:180). While it is often possible for individuals to participate in the organisations of global civil society, it is difficult to accept the assertion that 'signing petitions for and donating charitable contributions to such organisations must surely count as acts of world citizenship' (Heater 1999:144).

With regard to the South, the idea that NGOs and grass roots organisations (GROs) can represent the interests of the most marginal and isolated individuals has been challenged through empirical case studies, which highlight Southern NGOs' dependency on Northern partners and donors, and pressures to devote resources towards external funding sources (see Hudock 1999 for an excellent study; Sali-Terzić 2001; Chandler 1998). In fact, several studies suggest that the growth of community- and grassroots-based organisations, dependent on external funding, is as much as a sign of disempowerment and new forms of dependency as any positive indication of 'voice' or participation (see, for example, Chandhoke 2002:46–7; Maina 1998; Stirrat 1996; Weber 2002). Southern 'voices' which are 'heard' are inevitably in a minority as global civil networks have been shown to be highly asymmetric with over-representation of Northern NGOs reinforcing rather than challenging hierarchical relations (Edwards 2001:9; Edwards and Gaventa 2001; see also the statistical data in Glasius, Kaldor and Anheier 2002:318–23).

The opportunity for participation depends on the organisation concerned. For example, many of the global civic actors most active and influential in defending rights, like Human Rights Watch, the International Crisis Group or the International Commission of Jurists, have no mass membership and concentrate on elite advocates to enable them to gain admittance to government and international officials (Forsythe 2000:167–8; Charnovitz 1997:270; de Waal 1997b:3–4). The extent of any participation differs between organisations and even where there are high levels of participative involvement this generally stops short of having any say over policy. As Jenny Bates, at the Progressive Policy Institute, states: 'NGOs are not elected and, unlike governments, need not answer to the broad public they claim to represent.' (Cited in Bosco 2000) James Heartfield highlights the point:

> In an informal network, decisions cannot be tested, nor members held accountable for their actions. The environmentalist campaign Greenpeace has had considerable success intervening in the meetings of industry share holders to protest over genetic modification and pollution. It is pointed that Greenpeace itself could never be the target of such an intervention. The organisation has a tiny staff, and an unelected board. The millions of Greenpeace subscribers who pay standing orders to Greenpeace have no rights over policy. (Heartfield 2002:148)

There is no direct link between (non)participation and any conception of citizenship rights which can be given content through formal mechanisms of democratic accountability. We are not all equally involved in global civil society, we do not vote for global civil society policies and we cannot hold global civil society actors to account.

Thirdly, the rejection of state-based civil society activity, which was assumed to be central to global civil society's role in promoting democracy, is often more apparent than real (Kaldor 2003:6). Global civil society is no less shaped by national governments and state-based political structures than national political parties and other representative institutions. In fact, surveys demonstrate that the international human rights movement relies more heavily on 'insider' tactics which depend on access to state institutions, than other, less 'radical' non-state actors (Smith, Pagnucco and Lopez, 1998:394–5). As Martin Shaw notes:

> From the viewpoint of many groups in non-Western society...being involved in global civil society is in fact a way of connecting to Western civil society and hence securing some leverage with the Western state which is at the core of global power... The question that arises is whose voices are heard and how?  (Shaw 1999:223)

Without a global state or a global political framework, it is debatable whether it is possible to talk about a 'global' civil society beyond the nation-state. There are no genuinely transnational institutions and international institutions, from the IMF and the World Bank to the OSCE and NATO to the EU and the UN, are all composed of state actors and representatives. Martin Köhler, for example, argues that it is misleading to talk of a 'global civil society' in the same way as the independent realm of civil society within the domestic sphere:

> [T]he transnational public sphere itself cannot be conceived of simply as the extension of the national one. The very concept of the public sphere is intrinsically bound up in structures of authority and accountability which do not exist in the transnational realm... [A]s long as the state continues to be the only site of political authority in international relations, it is impossible for a transnational public sphere...to emerge.  (Köhler 1998:233)

In the cosmopolitan framework, it would appear problematic to talk about the exercise of rights, or of democracy, outside the framework of nation-states. Some leading analysts and advocates argue speculatively that 'NGOs will lead the way towards greater accountability by governments' or normatively insist that 'states should be accountable to international civil society' (Posner 1997:630; Otto 1996:140). However, as Jan Arte Scholte correctly notes, it is states which have to establish structures for the involvement of global civic actors and decide the methods of consultation (Scholte 2002:300). Steve Charnovitz highlights that even the involvement of international NGOs in policy-making cannot make nation-states more accountable, the establishment of NGO advisory committees actually gives nation-state governments greater control over decision-making as the real power belongs to the international officials who determine which NGOs to appoint (Charnovitz 1997:283; see also Dodds 2001; Colás 2002:154–5).

This reality of dependency is acknowledged in the frameworks articulated by Archibugi and Held, and in similar reform proposals forwarded by the Commission on Global Governance. These allow citizens and global civil society groups to participate in global or regional institutional forums where they have specific competencies, for example, in those that deal with the environment, population issues, development or disarmament. However, this participation 'would supplement but not replace existing inter-governmental organisations'. Archibugi stresses that: 'Their function would be essentially advisory and not executive.' (Archibugi 1998:219)

Despite the desires of cosmopolitan advocates, there appears to be little evidence of the claims of any 'new' levels of democracy or political accountability, promised to the global citizen, through membership of global civil society, as opposed the humble citizen of the nation-state, who can formally hold their government to account.[2] In fact, any search for the formal democratic rights of the cosmopolitan citizen would be a fruitless one. The new rights that the cosmopolitan citizen possesses cannot be located within the liberal democratic rights tradition, which equates the rights-holder and the duty-holder within the same legal subject. These new 'rights' do not manifest themselves at the level of the citizen or at the level of global civil society but rather at the level of international institutions:

> Rights ought to relate, in the first instance, to the sphere of survival and to issues which cross national boundaries. In relation to these rights, world citizens undersign certain duties which enable global institutions to perform a function of temporary replacement, subsi-

darity and substitution *vis-à-vis* national institutions. (Archibugi 1998:219)

The new 'rights' of global citizens and global civic actors are not exercised by the rights-holders but by international institutions, which have new 'duties' corresponding to the new rights created. As shall be highlighted below, the duties and rights created in the cosmopolitan discourse are of a qualitatively different nature to those established under the domestic framework of the rule of law and enforced through the police and the courts. The equation of the 'right' of the global citizen or global civil society with the 'duty' of international institutions creates a new level of rights on paper but is problematic in practice. This is clearly demonstrated in the fundamental area of the prevention of wide-scale abuses of human rights:

> The institutions of global civil society would exercise direct control in one essential area: the prevention and impediment of acts of genocide or domicide. To do so they would be entitled to demand the immediate intervention of the governments of all states. (Archibugi 1998:219)

The exercise of this right of protection or prevention is dependent on the actions of international institutions and major powers, which have the economic and the military resources to intervene. The new rights of global citizens, additional to their territorial citizenship rights, are ones which they cannot act on or exercise themselves, and in this crucial respect the new rights are highly conditional. While there may be a duty to protect the new rights of the cosmopolitan citizen the cosmopolitan framework provides no mechanism of accountability to give content to these rights. There is no link between the 'right' and the 'duty' of its enforcement. The additional rights upheld in the cosmopolitan framework turn out to be a chimera. As David Beetham notes: 'the weak point in this regime of course remains enforcement' (Beetham 1999:140). Archibugi concedes:

> There is undoubtedly a contradiction here: the cosmopolitical project would delegate to structures devoid of coercive powers (...institutions of the world's citizens) the job of establishing when force should be used, while asking states, who monopolize the means of military might, to acquiesce in their decisions. (Archibugi 2000:149)

As Neil Stammers writes, the imperative of action to defend the human rights of cosmopolitan citizens ironically entails a *realpolitik* which is highly state-centric (Stammers 1999:992). The onus for taking corrective action always lies with official bodies rather than civil society organisations (Scholte 2002:300; see also Hopgood 2000; Linklater 1998:45; Falk 1995; Baker 2002a:119). At the end of the day, the duty or responsibility to act (as considered in Chapters 3 and 4) falls to states. Rather than exercising 'direct control' the global citizens and global civil society groups are dependent on nation-states to accede to their claims. It is states, specifically Western states, rather than individuals that are the active subjects of cosmopolitan citizenship, and cosmopolitan citizenship rights are no more than 'vague and ultimately unenforceable moral responsibilities' of these states (see Linklater 1998:205). The concrete rights of democratic accountability remaining restricted to the 'limited' sphere of the national *demos*.

## The ethical approach

While the previous section considered the limited and conditional nature of the new rights of the cosmopolitan citizen, this section seeks to outline the consequences of this approach for the rights of state sovereignty and representative democracy. If the cosmopolitan framework merely held out the promise of additional rights, but still needed to further develop the theory to establish mechanisms through which these rights could be realised, there would be little problem with this form of normative global civil society theorising. In which case, one could sympathise with Falk's problem that the scheme 'might seem utopian from the outlook of the present', with what Held terms the 'embedded utopianism' inherent in the project, or with Mary Kaldor's defence of the need for a 'ridiculously utopian project', Archibugi's advocacy for the 'politics of cosmopolitan dreams', and with Linklater's 'utopian aspirations' (Falk 1995:4; Held 1995:286; Kaldor 1999b:212; Archibugi 2002:38; Linklater 1998:219). This seems to be the dominant approach taken by commentators, who have erred towards sympathy and understanding of the ambitious programmes set by normative theorists. We are often reminded that many social visionaries achieved a huge influence despite the apparently unrealistic nature of their demands at the time. McGrew, for example, argues: 'To discount normative theory simply on the grounds that it trades in ideas or projects which, under existing historical conditions, may appear politically infeasible is to accept a deterministic view of history.' (McGrew 1997:241)

The unwillingness of academic commentators to challenge cosmopolitan thinking despite its apparent 'infeasibility' has problematic repercussions, which will be drawn out in the rest of this chapter. Rather than being sensitive and supportive towards what may, or may not, turn out to be an illusory ideal of empowering global citizenship it is the consequences which this framework has for the defence of existing sovereign and democratic rights which needs to be highlighted. While the new rights may be difficult to realise, this is in many ways a secondary question. Of greater concern is the fact that the cosmopolitan cause has helped cohere and legitimise a powerful consensus on the need to recast the relationship between international institutions and the nation-state.

For its advocates, cosmopolitan theories of global civil society reflect the historical development of 'moral-practical learning' or the realisation of 'the unfinished project of modernity' (Linklater 1998:121–3). However, there is an alternative historical backdrop which can shed light on the popularity of the concept. Far from a utopian theory of hope in progress and the development of democracy, cosmopolitan theory appears to be a reflection of a growing disillusionment with politics at both the international and domestic levels. Cosmopolitan theorists are disappointed that after the end of the Cold War the resources of international society have not been devoted towards resolving outstanding 'global concerns'. Liberal international relations theorists often display a teleological or idealistic view of progress at an international level, assuming that the creation of international institutions, such as the United Nations or World Trade Organisation, is in itself enough to establish a framework through which national and regional differences could be put aside and new means developed for the neutral resolution of global problems. In this idealised view of the international sphere, it appears that the only thing stopping progress today, after the 'diversion' of the Cold War, is the narrow preoccupation of nation-states with appeasing their electorates as opposed to addressing global concerns.

Richard Falk, drawing on Held and Archibugi's emphasis on the agency of global civil society, suggests that 'normative democracy' may be the best description of a unifying cosmopolitan ideology which can galvanise social change. He states that: 'I prefer normative to substantive democracy because of its highlighting of ethical and legal norms, thereby reconnecting politics with moral purpose and values...' (Falk 2000a:171). Global or cosmopolitan democracy is held to provide these moral norms in a way which local territorially-tied democracy apparently cannot:

> It challenges an uncritical reliance on democracy at the local level. It questions whether deference to tradition and cultural diversity is appropriate under all conditions. It suggests that non-Western cultural traditions, as well as Western traditions, can be oppressive.   (Falk 1995:65)

This chapter suggests that the self-acknowledged utopian aspects of cosmopolitan theory stem from the fact that there is more attention to the ethical ends of cosmopolitan democracy than there is to the mechanisms and means of ensuring these. The irony is that, despite the talk about extending and deepening democracy, cosmopolitan theory is not really concerned with establishing new frameworks for democracy on the international level. As Falk argues:

> It is now evident that democracy, at least as constituted in liberal democratic societies, is not by itself a sufficient precondition for a peaceful and just world. Democracy as an operative political form seems quite compatible with certain types of militarism and racism, perhaps resting in turn on patriarchal practices and hidden assumptions.   (Falk 1995:24)

The question that cosmopolitans seek to address appears to be rather how to legitimise moral and ethical policy ends against the apparently 'narrow limits' of liberal democratic frameworks and of sovereign government. The cosmopolitans and global governance advocates are hostile to sovereignty, and strongly in favour of international regulation of the sovereign sphere, but not in order to strengthen the mechanisms of democratic accountability. They challenge the existing order because they represent a growing belief that progressive ends – such as the protection of human rights, international peace or sustainable development – would be more easily achieved without the institutional constraints of democratic accountability or the formalised rights of state sovereignty. In Falk's words, the problem is: 'the reluctance of national citizenries for emotive and self-interested reasons to endorse globalizing initiatives' (Falk 1995:216).

In fact, the moral and ethical premises of cosmopolitan democracy necessarily lead advocates of this perspective to downgrade the importance of the rights framework of democracy and political equality. For cosmopolitans, the artificial construction of the global citizen-subject, given voice through global civil society, is the key to their attempt to privilege the sphere of morality and ethics over that of politics. The cosmopolitan, or non-national, democratic subject is defined through being freed from any political framework which institutionalises liberal democratic norms of formal accountability. The global citizen, by definition, has no fixed territorial identity and thereby no place within any institutionalised framework of legal and political equality from which to hold policy actors to formal account. Freed from any such framework, the 'rights' of the cosmopolitan citizen become dependent on the advocacy of an external agency. By default, the cosmopolitan subject becomes concrete only through 'representation' on a particular issue through the agency of global civil society advocates who also have an existence 'free' from the institutionalised political framework of the nation-state.

Without the institutionalisation of mechanisms of accountability, global civil society claims to 'represent the people' remain unsubstantiated (Edwards 1999:180). Whereas the claim for representation is inevitably contested, global civil society actors and movements often assert that the crucial role which they perform is that of 'articulation' of the needs of global citizens. Because the global citizen cannot directly hold policy-makers to account, the role of global civil society interlocutors becomes central to give content to claims of democracy without formal representation. Mary Kaldor argues that 'the role of NGOs is not to be representative but to raise awareness', adding that the 'appeal is to moral conscience' not to political majorities (Kaldor 2001). Johan Galtung, similarly, gives support to this form of 'empowerment', which he terms 'democracy by articulation, not by representation' (Galtung 2000:155). Advocacy politics today appears to be more legitimate than instrumental politics: 'Civil society provides a legitimising platform for discordant and radical demands – a name which explains why authorities have to take these demands seriously' (Kaldor 2003:107). For Kaldor, the claim to be part of '"global civil society" holds out some promise of being heard' (Kaldor 2003:107).

The lack of accountability involved in 'representation' by agents of global civil society is not seen as a problem by normative theorists, it can be an advantage, as moral claims do not need to be compromised by building representative constituencies of support. In fact, because global civil society groups are claimed to be non-instrumental they are held to have a legitimacy lacking from political actors reliant on democratic legitimation:

> Global civil society…represents a new form of global politics that parallels and supplements formal democracy at the national level. These new actors do not take decisions. Nor should they have a formal role in decision-making since they are voluntarily constituted and represent nobody but their own opinions. The point is that through access, openness and debate, policy-makers are more likely to act as a Hegelian universal class, in the interests of the human community. (Kaldor 2003:108)

In this respect, cosmopolitan theorists reflect broader political trends towards the privileging of advocacy rights over the representational democracy of the ballot box. Political activity is increasingly undertaken outside of traditional political parties and is becoming a sphere dominated by advocacy groups and single-issue campaigns who do not seek to garner votes but to lobby elites directly. Today, groups which campaign on a minority cause often support their case by exaggerating their moral claim to make up for political weakness. For example, if a group opposes the construction of a hydro-electric dam in another country or the construction of a motorway or the building of an out-of-town superstore closer to home, they do not say they are just representing the personal views of those involved. Instead, they argue that they have a greater claim, not as individuals but as advocates for the rights of others, such as the rights of rare butterflies or the natural diversity that would be destroyed if these developments went ahead. They are, in fact, arguing against formal democracy; that democracy should come second to the ethical or moral concerns which they champion.

Groups that disapprove of mass production, today often argue that democracy must be overridden by the 'rights' of the environment or the 'rights' of future generations. These rights are fictitious rights. The subjects of these rights cannot speak or act for themselves.[3] Often it is radical critics, who oppose the injustices of the world, who bolster their cause through the reliance on fictitious rights. Cosmopolitan theorists start from a radical critique of existing norms in international relations, but it is a critique based on moral advocacy. The subject of this advocacy is the citizen as a moral abstraction rather than a politically- and legally-embedded subject. As Linklater states:

> ...the idea of citizenship...provides the moral resources with which to build still wider frameworks...that can be used to envisage new conceptions of community and citizenship which are freed from the constraints of national sovereignty.   (Linklater 1998:177–8)

The essence of cosmopolitan democracy vis-à-vis traditional views of liberal democracy, is that the new citizenship 'rights' it calls for are not democratic rights but are moral claims.[4] Andrew Linklater's assertion that he derives the 'moral principles', which should guide international policy-making, from the rights of cosmopolitan citizenship, is open to question (Linklater 1998:207). This chapter suggests that the actual relationship is inversed. The cosmopolitan impulse is, in fact, to forward moral principles in the form of the 'rights' claims of cosmopolitan citizens. This inversion of the relationship between rights and their subjects relies on the legitimacy of fictitious rights. In which case, there is a fixed separation between the subjects of these rights and the enforcing agency. Because there is no political collective mediation between the individual and the social, the individual is transformed into a political object rather than a political subject (see further, Chapter 5).

### New rights for old

Fictitious rights separate rights from their subject. The rights of the cosmopolitan citizen are outside the control of their subject in much the same way as animal rights or environmental rights cannot be acted upon by their subjects. The problem with rights without subjects is that they may become a licence for undermining (limited but nevertheless important) existing rights, such as those of democracy and self-government. The proposed framework of cosmopolitan regulation, based on the fictitious rights of global citizenship, rather than the expression of rights through the political framework of the nation-state, recognises neither the democratic rights of citizens nor the collective expression of these rights in state sovereignty. It is important to stress the qualitative difference between the liberal-democratic approach, which derives rights from self-governing human subjects, and the cosmopolitan approach of claiming rights on the behalf of others (see further, Heartfield 1996b; Chandler 2002:103–5).

This central distinction in approach to the rights-subject explains why the two different rights approaches have an opposing conception of the importance of the political sphere and its institutions at the level of the state and international society. In the work of cosmopolitan theorists this distinction, and the consequent undermining of traditional liberal democratic rights, is clear. In reinterpreting rights as a moral category, as opposed to a legal and political one, a contradiction appears between the enforcement and guarantee of cosmopolitan rights and the formal equality of the liberal democratic legal and political framework. Within the normative framework of cosmopolitan theory, vital areas of formal accountability, at both the domestic and international level, are questioned while new and increasingly ad hoc frameworks of decision-making are seen to be positive and 'emancipatory'.

Firstly, the formal right of sovereign equality under international law. The UN Charter regime was a radical break from the pre-World War Two system of legitimate Great Power domination. For the first time non-Western states had the same legitimacy and international rights as the more developed Western states, despite the inequality of economic and military power. Unlike the UN, which formally recognises the equality of nation-states regardless of political regime, cosmopolitans argue that many regimes are illegitimate. The right to equality under international law, the central pillar of the post-colonial international system, would be a conditional or residual right under the cosmopolitan framework. As Held notes, 'sovereignty *per se* is no longer a straightforward guarantee of international legitimacy' (Held 2000:24). Archibugi argues that it is a matter of urgency that 'democratic procedures should somehow be assessed by external agents' (Archibugi 1998:210). Beetham has developed a 'democratic audit' framework to undertake such assessments (Beetham 1999:151–94). States that fail the assessments of their legitimacy will no longer have equal standing or full sovereign rights and could be legitimately acted against in the international arena.

Cosmopolitan regulation is in fact based on the concept of sovereign inequality, that not all states should be equally involved in the establishment and adjudication of international law. Ironically, the new cosmopolitan forms of justice and rights protection involve law-making and law-enforcement, legitimised from an increasingly partial, and explicitly Western, perspective. David Held, for example, argues:

In the first instance, cosmopolitan democratic law could be promulgated and defended by those democratic states and civil societies that are able to muster the necessary political judgement and to learn how political practices and institutions must change and adapt in the new regional and global circumstances. (Held 1995:232)

Martin Shaw explains that behind the language of cosmopolitan universals lies the reality of legitimisation through 'economic, political and military resources' which gives the Western powers a new 'duty' or 'right' to assert 'global leadership':

> This perspective can only be centred on a new unity of purpose among Western peoples and governments, since only the West has the economic, political and military resources and the democratic and multinational institutions and culture necessary to undertake it. The West has a historic responsibility to take on this global leadership... (Shaw 1994a:180–81)

The special 'ethical duties' of the powerful, runs through the case for cosmopolitan normative regulation. Andrew Linklater argues:

> Affluent societies have special duties to involve relevant outsiders in dialogue about the principles which should govern the distribution of membership and about global responses to the plight of the world's refugees. It is incumbent upon them to constitute themselves as world citizens and act as local agents of a world common good. (Linklater 1998:104)

Secondly, the right of sovereign autonomy or self-government. Cosmopolitans assert that despite adherence to all internationally accepted formal democratic procedures, a state's government may not be truly democratic. For Archibugi: 'The governments of states do not necessarily represent global interests. On the contrary, they tend to privilege the particular interests of their own political quarter'. (Archibugi 1998:213) Because of this 'bias' of self-interest a decision or choice made by the *demos*, or the people, even with full information and full freedom of decision-making, would not necessarily have cosmopolitan democratic legitimacy. In the cosmopolitan framework a decision by popular vote could be as flawed as national governments having the final say. The *demos* cannot necessarily be the final arbiter of democracy because:

> ...the choices of a people, even when made democratically, might be biased by self-interest. It may, for example, be in the interests of

the French public to obtain cheap nuclear energy if they manage to dispose of radioactive waste in a Pacific isle under their control, but this will obviously be against the interests of the public living there.   (Archibugi 1998:211)

For cosmopolitan theorists, the ethical ends for which they advocate are privileged above the sphere of democracy. As Andrew Linklater argues, this means a 'break with the supposition that national populations have the sovereign right to withhold their consent' if cosmopolitan demands 'clash with their conception of national interests' (Linklater 1998:192). In this framework, a small minority may be more 'democratic' than a large majority if they have an outlook attuned to cosmopolitan aspirations.[5] Mary Kaldor draws out the implications of the argument when she suggests that the international community should not necessarily consult elected local representatives but seek 'to identify local advocates of cosmopolitanism' where there are 'islands of civility' (Kaldor 1999a:120). Just as states cannot be equally trusted with cosmopolitan rights, neither can people. Instead of the 'limited' but fixed *demos* of the nation-state there is a highly selective *'demos'* identified by international institutions guided by the cosmopolitan impulse.

## Good governance

If governments and people cannot be trusted to overcome their narrow 'political' differences and prejudices, then a new authority is needed to act in important international situations. This authority must be 'independent' of established political mechanisms of democratic accountability. Cosmopolitan theorists favour an independent and 'higher' mechanism of international regulation in the belief that under such a system the ethical ends of cosmopolitan liberalism can be enforced. The authority they wish to establish, without democratic accountability but with the legitimacy to overrule popular opinion and elected governments, is that of cosmopolitan governance. The essential attribute of 'governance' is that it is regulation freed from the formal restrictions of 'government'. Cosmopolitan governance, the less accountable power of international regulation, is the ideological counterpart to the cosmopolitan citizen, who has less rights of democratic accountability. In exchange for new 'rights' for the global individual, the cosmopolitans want to sacrifice the old rights of sovereignty, which are seen to restrict the benign and protective actions of international institutions. Mary Kaldor suggests:

> [T]he term cosmopolitan, when applied to political institutions, implies a layer of governance that constitutes a limitation on the sovereignty of states and yet does not itself constitute a state. In other words, a cosmopolitan institution would co-exist with a system of states but would override states in certain clearly defined spheres of activity.   (Cited in Archibugi 1998:216)

For David Held, the framework of global governance is 'cosmopolitan democratic law' a 'domain of law different in kind from the law of states and the law made between one state and another, that is, international law' (Held 1995:227). This law 'transcends the particular claims of nations and states' and would be upheld by a framework of 'interlocking jurisdictions' (Held 1995:232). While there is no world state that is constituted politically, there are international and transnational institutions which have the authority to undermine sovereignty when the need arises regarding an issue of 'global concern'.

   Global governance, free from the restrictions of political ties of representation and accountability, is the flip side of the 'freedoms' and 'autonomy' of the global citizen celebrated by the normative project of global civil society. As Falk explains: 'To associate citizenship with humane governance...would provisionally shift the location of political identity...and further undermine the hold of sovereignty on the political imagination.' (Falk 1995:93) 'Citizenship' is here redefined as its opposite – as the denial of political accountability – through the promise of inclusive and cooperative mechanisms of governance which can only include global civic actors through removing sovereign restrictions. As Leon Gordenker and Thomas G. Weiss note: 'like the NGO universe, global governance implies the absence of central authority' (Gordenker and Weiss 1996:17). While the individual is freed from the 'constraints' of the political sphere so, of course, is government. Linklater argues that the European Union could evolve into a model for cosmopolitan governance:

> What would eventuate as a result of this... [would be] a system of multi-tiered authority which corresponded with the multiple loyalties of European citizens. No authority would claim absolute sovereignty or 'superior jurisdiction', and none would seek to monopolise political loyalties of groups or individuals. Should this ever occur, a

'genuine innovation' in the nature of European international society involving significant progress beyond the nation-state would
have taken place.   (Linklater 1998:194)

In fact, European governments appear increasingly keen on avoiding
responsibility and accountability for policy-making and all too happy
to blur the boundaries of 'absolute sovereignty' amidst the unaccountable chambers of Brussels. A person in Glasgow, in Linklater's example,
would have the freedom from 'exclusive or overriding loyalty' to political authority in Edinburgh, London or Brussels (Linklater 1998:195).
However, they would find that the governing elites are also free from
direct political accountability to them.

The assumption that the 'totalising project' of the state could be
restricted by such alleged 'freedoms' seems ludicrous. In fact, the
highly regulative norms proposed by the cosmopolitan theorists
suggest the opposite. Rather than freeing the individual, overlapping
conceptions of sovereignty are favoured to overcome localised resistance. Falk makes this clear in his discussion of Salman Rushdie's
*Satanic Verses* which incited the ire of the Muslim community in
Britain. His explicit argument is that overlapping 'loyalties' would
mean more sites of regulation rather than more freedoms. Essentially
this is the picture of a draconian police-state where the consideration
of the rights of others is continually extended at the price of individual
freedom:

> Such overlapping conceptions of sovereignty would not pose serious
> problems if their underlying ethos was shared. The problems in this
> setting arise because the West regards freedom of artistic expression
> as almost an absolute right of the individual, even if the results
> prove offensive to the community or parts of it and even if the work
> in question is deemed of little artistic content.   (Falk 1995:68)

For Falk, the regulative focus of global governance regimes would
stretch down to include oversight of 'serious adjustments in lifestyle'
and possibly even dietary regulations, in order to ensure sustainable
and equitable global development (Falk 1995:168).

While Falk and Held's fantasy of a global patchwork of normative
micro-regulation appears to be far-fetched, their prescription for a new
form of flexible law-making, no longer formally restricted by traditional domestic or international frameworks of accountability, in fact,
reflects the evolving practice of leading Western states in international

regulation. The theorists of cosmopolitan democracy feed into and reflect broader trends for Western governments to prefer ad hoc 'quasi-legal' international regulatory regimes which increasingly avoid formal accountability (see Gill 1995). The example of international intervention is considered above (in Chapter 4) but the preference for informal mechanisms of governance can be seen in the power and authority given to institutions such as the Peace Implementation Council, an ad hoc body overseeing the Bosnian protectorate, or the Stability Pact for South-East Europe (see for example, Chandler 2000a; 2003b). Despite the rhetoric about the transformation of sovereign power among members of the European Union, it is beyond the borders of the EU that the patchwork of 'overlapping' regulative bodies and the denigration of sovereignty is becoming a reality as Western power is informally institutionalised in relation to non-Western states.

As David Williams notes, the emergence of the doctrine of 'good governance' is 'best understood as a return to pre-World War Two patterns in the relationship between the West and others' (Williams 1997:227–8). More direct patterns of domination are eroding the formal sovereign equality of post-colonial states. Rita Abrahamsen, argues that the good governance agenda, decided upon by Western states and international institutions, proposes to empower individuals in the South and to extend democracy, but has increasingly transferred power and influence over policy matters to external actors (Abrahamsen 2000:144–5).

Underneath the moral veneer of the extension of democracy there is a deeply elitist core at the heart of the cosmopolitan democratic impulse. This is captured well by one of the co-originators of the concept of cosmopolitan democracy, Richard Falk, who argues the struggle to establish cosmopolitan democracy:[6]

> ...depends heavily on...a critical posture directed at identifying and challenging deformed cultural dispositions and practices that manifest themselves through militarist or environmentally irresponsible positions, and can flourish in democratic frameworks that endow leaders with a genuine popular mandate. A further danger is that 'the people' may embody violent or racist or sexist dispositions. In such settings the government may interpose restraining limits on public opinion, serving as a vehicle of moderation in relation to regressive populism.   (Falk 1995:119)

Ironically, the normative drive, ostensibly promoted as a method of extending democracy beyond the borders of states, legitimises restrictions on the democratic process at both domestic and inter-national levels. Far too many commentators lazily argue along the lines of Colás, that: 'In so far as incremental change and the 'plural-ization' of governing structures bear some promise for the improve-ment of people's lives across the world, they are obviously worth struggling for.' (Colás 2002:157) Perhaps counter-intuitively, rather than constraining unregulated global institutional decision-making, the emphasis on overlapping plural regulatory regimes, with no focal point of sovereignty, legitimises precisely the unaccountable mechanisms of regulation its advocates set out to criticise (see further, Laxer and Halperin 2003).

The problem is not the limited nature of the incorporation of global civil society actors into the new structures of global governance, but rather the failure to hold elected governments to account. Blurring the distinction between the citizen, with rights of formal democratic accountability, and the merely moral claims of the non-citizen, cannot further democracy under any normative framework, no matter how 'utopian'. The early normative critics of liberal democracy's limita-tions, like Ernest Gellner, argued that 'civil society' was a far better concept to describe liberal society because 'democracy' merely high-lighted procedural questions and the preference for consent over coer-cion (Gellner 1994:211). In the increasingly hierarchical international sphere it seems clear that a preference for global civil society has gone along with a preference for coercion over consent and a downgrading of the procedural rules of international law. This seems less the path of 'emancipatory' progress and more that of increasingly unaccountable ways of exercising political power (see further, Chapter 4).

## Conclusion

Cosmopolitan theorists have highlighted a crucial need for the exten-sion of democracy to the international sphere. This is of particular importance in the post-Cold War world where it is increasingly argued that the new 'duties' created by 'globalised interconnectedness' neces-sitate a new framework by which international institutions can be held accountable for their actions (and inaction). David Beetham stresses the 'duties to strangers that we all owe' arguing that global interdepen-dence means we must 'expand our definition of the stranger who merits are concern' (Beetham 1999:138–9). Mary Kaldor takes the point to its logical conclusion, stating that 'there is no such thing as non-intervention'. We are so interconnected that we have a duty to take responsibility for events which affect citizens in any country in the world: 'The failure to protect the victims is a kind of tacit intervention on the side of those who are inflicting humanitarian or human rights abuses.' (Kaldor 1999:118) In these circumstances, the gap between power and accountability at the international level becomes an ever more pressing problem.

By bringing the need for new forms of democracy to the fore, the cosmopolitan thesis has highlighted important institutional barriers to the extension of democracy from the level of the nation-state to that of the international. However, the artificial creation of global 'citizens', without the rights of accountability, and exaggerated claims for global civil society, do little to bridge this gap. While global citizenship remains a positive aspiration, it is only an inherent possibility without the development of a broader framework of political and legal equality. Attempts to posit cosmopolitan rights of citizenship in the absence of such a framework have, in fact, taken the cosmopolitan argument a full circle.

Their starting point was that democracy was too restrictive because it excluded non-citizens who would be affected by decisions of foreign national governments. While this is undoubtedly a limitation, it is clear that allowing more leeway for international institutions to act on behalf of global subjects, has merely allowed the affairs of these non-citizens to be brought more directly under the control of powerful foreign powers. While the non-citizens have gained no more power to influence the policy-making of the major Western states they have lost the right to hold their own governments to account. Rather than furthering democracy, the premature declaration of a framework of universal cosmopolitan rights can, in fact, result in the rights people do have being further restricted.

# 8
# Conclusion

## Actually existing global civil society

The focus of Part I of this book was the constructivist vision of an actually existing global civil society, which was held to explain change in the international sphere, which realist, rationalist and materialist approaches had allegedly failed to grasp. Advocates of this approach hold that ideas, particularly 'principled', 'ethical' and 'moral' ideas, articulated through the agency of global civil society, were responsible for major international changes in the 1990s. New developments, such as the decline of sovereign equality, the end of the UN Charter principle of non-intervention, the declining importance of inter-state consensus and international law, and growing regulatory powers for international institutions such as the International Criminal Court were read to herald the declining importance of the nation-state and the influence of both the activist campaigning and the normative values of global civil society on the international sphere.

In Chapter 3 it was argued that the constructivist attention to ideas and norms and the actions of non-state actors reflected the apparent inability of leading Western states to assert power internationally in a legitimate and meaningful way, in the new international context at the end of the Cold War. In the collapse of the old framework of the UN Charter and the absence of any new shared framework of meaning it appeared that nation-states had lost a coherent framework for understanding and managing 'national security' and that non-state 'moral entrepreneurs' were central to shaping a more norm-driven international agenda.

The central argument forwarded was that recognising the limitations of the realist approach and the problems with materialist explanations, that attempt to crudely read economic interests directly into policy decisions, is not at all the same as accepting the constructivist framework. For constructivist commentators, the gap between 'rational' state interests and policy appearances can be explained by the actions of non-state actors and 'norm entrepreneurs'. Unfortunately, the constructivist approach has not been challenged by any alternative theoretical explanations of the type developed here, but rather by events themselves, which have, at least in part, exposed the claims of morality walking hand-in-hand with power in a new global normative order.

In 2004 there would appear to be fewer grounds for optimism over the power of norms and shared values dictating the international agenda. Idealist theorists, like the English School social constructivist Nicholas Wheeler, argue that perhaps the hope that new global norms could inhibit US power has been misplaced. It appears that rather than global humanitarian norms restraining the 'war on terror', US unilateralism has been able to use 'token humanitarianism' to 'nullify dissent at home' (Wheeler forthcoming). Mary Kaldor ends her 2003 book *Global Civil Society: An Answer to War?* on a downbeat note, asking: 'Will we look back on the last decade as the "happy nineties"? Was it an interregnum between global conflicts when utopian ideas like global civil society, human rights, a global rule of law, or global social justice seemed possible?' (Kaldor 2003:149)

While global civil society was alleged to rule the roost during NATO's formally illegal bombing campaign over Kosovo in 1999 it appeared as if global civil society had somehow been marginalised, and that 'global consciousness' had declined, by the time of the US war on Iraq in March 2003. Kaldor was disillusioned that neither the European governments, who were opposed to the war, nor the anti-war movement appeared to support her 'global civil society' position: 'There is no strong constituency for an international law enforcement position. It is very difficult to imagine a return to the global politics of the 1990s...' (Kaldor 2003:155). It appeared that actually existing global civil society was now no more than a refuge for those, like Mary, isolated by events, who could at least have some 'space' to engage in 'civilized conversation' and hope, at the most, 'to create some new "islands of engagement"' during the dark days of Bush's unilateralism (Kaldor 2003:160).

The reason for this malaise, as was made clear in Chapter 4, has been the apparent return of the nation-state and of an inter-state framework for viewing the world with the post 9/11 'war on terror'. The global transformation which apparently had brought about the decline of nation-states and the rise of global civil society has allegedly been challenged by George W. Bush's attempt to hold back the tide and 'to re-impose international relations' (Kaldor forthcoming). So introspective is the global civil society perspective that the major transformations of the international sphere – the lack of a stable framework for managing international relations, the post-Cold War abandonment of sovereign equality, and the creation of a much more hierarchical and coercive global order – are an irrelevancy compared to this perceived setback to the ideal prescriptions advocated by the liberal academics. As long as they felt they had the ear of the policy-makers, it would appear that, for them, the end of the UN Charter guarantees and safeguards of international law were of little importance. Now that the courtly liberal advocates would appear to have less influence (particularly in the US and Britain) they wrongly perceive that it is 'business as usual', with US 'national interests' at the forefront (see, for example, Jacques 2004).

While global civil society advocates have varied widely in their estimations of the strength of actually existing global civil society, always tending to generalise from superficial readings of the present, this book has attempted to steer an alternative path, avoiding both the narrow realist perspectives of the past and the idealist social constructivism of the late 1990s. The empirical project of actually existing global civil society has, even for its keenest advocates, been severely tested by events since 9/11. However, the attraction of the constructivist framework was not founded upon the empirical strengths of the global civil society thesis, but rather its normative implications.

These normative concerns were not always explicitly raised because many of the constructivist theorists – working mainly in the US, where a positivist tradition in international relations has long been dominant – preferred to argue that their positions were fact-, rather than norm-, based (Reus-Smit 2002). Due to the strength of this normative drive it seems unlikely that promoters of global civic values will stop exhibiting the tendency 'to allow their wishes for shifts in powers, influence, and status...to be treated as already established' facts (Falk forthcoming). Bearing this in mind, it is with the normative claims for global civil society that this book concludes.

## The normative project

In the Introduction, the three key claims for the normative global civil society project were highlighted: firstly, the claim that global civil society extended the bounds of political community beyond the territorial borders of the nation-state; secondly, that global civil society theorising restored the centrality of human agency to international political theorising; and finally, that global civil society facilitated the radical extension of democracy and 'active citizenship' from the local and national levels to the global. These three claims are re-engaged with below on the basis of the factual and theoretical analysis forwarded in the preceding chapters.

## Extending political community?

In the foregoing chapters it has been suggested that the critical normative project of global civil society reflects the undermining of social and political bonds essential to the constitution of political community. Andrew Linklater, for example, raises but dismisses the problem of the destruction of social ties:

> Discourse ethics takes a critical stance towards all systems of exclusion and places the considerations which are decisive in preconventional and conventional moral reasoning in doubt. This is not to imply that all special ties and all modes of exclusion are suspect from the vantage-point of discourse ethics; all it suggests is that discourse ethics generates the concern that participants in any bounded association may not have been moral enough... (Linklater 1998:92–3)

Linklater's concern with the morality of exclusion and the ethic of radical questioning of any claims to trust and certainty, necessary for strong social ties, would, in fact, question the morality of any social institution, from the private sphere of marriage and friendship networks to the public sphere of collective association and government. He argues that 'although the universal communication community may never be realised completely, it is an important ethical ideal which permits the critique of defective social arrangements' (Linklater 1998:123). However, as consistently highlighted here, the radical critique of these 'defective social arrangements' privileges the standpoint of the abstract, isolated individual. This is captured well by Mary Kaldor, in her description of global civil society as 'a move away from state-centred approaches' and towards 'more concern with individual empowerment and personal autonomy' (Kaldor 2003:6).

The freeing of the individual from collective responsibility and from the ties of social engagement is celebrated, in the normative language of global civil society theorists, as a gesture of radical empowerment or democratisation. Kaldor argues that the popularity of the term 'civil society', since 1989, has led to some conceptual confusion, particularly prevalent in debates about the meaning of the concept which turn to classic texts of political theory for a 'legitimizing narrative' (Kaldor, 2003:2). She argues that the focus on past meanings and uses has 'imposed a kind of straitjacket' which has tended to obscure what she sees as the 'radical contemporary implications' of the concept, particularly 'the implications of the break with territorially bound civil society' (Kaldor 2003:3). Kaldor is right to highlight the radical nature of this break, which separates normative global civil society theorising from the liberal democratic tradition which, from the time of Thomas Hobbes and John Locke, assumed the existence of a separate, institutionalised, political sphere.

Global civil society lacks a clearly defined sphere of the political. Without a prior relationship of collective aspirations and engagement, individual activism loses any sense of collective meaning. Naomi Klein describes well how, without a collective sense of purpose, derived from a shared project, there can be no political debate and no testing of ideas. She describes being invited to a post-Seattle New York conference on 'Re-Imagining Politics and Society' and being:

> ...struck by the futility of this entire well-meaning exercise. Even if we did manage to come up with a ten-point plan – brilliant in its clarity, elegant in its coherence, unified in its outlook – to whom, exactly, would we hand down these commandments?... [T]he ideas and plans being hatched...weren't irrelevant exactly, they just weren't important in the way that was hoped... [T]hey were destined to be swept up and tossed around in the tidal wave of information – Web diaries, NGO manifestos, academic papers, homemade videos, *cris de coeur* – that the global anti-corporate network produces and consumes each and every day.   (Klein 2002:15)

There is no need to win an argument or convince an audience or reach any form of consensus. As Klein notes: 'If somebody feels that he or she doesn't quite fit into one of the thirty thousand or so NGOs or thousands of affinity groups out there, she can just start her own and link up.' (Klein 2002:20) As critics of the normative approach of global civil society argue, the privileging of the individual above the social makes any form of politics impossible. Political life depends on collectivities, on a shared project of political engagement. As Kimberly

Hutchings notes, to take part in political life it is necessary to have 'a strong identification between competing participants' (Hutchings 2000:45). Chantal Mouffe also makes this vital point about the importance of collectivities and stresses the importance of two levels of collective identification, the politics of political contestation between an 'us' and a 'them' (Mouffe 1993). Mouffe emphasises the importance of disagreement, but the prior factor, which should not be underemphasised, is that of a shared view of political community and political responsibility that makes these disagreements worth pursuing.

The belief that it is not necessary to have any allegiances beyond the autonomous individual is an appealing one for many people, disillusioned and frustrated with the formal political process. However, rather than challenge this retreat into individualism, the political parties often seek to gain a sense of connection to society through pandering to these prejudices. For example, Fausto Bertinotti, national secretary of Italy's Refounded Communist Party (*Rifondazione Comunista*) argues that the 'only possibility' of challenging neo-liberalism is not through 'defending democracy as it currently exists' but 'starting from the main resource available, which is the movement against capitalist globalisation' (Bertinotti 2003). He argues that this movement has:

> ...tackled the theme of power, in terms not of achieving and keeping it, but of transforming, dissolving and reconstructing power through self-government. And it has challenged the model of a party leading the movement, proposing instead the notion of networks and links among groups, associations, parties and newspapers. (Bertinotti 2003)

For Bertinotti, and other commentators of the 'old' left, the political challenge is to 'build out of the anti-globalisation movement a real democratic power' which can re-energise left institutions. The problem, which Bertinotti avoids facing, is that it is likely to prove impossible to transform a 'movement' that has rejected 'democracy as it currently exists', i.e., popular electoral contestation, into a traditional political project of the past. In fact, attempts to celebrate the potential of new social movements threaten to further undermine the traditional political process. For example, Luca Casarini, leader of the group Disobbedienti, veteran of Seattle and Genoa with the group Tute Bianche (white overalls), typically asserts that the movement rejects electoral politics on the basis that taking power is 'a political category of the 20th century left that we reject' (Casarini 2003). He further argues that joint activity with Bertinotti should not be supported because: 'We are different. For us ethics and principles are more important than a round of elections. You are talking on the phone with someone who is not sitting in a political party's or a union's headquarters, nor in the foyer of a Holiday Inn. But in a squat in Marghera [a town in the north of Italy].' (Casarini 2003) What is popular about radical politics is precisely its hostility to the old projects of the left and politics as a formal process of engagement. This lies behind the 'deep distrust of the state' highlighted by Naomi Klein as the central difference between radicalism today and in the past (Klein 2002:229).

It seems that rather than reconstructing political society and progressive politics on the international stage, global civil society activism can easily retreat into a distrust of popular processes which are held to threaten individual autonomy. As William Connolly argues, there is no reason for any allegiance to the state or any collectivity beyond the individual:

> Today, pluralisation of identifications and allegiances with the state need to be matched by a pluralisation that exceeds it. So the first answer to the question of the locus of final political loyalty is: 'it depends'... In a multi-dimensional, pluralist world, every particular allegiance is contingent because the occasion might occur when it collides with another one you have found to be even more fundamental at this *time*.   (Connolly 1991:480)

This is the politics of self-expression and narcissism, rather than the construction and extension of political community. As the February 2004 study *Conspicuous Compassion* from the think tank Civitas suggests, the politics of Drop the Debt or Not in My Name are more about individual statements than any collective political engagement orientated towards social change: 'Our culture of ostentatious caring concerns...[involves] projecting one's ego, and informing others what a deeply caring individual you are' (West 2004). Gideon Baker, in fact suggests that rather than engagement in politics, the 'practice of freedom' is 'a practice of the self on the self' (Baker 2003:18). By placing the autonomy of the self at the centre of its ethical code, global civil society approaches tend to reduce political community to the individual rather than extend it.

### The centrality of agency?

Throughout this study it has been observed that the emancipatory promise of the global civil society project is an abstract, hollow and idealised view of progress. There can be no agency as long as there is no connection or mediation between the individual and the social. Where there is agency in the accounts of global civil society it is to be found in external authorities, which endow global civic actors or global citizens with recognition and act to enforce and empower.

The critique of existing frameworks of political community celebrates the collapse of the boundaries between the 'inside' and the 'outside', between the domestic and the international, and in effect the end of political agency. As Hardt and Negri correctly assert: 'The end of the outside is the end of liberal politics.' (Hardt and Negri 2001:189) They argue that with the end of the salience of sovereign divisions 'there is no place of power – it is both everywhere and nowhere', making marginal struggles immediately radical (Hardt and Negri 2001:190). Once power has no focal point it is effectively written out of the equation. This then enables a focus on claims for 'recognition' which call for external agency and are ultimately disempowering.

Despite the talk of agency, in the normative project of global civil society advocates, it is not the disempowered or excluded who have agency but their network advocates and the 'enlightened' Western states themselves. Linklater, for example, emphasises that: 'The central task is to set out some of the primary duties and responsibilities of the post-Westphalian state.' (Linklater 1998:183) This problem is highlighted in the South, where the 'boomerang' politics of global civic actors (considered in Chapter 2) has encouraged external regulation and weakened community engagement in policy-making. As Michael Edwards notes:

> There is always a temptation to 'leap-frog' the national arena and go direct to Washington or Brussels, where it is often easier to gain access to senior officials and thus achieve a response. This is understandable but in the long term it is a serious mistake. It increases the influence of multilateral institutions over national development and erodes the process of domestic coalition building... (Edwards 2001:8–9)

Normative global civil society theorists reject the collective agency of mass political movements, preferring to highlight the self-constituting nature of 'global space' and 'new' movements that derive power from the fact of their existence rather than their transformative capacities. The radical rejection of collective engagement is summed up in Mary Kaldor's approving view of the model of Central European dissidents:

> Anti-politics is the emergence of forums that can be appealed to against political power; it is a counter power that cannot take power and does not wish to. Power it has already, here and now, by reason of its moral and cultural weight.   (Kaldor 2003:56)

There is no need for agency if 'power' is a self-constituting product of moral and cultural values, which is never socially tested. Rather than challenging domestic political quietism and posing a political alternative, the radical critique of the global civil society theorists, in fact, reflects and reproduces an underlying sense of incapacity. The moral perfectionism of the Habermasian ideal speech situation – the neglect of the simple fact that, in Chris Brown's words: 'All political arrangements rest on inclusion and exclusion' – means that global civil society can be profoundly disempowering (Brown 2002:10). The moralism at the heart of the radical challenge to the political is also its greatest problem when it comes to placing agency at the centre of political theorising:

> The feature of liberal, cosmopolitan, social theory which generates this difficulty is, arguably, its reduction of political theory to moral theory – the insistence that a *legitimate* account of the political is a *moralized* account of the political. Thus, politics becomes equated to a search for legitimacy in which all social arrangements are regarded as in need of...justification.   (Brown 2002:184)

The discourse provides a moral critique of power but can never constitute a collective political challenge to it. As Linklater highlights, global civil society theorising reflects the fact that: 'increasingly, the central questions of international relations concern the ethical foundations of political community' (Linklater 1998:34). The radical critique of the political is an excuse for refusal rather than grounds for collective agency. English School international relations theorist, Martin Wight, foresaw just such a consequence in the moralist critique of the political sphere:

> It is the total withdrawal into the sphere of the private ethic, and repudiation of the political sphere altogether. It involves a passive attitude towards life...and abandonment of the will...and is very attractive to the intelligent and sensitive person today; the political sphere obviously offers nothing but insoluble predicaments; ...for political incompetence and buffoonery there is nothing to choose between the political parties so there is no point in exercising one's

vote; all one can do is to retire within the sphere of private life and personal relationships...   (Wight 1991:256–7)

The other side of the agency coin is the lack of impact of private moral protest, driven by personal conscience rather than collective political ends. For example, the anti-Iraq war movement in Britain was hailed as a success for global civic activism, and has certainly reflected widespread cynicism and luck of trust in the British government. Opinion polls in August 2003 showed that only six per cent of voters trusted the government more than the BBC over the weapons of mass destruction claims (Hall, 2003). Yet the lack of political alternatives meant that, while cynicism and lack of trust in the government were at record levels, the government's lead over the opposition had more than doubled since the previous month (Hall, 2003).

Without an alternative collective focus, the activism of individuals is more likely to be inwardly orientated towards self-awareness and 'personal growth' rather than projected socially in engagement with others. The end of agency in the cultivation of individual identity as an end in-itself is well captured by the individualised activity of leading global civil society activists who are on a self-centred journey of discovery, personally travelling around the world to 'make the links' between the Israeli occupation of the West Bank, the WTO in Seattle and Cancun, and US privatisation in Iraq (Klein 2003).

## Extending democracy?

For Mary Kaldor: 'It is not possible to breathe new life into traditional representative democracy through unilateralism, or a reversal of globalisation, nor is it feasible to reconstitute this type of democracy at global levels.' (Kaldor 2003:148) This critique of liberal democracy, at the heart of global civil society theorising, is given a radical edge by claims that rather than being elitist, normative global civil society advocates wish to see new and better forms of global democracy and global citizenship. As considered in Chapter 7, the promise of empowerment of global civil society is an illusory one. While there is support for abstract political autonomy out in 'global space' there is nothing but hostility to collective political projects down on 'territorial' planet Earth.

In fact, the popularisation of concepts such as 'global citizenship' stems from the normative desire to restrict, rather than extend, civil and political rights. The meaning of citizenship has been transformed and hollowed out. As John Gaventa argues:

> An understanding of citizenship as participation puts less emphasis on rights as entitlements, to be bestowed by a nation-state or another form of government, and more emphasis on citizenship as something that is realized through responsible action.   (Gaventa 2001:278)

Every normative claim for global civil society posits the importance of normative regulation above the rights claims of the subject. The cosmopolitan claims of extending democracy are not about protecting rights claims of autonomy but promoting duties and new forms of less accountable regulation. As Naomi Klein notes:

> This is what sets the young protesters in Seattle apart from their sixties predecessors. In the age of Woodstock, refusing to play by state and school rules was regarded as a political act in itself. Now, opponents of the W[orld] T[rade] O[rganisation] – even many who call themselves anarchists – are outraged about the lack of rules being applied to corporations, as well as the flagrant double standards in the application of existing rules...   (Klein 2002:5)

The concern here is not about autonomy but regulation. This reflects the problem at the heart of much of global civil society theorising, the desire to regulate to overcome the problems of autonomous political, economic and social activity. In this context democracy is always seen as a problem rather than a solution. Richard Falk argues:

> ...to the extent that democratisation infringes upon basic normative objectives by way of militarism and consumerism, there is present a need for supervening constraints on political behaviour of governments by way of international law... Such expanded applications of international law need to be supplemented by cultural pedagogy and socialization practices that are orientated around the spread of an ethos of non-violence, ecological sustainability, and human rights, that is, in effect an offset to consumerism and militarism, a reorienting of citizenship toward the priorities of global civil society.   (Falk 1995:1118)

Rather than global civil society representing the 'voices' of the excluded and marginal through expanding democracy, Falk, one of the leading theorists in the field, argues that elected governments should be coerced into following the values of global civil society through the edicts of transnational lawyers while the citizens need to be reformed from the errors of their ways by 'cultural pedagogy and socialisation practices'.

The global civil society perspective tends to be an elitist and regulatory one which seeks to avoid establishing political legitimacy through democratic and representative means. Bearing this in mind, the widespread claim that one of the main reasons why global civil society is allegedly a growing force and politically necessary – because it is the only alternative to unaccountable and undemocratic mechanisms of global governance – appears to be an unsubstantiated one.

Rather than challenge attempts to remove political decision-making from democratic accountability, the global civil society project can only legitimise these shifts in regulatory power, firstly by critiquing the legitimacy of formal political mechanisms, and secondly, by suggesting that moral advocacy and the politics of recognition are an adequate response to the undermining of democracy. As considered in Chapter 7, national governments, let alone international institutions, are more than happy to swap the pressures of democratic accountability for the courtier politics of 'communicative engagement' with the 'representatives' of global civil society.

## Conclusion

It would appear that the attraction of global civil society lies less in its ability to grasp or create change in the international realm than in its role in shaping responses to problems of the domestic sphere. In the past, international relations theory was predicated on the strict divide between the institutionalised domestic arena where political progress and social transformation was seen to be possible and the 'anarchic' international sphere where the highest goal was peaceful co-existence. Today, the domestic and international spheres appear indistinct, not because the international has been transformed and 'domesticated' but because domestic political progress no longer appears possible. Global civil society theorising is predicated on the rejection of domestic political engagement by disillusioned radical and liberal commentators and their search for new 'spaces' of politics and new 'communities' where they can project their radical demands without having to engage with society.

Radical commentators assert that 'until citizens can seize control of global politics, we cannot regain control of national politics' (Monbiot 2003). This desire to solve the problems of politics at the global level, before addressing questions at the national or local level, and the perception that problems are easier to negotiate globally, where we can 'make a difference' (rather than nationally where we allegedly cannot) are unique aspects of our deeply estranged political times. This estrangement from our own political circumstances is crucial to any explanation of the current theorising of morality and power in international relations.

The aspiration to look to the global for easy solutions to the political problems of social disengagement and the perceived lack of any collective political meaning is not just a radical fashion. Governments across the West similarly view domestic problems of legitimacy, trust and collective engagement as potentially resolvable through global or international activism rather than domestic initiatives. Today, it appears that the 'global sphere' has the answers to the existential political vacuum left by the lack of certainty, mission, political ideologies and 'big ideas', which has been particularly deeply felt by governments and individuals since the start of the 1990s.

This book has suggested that the attraction of the global sphere has little to do with changes at the international level. The focus on morality and values in international relations is not the product of an actually existing global civil society, of the campaigns and work of NGOs, 'moral entrepreneurs', or any other providers of information or ethical ideas. The 'idealist turn' in international relations, and global civil society theorising in particular, stems largely from the difficulty of finding shared meaning though the domestic political process.

It would appear that the more our connections with other members of society break-down, the more we find 'imagined communities' in global space. The idealised normative community and 'thick interconnections' of global civil society invoke the Christian imagery of an ideal harmony as a counterpart to our fragmented, estranged and profane earthly existence. It is precisely the fictional, fantasy aspect of 'global space' that allows individuals, organisations and institutions, from NGOs to leading Western governments, to project their idealised visions of themselves onto the global plane.

Just as the rejection of an earthly paradise for a heavenly one leaves untouched the problems which create the demand for an idealised solution, the fantasy internationalism of global civil society can do little to address the problem which provides it's dynamic: the political malaise haunting Western societies. Instead of seeking to avoid political responsibility and accountability, the task of those who wish to engage in the normative project of emancipatory politics is surely to start to restore relations of trust and collective responsibility, rather than seek to escape or to undermine them. If we cannot politically, socially and intellectually engage with those closest to us we are never going to be able to construct a broader sense of shared community or revitalise the political. We should perhaps ask less of global civil society and more of ourselves.

# Notes

## Chapter One – Introduction

1. The historical and sociological aspects of the inter-state system were the focus of the English School thinkers during the Cold War but have recently been developed in postmodernist accounts and those of historical sociologists. For the English School, see, for example, Bull 1995, Bull and Watson 1984; for postmodernist accounts, see for example, Ashley 1988; Walker 1994; 1995; for historical sociological accounts see, for example, Mann 1988; Tilly 1990; Hobden and Hobson 2002.

2. Because this book deals with the construction of global civil society as a normative and empirical project it gives little consideration to neo-Gramscian or traditional Marxist approaches to global civil society. These commentators use the concept in an analogous way to domestic civil society, in line with classical political thought, as the private sphere of autonomy in contrast to the public sphere of the state. In these readings, global civil society is a sphere of ideological contestation between the forces of hegemony and those of progress but no particular moral significance is attached to the concept of global civil society itself, and it is not seen as being independent of power relations that characterise the state or the market (see Colás 2002:42–3).

## Chapter 2 – The Constructivist Thesis

1. As Alexander Wendt suggests, constructivism is an approach to international relations which focuses on how actors are socially constructed, rather than a theory which tells us which actors are important: 'Constructivism is not a theory of international politics.' (Wendt 1999:7)

2. The question of the 'reinterpretation' of the 'national interest', central to the constructivist approach, will be the focus of the following chapter.

## Chapter 3 – The Decline of 'National Interests'

1. This chapter concerns the shift in government emphasis and public perceptions. As Chris Brown notes, foreign policy-making has always been shaped by broader concerns than those of narrow self-interest. The framework of international law and diplomacy, for example, depend on states upholding shared international norms and values (Brown 2001:24–26).

2. As Hedley Bull noted, international law and the system of the reciprocal rights of state sovereignty 'assume a situation in which no one power is preponderant in strength'; otherwise international law and sovereign rights could be disregarded with impunity (Bull 1995:112; see also Holbrook 2002:140).

3. One exception is David Campbell's *Writing Security* (1998a) which uses Foucault's insights on regulation to focus on the regulatory subject rather than the object of regulation. Whereas realist and liberal approaches often read-off the interests of states from the object being regulated – territories which have oil or other natural resources or human rights victims, for example – Foucault insisted that it was the regulatory practices themselves which were of primary importance (Foucault 2003:30–33). By focusing on the regulatory body rather than the object of regulation, Campbell brings domestic politics to the centre of international policy-making:

> In reorienting analysis from the concern with the intentional acts of pre-given subjects to the problematic of subjectivity, this argument proposes that United States foreign policy be understood as a political practice central to the constitution, production, and maintenance of American political identity.   (Campbell 1998a:8)

4. David P. Forsythe notes that: 'Analysts concluded that there was considerable American popular support for pragmatic internationalism, but not a great deal of support for moral internationalism' (Forsythe 2000:143). See further, Holsti (2000).
5. The International Commission on Intervention and State Sovereignty recommends rejecting the concept of 'humanitarian intervention' on the basis that success is easier to achieve if military action is legitimised for 'protection' rather than humanitarian purposes. Otherwise intervention can easily be discredited through the 'tough choices' and 'short- and long-term trade offs' which have to be made between effective military action and humanitarian assistance (see, for example, ICISS 2001a:61; ICISS 2001b:368). For an example of the disillusionment of humanitarian agencies see Vaux (2001:202).
6. In relation to the 'war on terror' this was highlighted again by the shifting responses of Washington to North Korea. In January 2002, in his State of the Union address President Bush named North Korea as part of the 'axis of evil' and a 'threat to world peace' alongside Iran and Iraq (Bush 2002a). The US cut fuel aid that had been promised to ease the North's energy needs and, in response, North Korea defended its right to restart its nuclear weapons programme, making the focus on Iraq as the main danger of supplying weapons of mass destruction appear increasingly irrational. Washington could not sustain its hard line and in January 2003 was forced to publicly back down, offering food and energy aid to North Korea as an incentive to dismantle its nuclear weapons programme (Goldenberg and Watts 2003).

## Chapter 4 – Morality and Power

1. The global civil society thesis' emphasis on shared international moral norms is often traced back to the Enlightenment and Immanuel Kant's essay *Perpetual Peace: A Philosophical Sketch* (Kant 1795). Kant argued that as democratic consciousness developed liberal states would emerge and band together to form a 'league of peace' to protect their own security and also to

encourage the spread of liberal ideas and promote individual rights internationally (see further, Waltz 1962; Doyle 1983; Brown, Nardin and Rengger
2002:428–455).

2. The Commission was launched on 14 September 2002. The Canadian
Government invited the Honourable Gareth Evans, AO QC, President of the
International Crisis Group and former Australian Foreign Minister, and His
Excellency Mohamed Sahnoun of Algeria, Special Advisor to the UN
Secretary-General and formerly his Special Representative (SRSG) for
Somalia and the Great Lakes Region of Africa to jointly head the ICISS. In
consultation with the Co-Chairs, 10 other distinguished Commissioners
were appointed: Gisèle Côté-Harper; Lee Hamilton; Michael Ignatieff;
Vladimir Lukin; Klaus Naumann; Cyril Ramaphosa; Fidel Ramos; Cornelio
Somaruga; Eduardo Stein; and Ramesh Thakur. Canada's Minister for
Foreign Affairs, the Honourable John Manley, also appointed an interna-
tional Advisory Board of serving and former foreign ministers from Canada,
Chile, the Palestinian National Authority, the UK, Poland, Mexico, the US,
Egypt, Greece, Thailand, South Africa and Argentina, as well as other
eminent individuals, to help ground the report in current political realities
and to assist in building up political momentum and public engagement to
follow up its recommendations. As well as meetings with the Advisory
Board the Commissioners held five full meetings and eleven regional
roundtables and national consultations were held around the world at
Ottawa, Geneva, London, Maputo, Washington, Santiago, Cairo, Paris, New
Delhi, Beijing and St. Petersburg. At these meetings a variety of national
and regional officials, representatives of civil society, academic institutions
and think tanks joined some of the Commissioners and one, but usually
both, of the Co-Chairs in deliberations. The Commission also met with
interested governments, representatives of Permanent Missions, heads or
senior representatives of major international organisations and UN agencies
and with the Secretary-General Kofi Annan and key members of the UN
Secretariat. Alongside this process, an extensive research programme was
organised in support of ICISS's work and an international research team
created, led jointly by Thomas G. Weiss, Presidential Professor at The CUNY
Graduate Centre, and Stanlake J. T. M. Samkange, a lawyer and former
speechwriter to UN Secretary-General Boutros Boutros-Ghali.

3. The Report notes: 'There is little reason to invest much hope that global
civil society can systematically ensure human security.' NGOs can play
important roles in standard-setting and monitoring but states remain the
only actors with the resources and power to ensure human protection measures are enforced (see ICISS 2001b:136).

4. Participants at the Maputo regional roundtable, for example, believed that
Africa had been marginalised by the Security Council, comparing the bil-
lions of dollars expended on the Balkans with the case of Liberia where UN
members failed to meet pledges of $150 million in support of subregional
efforts. The discussion stressed the 'strong nexus between poverty and
conflict' and complained that in relation to poverty international responses
have ranged from inadequate to entirely absent. Of particular concern was
the increasing deterioration in the terms of trade and the sharp reduction
in the disbursement of bilateral aid (see ICISS 2001b:363).

5. The Report itself states that: 'the "responsibility to protect" is more of a linking concept that bridges the divide between intervention and sovereignty; the language of the "right or duty to intervene" is intrinsically more confrontational' (ICISS 2001a:17). Whereas the language of the 'right of intervention' highlights the challenge to established rights of sovereign equality, the language of the 'responsibility to protect' attempts to minimise the importance of this proposed shift in legal perspective.

6. For example, the majority of participants at the Cairo regional roundtable felt that the Security Council lacked legitimacy with Arab public opinion following its perceived double-standard approach in dealing with the region and was 'unrepresentative and undemocratic' (ICISS 2001b:376–7). Many participants at the New Delhi regional roundtable called for a review of the structure and composition of the Security Council to make it more representative and increase its legitimacy (ICISS 2001b:389).

7. Participants at the Maputo regional roundtable were concerned that intervention would reflect the needs of powerful states intervening and wished to avoid the Western view of Africa 'as a problem to be solved' (ICISS 2001b:362–4). The New Delhi regional roundtable raised similar concerns that 'the morality and claimed legitimacy of interventions have in reality only been those of dominant nations or groups of nations'. These fears were held to be as relevant today as in the past as 'international society still lacks...an authoritative, objective decision maker to adjudicate the applicability of intervention' (ICISS 2001b:388). The majority of the participants at the Cairo regional roundtable agreed that the use of force should be strictly in conformity with the UN Charter. Nabil Elarby from the Egyptian Council of Foreign Affairs, the Chair of the meeting, concluded the session with a ringing endorsement of UN Charter's prohibition of the use of force 'as the greatest achievement of the contemporary international legal order in the 20th century' (ICISS 2001b:376–8). In Beijing, Chinese participants at the regional roundtable strongly emphasised that the interventionist liberal thesis was flawed on the basis of law, theory and practice, concluding that 'using force for moral or conceptual reasons is questionable and dangerous' (ICISS 2001b:392). A similar response greeted the Commissioners at the St. Petersburg regional roundtable, which raised concerns over Western unilateralism and double standards, highlighting that the ICISS thesis 'risks undermining the whole international system' (ICISS 2001b:394–8).

8. For example, participants at the Cairo roundtable rejected the ICISS Commissioner's suggestion that an international board of eminent persons make recommendations to the Secretary-General or president of the Security Council as to when intervention may be required: 'They noted that for the majority of the Third World, the General Assembly, while flawed, is still the most democratic of the existing international bodies, and it is, at the very least, a better reflection of world public opinion.' (ICISS 2001b:377)

9. In the Cold War era the UN Security Council, hamstrung by the veto of one or other of the Great Powers, played a minor role in the authorisation of military intervention. It is in the context of UN Security Council activism over the past decade that the question of the enforcement of UN mandates has become increasingly problematic. This was apparent in the case of Iraq

after the 1991 Gulf War when there was no consensus on whether UN Security Council resolution 688 authorised the air-exclusion zones restricting Iraqi sovereignty in North and South Iraq. There was similarly little agreement over whether UN Security Council resolution 1441 authorised the use of military force in the run up to the war on Iraq in 2003. For an excellent study of how the UN has 'passed the baton' of authorisation for intervention and the enforcement of UN Security Council resolutions over to major powers see Simon Chesterman's *Just War or Just Peace?* (2001).

10. The Report states that 'military action can be legitimate as an anticipatory measure in response to clear evidence of likely large scale killing' (ICISS 2001a:33). I am grateful to Michael Byers for highlighting this link at the British International Studies Association 47th annual conference, London School of Economics, 16–18 December, 2002. See also The National Security Strategy of the United States of America (US 2002).

11. As Chris Brown notes, today, all but a few 'hyper-realist' international relations theorists would agree that normative principles are intimately bound up with definitions and understandings of the national interest (Brown 2001:24).

12. See, Note 2, Chapter 3.

13. For example, the UK House of Commons Foreign Affairs Committee concluded that although the war was of 'dubious legality' it was, however, 'justified on moral grounds' (UK 2000:§138); the UN's Independent International Commission on Kosovo concluded that 'the intervention was legitimate, but not legal' (IICK 2000:289).

14. See, for example, Tony Blair's statements in the face of the largest anti-war political demonstrations ever seen in Britain, on 15 February 2003. While he did not openly reject the legal standing of the UN, the justification for conflict and explicitly for 'regime change', for which there is no basis in international law, was made in moral terms: 'the moral case against war has a moral answer: it is the moral case for removing Saddam. It is not the reason we act... But it is the reason, frankly, why if we do have to act, we should do so with a clear conscience.' (Blair 2003)

15. For further information see the Commission's web page: http://www.iciss. gc.ca/.

# Chapter 7 – The Cosmopolitan Paradox

1. The work of cosmopolitan theorists, for example, that of David Held, Daniele Archibugi, Mary Kaldor, Richard Falk, Andrew Linklater, Martin Shaw, Ken Booth and David Beetham, differs in focus and emphasis, however, for the purposes of this brief survey, the similarities in their approach to the questions of democracy and rights are highlighted.

2. The limits of formal political accountability and the possibilities for the 'will of the majority' to be constrained and circumscribed even within the most highly developed constitutional frameworks have been well documented over the past one-and-a-half centuries. Nevertheless the epistemological premise of democracy – that there are no final truths about what is good for society that can be established through the powers of revelation or special

knowledge – and the underlying principle of equality – that in any process of deciding the good 'everyone counts for one and none for more than one' – has maintained a legitimacy which has yet to be matched by any contending theory (see Beetham 1999:35–6).

3. The question of enforcing universal children's rights, raised by the UN Convention on the Rights of the Child, provides an excellent illustration of some of the problems with advocacy rights in the international sphere (see further, Lewis 1998; Pupavac 2001).

4. Moral claims have always been a vital component of political struggles, including those for the extension of rights, for example, the campaign to abolish slavery. There is however a qualitative distinction between using moral arguments to extend the framework of political and legal equality, for example, through the abolition of slavery, and campaigning to subordinate political and legal institutions to moral ends.

5. This critique of 'narrow' or 'thin' democracy based on equal representation, and the privileging of normative or ethical views of democracy, is not unique to cosmopolitan theory and can also be found at the national level (see for example, Guinier 1995).

6. Richard Falk, David Held, Daniele Archibugi and Mary Kaldor jointly conceived the concept of cosmopolitan democracy (Archibugi and Koenig-Archibugi 2003:271 n.5).

# References

Abrahamsen, R. (2000) *Disciplining Democracy: Development Discourse and Good Governance in Africa* (London: Zed Books).

Alkire, S., Bebbington, A., Esmail, T., Ostrom, E., Polski, M., Ryan, A., Van Domelen, J., Wakeman, W. and Dongier, P. (2001) *Community Driven Development*. Available from: http://www.worldbank.org/poverty/strategies/chapters/cdd/cdd0427.pdf.

Allott, P. (1999) 'The Concept of International Law, *European Journal of International Law*, Vol. 10, pp. 31–50.

Anderson, B. (1991) *Imagined Communities: Reflections on the Origin and Spread of Nationalism* (rev. ed.) (London: Verso).

Anheier, H. (2001) 'Measuring Global Civil Society', in H. Anheier, M. Glasius and M. Kaldor (eds) *Global Civil Society 2001* (Oxford: Oxford University Press).

Anheier, H., Glasius, M. and Kaldor, M. (2001a) *Global Civil Society 2001* (Oxford: Oxford University Press).

Anheier, H., Glasius, M. and Kaldor, M. (eds) (2001b) 'Introducing Global Civil Society', in H. Anheier, M. Glasius and M. Kaldor (eds) *Global Civil Society 2001* (Oxford: Oxford University Press).

Anheier, H. and Themudo, N. (2002) 'Organisational Forms of Global Civil Society: Implications of Going Global', in M. Glasius, M. Kaldor and H. Anheier (eds) *Global Civil Society 2002* (Oxford: Oxford University Press).

Appleton, J. (2003) 'Suicidal Tendencies', *Spiked Online*, 7 May. Available from: http://www.spiked-online.com/Articles/00000006DD8B.htm

Archibugi, D. (1998) 'Principles of Cosmopolitan Democracy', in D. Archibugi, D. Held and M. Köhler (eds) *Re-imagining Political Community: Studies in Cosmopolitan Democracy* (Cambridge: Polity).

Archibugi, D. (2000) 'Cosmopolitical Democracy', *New Left Review*, Vol. 2, No. 4, pp. 137–150.

Archibugi, D. (2002) 'Demos and Cosmopolis', *New Left Review*, Vol. 2, No. 13, pp. 24–38.

Archibugi, D. and Koenig-Archibugi, M. (2003) 'Globalization, Democracy and Cosmopolis: A Bibliographical Essay', in D. Archibugi (ed.) *Debating Cosmopolitics* (London: Verso).

Ashley, R. K. (1988) 'Untying the Sovereign State: A Double Reading of the Anarchy Problematique', *Millennium: Journal of International Studies*, Vol. 17, No. 2, pp. 227–262.

Aziz, N. (1995) 'The Human Rights Debate in an Era of Globalization: Hegemony of Discourse', *Bulletin of Concerned Asian Scholars*, Vol. 27, No. 4.

Badiou, A. (2001) *Ethics: An Essay on the Understanding of Evil* (London: Verso).

Bain, W. (2003) *Between Anarchy and Society: Trusteeship and the Obligations of Power* (Oxford: Oxford University Press).

Baker, G. (2002a) *Civil Society and Democratic Theory: Alternative Voices* (London: Routledge).

Baker, G. (2002b) 'Problems in the Theorisation of Global Civil Society', *Political Studies*, Vol. 50, No. 5, pp. 928–943.

Baker, G. (2003) 'Unstable Subjects and Unknowable Others: Is Political Representation Possible?', paper presented to the 'Political Representation' workshop ECPR Joint Sessions of Workshops, Edinburgh, 28 March–2 April 2003.

Baker, G. and Chandler, D (eds) (forthcoming) *Global Civil Society: Contested Futures* (London: Routledge).

Baldwin, D. A. (1993) *Neorealism and Neoliberalism: The Contemporary Debate* (New York: Columbia University Press).

Barcz, J. (1992) 'European Standards for the Protection of National Minorities with Special Regard to the OSCE – Present State and Conditions of Development', in A. Bloed and A. de Jonge (eds) *Legal Aspects of a New European Infrastructure* (Utrecht: Europa Instituut and Netherlands Helsinki Committee).

Barlow, K. (2002) 'Courage under Fire', *Guardian*, 27 November.

Beaumont, P. and Wainwright, M. (2002) 'I Never Thought They Would Fire Live Rounds', *Guardian*, 3 April.

Beck, U. (2002) 'The Cosmopolitan Society and its Enemies', *Theory, Culture and Society*, Vol. 19, No. 1–2, pp. 17–44.

Beckman, B. (1993) 'The Liberation of Civil Society: Neo-Liberal Ideology and Political Theory', *Review of African Political Economy*, Vol. 20, No. 58, pp. 20–34.

Beetham, D. (1999) *Democracy and Human Rights* (Cambridge: Polity).

Bell, D. (1975) 'The End of American Exceptionalism', *The Public Interest*, Vol. 41, pp. 193–224.

Bellamy, A. J. (2003) 'Humanitarian Responsibilities and Interventionist Claims in International Society', *Review of International Studies*, Vol. 29, No. 3, pp. 321–340.

Bertinotti, F. (2003) 'Reformist Social Democracy is no longer on the Agenda', *Guardian*, 11 August.

Bianchi, A. (1999) 'Immunity Versus Human Rights: The Pinochet Case', *European Journal of International Law*, Vol. 10, pp. 237–277.

Black, D. (1999) 'The Long and Winding Road: International Norms and Domestic Political Change in South Africa', in T. Risse, S. C. Ropp and K. Sikkink (eds) *The Power of Human Rights: International Norms and Domestic Change* (Cambridge: Cambridge University Press).

Blair, T. (1999) 'A New Generation Draws the Line', *Newsweek*, 19 April.

Blair, T. (2001a) 'Speech to the House of Commons', 14 September. Available from: www.guardian.co.uk/Archive/Article/0,4273,4257319,00.html.

Blair, T. (2001b) 'Speech to the Labour Party Conference', 2 October. Available from: http://politics.guardian.co.uk/labour2001/story/0,1414,562007,00.html.

Blair, T. (2003) 'The Price of My Conviction', *Observer*, 16 February.

Blaug, R. (1999) *Democracy, Real and Ideal: Discourse Ethics and Radical Politics* (Albany: State University of New York Press).

Booth, K. (1991) 'Security in Anarchy: Utopian Realism in Theory and Practice', *International Affairs*, Vol. 67, No. 3, pp. 527–545.

Booth, K. (1995) 'Human Wrongs and International Relations', *International Affairs*, Vol. 71, No. 1, pp. 103–126.

Booth, K. (1999) 'Three Tyrannies', in T. Dunne and N. Wheeler (eds) *Human Rights in Global Politics* (Cambridge: Cambridge University Press).

Booth, K. and Dunne, T. (2002) 'Preface', in K. Booth and T. Dunne (eds) *Worlds in Collision: Terror and the Future of the Global Order* (London: Palgrave Macmillan).

Borger, J. (2003) 'Bush Rallies Troops for War', *Guardian*, 4 January.

Bosco, D. (2000) 'Dictators in the Dock', *American Prospect*, 14 August.

Brown, C. (1995) 'International Political Theory and the Idea of World Community', in K. Booth and S. Smith (eds) *International Relations Theory Today* (Cambridge: Polity).

Brown, C. (2001) 'Ethics, Interests and Foreign Policy', in K. E. Smith and M. Light (eds) *Ethics and Foreign Policy* (Cambridge: Cambridge University Press).

Brown, C. (2002) *Sovereignty, Rights and Justice: International Political Theory Today* (Cambridge: Polity).

Brown, C., Nardin, T. and Rengger, N. (eds) (2002) *International Relations in Political Thought: Texts from the Ancient Greeks to the First World War* (Cambridge: Cambridge University Press).

Brown, L. D. and Fox, J. (2001) 'Transnational Civil Society Coalitions and the World Bank: Lessons from Project and Policy Influence Campaigns', in M. Edwards and J. Gaventa (eds) *Global Citizen Action* (London: Earthscan).

Bull, H. (ed.) (1984) *Intervention in World Politics* (Oxford: Clarendon Press).

Bull, H. (1995) *The Anarchical Society: A Study of Order in World Politics* (2nd ed.) (Basingstoke: Palgrave Macmillan).

Bull, H. and Watson, A. (1984) *The Expansion of International Society* (Oxford: Oxford University Press).

Bunch, C. (2001) 'International Networking for Women's Human Rights', in M. Edwards and J. Gaventa (eds) *Global Citizen Action* (London: Earthscan).

Burbach, R. (1996) 'For a Zapatista Style Postmodernist Perspective', *Monthly Review*, Vol. 47, No. 10, pp. 34–41.

Burgerman, S. D. (1998) 'Mobilizing Principles: The Role of Transnational Activists in Promoting Human Rights Principles', *Human Rights Quarterly*, Vol. 20, pp. 905–923.

Bush, G. W. (2001a) 'Speech to the US Congress', 20 September. Full text available from: http://www.guardian.co.uk/Archive/Article/0,4273,4261868,00.html.

Bush, G. W. (2001b) 'President Bush Announces Military Strikes in Afghanistan', 7 October. Available from: http://www.globalsecurity.org/military/library/news/2001/10/mil-011007-usia01.htm.

Bush, G. W. (2002a) 'State of the Union Address', 29 January. Available from: http://www.whitehouse.gov/news/releases/2002/01/20020129-11.html.

Bush, G. W. (2002b) 'Remarks by the President at 2002 Graduation Exercise of the United States Military Academy West Point, New York', 1 June. Available from: http://www.whitehouse.gov/news/releases/2002/06/20020601-3.html.

Bush, G. W. (2002c) 'President's Remarks at the United Nations General Assembly', Office of the Press Secretary, September 12. Available from: http://www.whitehouse.gov/news/releases/2002/09/20020912-1.html.

Buzan, B. (1991) *People, States and Fear: An Agenda for International Security Studies in the Post-Cold War Era* (2nd ed.) (London: Longman).

Buzan, B. (1996) 'The Timeless Wisdom of Realism', in S. Smith, K. Booth and M. Zalewski (eds) *International Theory: Positivism and Beyond* (Cambridge: Cambridge University Press).

Callinicos, A. (2002) 'The Actuality of Imperialism', *Millennium*, Vol. 31, No. 2, pp. 319–326.

Camilleri, J. A. and Falk, J. (1992) *The End of Sovereignty?: The Politics of a Shrinking and Fragmenting World* (Brookfield, VT: Ashgate).

Cammack, P. (2002) 'The Mother of all Governments: The World Bank's Matrix for Global Government', in R. Wilkinson and S. Hughes (eds) *Global Governance: Critical Perspectives* (London: Routledge).

Campbell, D. (1998a) *Writing Security: United States Foreign Policy and the Politics of Identity* (2nd ed.) (Minneapolis: University of Minnesota Press).

Campbell, D. (1998b) *National Deconstruction: Violence, Identity and Justice in Bosnia* (Minneapolis: University of Minnesota Press).

Canovan, M. (2001) 'Sleeping Dogs, Prowling Cats and Soaring Doves: Three Paradoxes in the Political Theory of Nationhood', *Political Studies*, Vol. 49, No. 2, pp. 203–215.

Carr, E. H. (2001) *The Twenty Years Crisis, 1919–1939: An Introduction to the Study of International Relations* (new ed.) (Basingstoke: Palgrave Macmillan).

Carroll, R. (2003) 'Pop Star's Relations with Bush Turn Sour', *Guardian*, 18 September.

Casarini, L. (2003) 'Basta con le Ipocrisie Siamo Tutti Condannati Alla Violenza', *La Repubblica*, 31 October.

CGG (1995) The Commission on Global Governance, *Our Global Neighbourhood* (Oxford: Oxford University Press).

Chandhoke, N. (2001) 'The "Civil" and the "Political" in Civil Society', *Democratization*, Vol. 8, No. 2, pp. 1–24.

Chandhoke, N. (2002) 'The Limits of Global Civil Society', in M. Glasius, M. Kaldor and H. Anheier (eds) *Global Civil Society 2002* (Oxford: Oxford University Press).

Chandler, D. (1998) 'Democratization in Bosnia: The Limits of Civil Society Building Strategies', *Democratization*, Vol. 5, No. 4, pp. 78–102.

Chandler, D. (1999) 'The OSCE and the Internationalisation of National Minority Rights' in K. Cordell (ed.) *Ethnicity and Democratisation in the New Europe* (London: Routledge).

Chandler, D. (2000a) *Bosnia: Faking Democracy after Dayton* (2nd ed.) (London: Pluto Press).

Chandler, D. (2000b) 'International Justice', *New Left Review*, Vol. 2, No. 6, pp. 55–66.

Chandler, D. (2001a) 'The People-Centred Approach to Peace Operations: The New UN Agenda', *International Peacekeeping*, Vol. 8, No. 1, pp. 1–19.

Chandler, D. (2001b) 'The Road to Military Humanitarianism: How the Human Rights NGOs Shaped a New Humanitarian Agenda', *Human Rights Quarterly*, Vol. 23, No. 3, pp. 678–700.

Chandler, D. (2001c) 'Universal Ethics and Elite Politics: the Limits of Normative Human Rights Theory', *International Journal of Human Rights*, Vol. 5, No. 4, pp. 72–89.

Chandler, D. (2002) *From Kosovo to Kabul: Human Rights and International Intervention* (London: Pluto Press).

Chandler, D. (2003a) 'Rhetoric without Responsibility: The Attraction of "Ethical" Foreign Policy', *British Journal of Politics & International Relations*, Vol. 5, No. 3, pp. 295–316.

Chandler, D. (2003b) 'Governance: the Unequal Partnership', in W. van Meurs (ed.) *South Eastern Europe: Weak States and Strong International Support* (Opladen: Leske and Budrich/Bertelsmann Foundation).

Charnovitz, S. (1997) 'NGOs and International Governance', *Michigan Journal of International Law*, Vol. 18, pp. 183–286.

Chesterman, S. (2001), *Just War or Just Peace? Humanitarian Intervention and International Law* (Oxford: Oxford University Press).

Chesterman, S. (2002), *Tiptoeing Through Afghanistan: The Future of UN State-Building* (New York: International Peace Academy).

Chomsky, N. (1999) *The New Military Humanism: Lessons from Kosovo* (London: Pluto Press).

Christenson, G. A. (1997) 'World Civil Society and the International Rule of Law', *Human Rights Quarterly*, Vol. 19, pp. 724–737.

Clapham, C. (1999) 'Sovereignty and the Third World State', *Political Studies*, Vol. 47, No. 3, pp. 522–537.

Clark, D. (2003) 'Iraq has Wrecked our Case for Humanitarian Wars', *Guardian*, 12 August.

Clark, J. (1991) *Democratizing Development: The Role of Volunteer Organizations* (London: Earthscan).

Clark, J. (2001) 'Ethical Globalization: The Dilemmas and Challenges of Internationalizing Global Civil Society', in M. Edwards and J. Gaventa (eds) *Global Citizen Action* (London: Earthscan).

Clayton, A. (ed.) (1996) *NGOs, Civil Society and the State: Building Democracy in Transitional Societies* (Oxford: INTRAC).

Cohen, J. L. and Arato, A. (1992) *Civil Society and Political Theory* (Cambridge, MA: The MIT Press).

Coker, C. (2001) 'The United States and the Ethics of Post-Modern War', in K. E. Smith and M. Light (eds) *Ethics and Foreign Policy* (Cambridge: Cambridge University Press).

Colás, A. (2002) *International Civil Society: Social Movements in World Politics* (Cambridge: Polity).

Connolly, W. E. (1991) 'Democracy and Territoriality', *Millennium: Journal of International Studies*, Vol. 20, No. 3, pp. 463–484.

Cooper, R. (2002) 'The Post-Modern State', in M. Leonard (ed.) *Reordering the World* (London: The Foreign Policy Centre).

Cox, R. W. (1981) 'Social Forces, States and World Orders: Beyond International Relations Theory', *Millennium: Journal of International Studies*, Vol. 10, No. 2, pp. 126–155.

Cox, R. W. (1983) 'Gramsci, Hegemony and International Relations: An Essay in Method', *Millennium: Journal of International Studies*, Vol. 12, No. 2, pp. 162–175.

Cox, R. W. (1999) 'Civil Society at the Turn of the Millennium: Prospects for an Alternative World Order', *Review of International Studies*, Vol. 25, No. 1, pp. 1–28.

Cunninghame, P. and Corona, B. C. (1998) 'A Rainbow at Midnight: Zapatistas and Autonomy', *Capital and Class*, No. 66, pp. 12–22.

Debray, R. (1996) 'A Guerrilla with a Difference', *New Left Review*, No. 218, pp. 128–137.

de Tocquville, A. (1945) *Democracy in America*, Vol. 2 (New York: Vintage Books).

Deudney, D. (1993) 'Global Environmental Rescue and the Emergence of World Domestic Politics', in R. Lipschutz and K. Conc (eds) *The State and Social Power in Global Environment Politics* (Ithaca, NY: Columbia University Press).

de Waal, A. (1997a) *Famine Crimes: Politics and the Disaster Relief Industry in Africa* (London: Africa Rights/James Currey).

de Waal, A. (1997b) 'Becoming Shameless: The Failure of Human Rights Organizations in Rwanda', *Times Literary Supplement*, 21 February.

Diamond, L. (1994) 'Rethinking Civil Society: Toward Democratic Consolidation', *Journal of Democracy*, Vol. 5, No. 3, pp. 4–17.

Dodds, F. (2001) 'From the Corridors of Power to the Global Negotiating Table: The NGO Steering Committee of the Commission on Sustainable Development', in M. Edwards and J. Gaventa (eds) *Global Citizen Action* (London: Earthscan).

Donnelly, J. (1999) 'The Social Construction of International Human Rights', in T. Dunne and N. Wheeler (eds) *Human Rights in Global Politics* (Cambridge: Cambridge University Press).

Donnelly, J. (2000) *Realism and International Relations* (Cambridge: Cambridge University Press).

Dowd, M. (2002) 'Culture War with B-2s', *New York Times*, 22 September.

Doyle, M. W. (1983) 'Kant, Liberal Legacies and Foreign Policy', *Philosophy and Public Affairs*, Vol. 12, pp. 205–235 and pp. 323–353.

Doyle, M. W. (1986) 'Liberalism and World Politics', *American Political Science Review*, Vol. 80, No. 4, pp. 1151–1163.

Duffield, M. (1996) 'The Symphony of the Damned: Racial Discourse, Complex Political Emergencies and Humanitarian Aid', *Disasters*, Vol. 20, No. 3, pp. 173–193.

Duffield, M. (2001) 'Governing the Borderlands: Decoding the Power of Aid', *Disasters*, Vol. 25, No. 4, pp. 308–320.

Dunne, T. (1995) 'The Social Construction of International Society', *European Journal of International Relations*, Vol. 1, pp. 367–389.

Dunne, T. and Wheeler, N. J. (forthcoming) '"We the Peoples": Contending Discourses of Security in Human Rights Theory and Practice', in K. Booth (ed.) *Security, Community, and Emancipation: An Introduction to Critical Security Studies* (Boulder, CO: Lynne Rienner).

Economist (2000) 'Sins of the Secular Missionaries', *Economist*, 29 January, pp. 25–28.

Edwards, M. (1999) *Future Positive: International Co-operation in the 21st Century* (London: Earthscan).

Edwards, M. (2001) 'Introduction', in M. Edwards and J. Gaventa (eds) *Global Citizen Action* (London: Earthscan).

Edwards, M. and Gaventa, J. (eds) (2001) *Global Citizen Action* (London: Earthscan).

Edwards, M. and Hulme, D. (1995) 'NGO Performance and Accountability in the Post-Cold War World, *Journal of International Development*, Vol. 7, No. 6, pp. 849–856.

Edwards, M. and Hulme, D. (1996) 'Too Close for Comfort? The Impact of Official Aid on Nongovernmental Organizations', *World Development*, Vol. 24, No. 6, pp. 961–973.

Esteva, G. (1999) 'The Zapatistas and People's Power', *Capital and Class*, No. 68, pp. 153–182.

Esteva, G. and Prakash, M. (1998) *Grassroots Post-modernism: Re-making the Soil of Cultures* (London: Zed Books).

Evans, G. and Sahnoun, M. (2002) 'The Responsibility to Protect', *Foreign Affairs*, Vol. 81, No. 6, pp. 99–110.

Evans, T. (2001), 'Globalization, Human Rights and International Citizenship', *Alternatives*, Vol. 26, No. 1.

Falk, R. A. (1995) *On Humane Governance: Toward a New Global Politics* (Cambridge: Polity).

Falk, R. A. (1999a) 'Kosovo, World Order and the Future of International Law', *American Journal of International Law*, Vol. 93, pp. 847–857.

Falk, R. A. (1999b) 'The Challenge of Genocide and Genocidal Politics in an Era of Globalization', in T. Dunne and N. Wheeler (eds) *Human Rights in Global Politics* (Cambridge: Cambridge University Press).

Falk, R. A. (2000a) 'Global Civil Society and the Democratic Prospect', in B. Holden (ed.) *Global Democracy: Key Debates* (London: Routledge, 2000).

Falk, R. A. (2000b) 'A New Medievalism?' in G. Fry and J. O'Hagen (eds) *Contending Images in World Politics* (Basingstoke: Palgrave).

Falk, R. A. (forthcoming) 'The Changing Role of Global Civil Society', in G. Baker and D. Chandler (eds) *Global Civil Society: Contested Futures* (London: Routledge).

Falk, R. A. and Krieger, D. (2002) 'Subverting the UN', *The Nation*, posted 17 October. Available from: http://www.thenation.com/doc.mhtml?i=20021104&s=falk.

Falk, R. A. and Strauss, A. (2003) 'The Deeper Challenges of Global Terrorism: A Democratizing Response', in D. Archibugi (ed.) *Debating Cosmopolitics* (London: Verso).

FIL  (2002)  Fédération  Internationale  de  Ligues  des  Droits  de L'Homme/International Federation of Human Rights, *International Criminal Court (ICC): No to American Exceptionalism*. Available from: http://www.iccnow.org/documents/otherissues/impunityart98/FIDHPaperUSandICC.pdf.

Finnemore, M. (1996a) *National Interests in International Society* (Ithaca: Cornell University Press).

Finnemore, M. (1996b) 'Norms, Culture, and World Politics: Insights from Sociology's Institutionalism', *International Organization*, Vol. 50, pp. 325–347.

Florini, A. M. (1996) 'The Evolution of International Norms', *International Studies Quarterly*, Vol. 40, pp. 363–389.

Florini, A. M. (2001) 'Transnational Civil Society', in M. Edwards and J. Gaventa (eds) *Global Citizen Action* (London: Earthscan).

Fore, H. H. (1993) 'Lean Development and the Privatization of U.S. Foreign Assistance', *Washington Quarterly*, Vol. 17, No. 1, pp. 183–196.

Forsythe, D. P. (2000) *Human Rights in International Relations* (Cambridge: Cambridge University Press).

Foucault, M. (2003) *Society Must Be Defended: Lectures at the Collège De France, 1975–76* (London: Allen Lane/Penguin).

Fox, C. (2003) 'Thinking Global, Not Local', *Municipal Journal*, 10 July.

Füredi, F. (1994) *Colonial Wars and the Politics of Third World Nationalism* (London: I. B. Tauris).

Füredi, F. (1998) *The Silent War: Imperialism and the Changing Perception of Race* (London: Pluto Press).

Galtung, J. (2000) 'Alternative Models for Global Democracy', in B. Holden (ed.) *Global Democracy: Key Debates* (London: Routledge, 2000).

Gaventa, J. (2001) 'Global Citizen Action: Lessons and Challenges', in M. Edwards and J. Gaventa (eds) *Global Citizen Action* (London: Earthscan).

Gelb, L. H. and Rosenthal, J. A. (2003) 'The Rise of Ethics in Foreign Policy', *Foreign Affairs*, Vol. 82, No. 3, pp. 2–7.

Gellner, E. (1994) *Conditions of Liberty: Civil Society and its Rivals* (London: Hamish Hamilton).

Ghils, P. (1992) 'International Civil Society: International Non-governmental Organizations in the International System', *International Social Science Journal*, No. 133, pp. 417–431.

Giddens, A. (1992) *The Transformation of Intimacy: Sexuality, Love and Eroticism* (Cambridge: Polity).

Giddens, A. (1994) *Beyond Left and Right: The Future of Radical Politics* (Cambridge: Polity).

Giles, M. and Stokke, K. (2000) 'Participatory Development and Empowerment: The Dangers of Localism', *Third World Quarterly*, Vol. 21, No. 2, pp. 247–258.

Gill, S. (1995) 'Market Civilization and Global Disciplinary Neoliberalism', *Millennium: Journal of International Studies*, Vol. 25, No. 3, pp. 399–423.

Glasius, M., Kaldor, M. and Anheier, H. (eds) (2002) *Global Civil Society 2002* (Oxford: Oxford University Press).

Goldenberg, S. and Borger, J. (2003) 'How Cheney's Revelation Led to the Point of No Return', *Guardian*, 17 January.

Goldenberg, S. and Watts, J. (2003) 'Bush Does U-turn in Effort to End Korea Crisis', *Guardian*, 15 January.

Gordenker, L. and Weiss, T. G. (1996) 'Pluralizing Global Governance: Analytical Approaches and Dimensions', in T. G. Weiss and L. Gordenker (eds) *NGOs, the UN, and Global Governance* (Boulder, CO: Lynne Rienner).

Gowan, P. (1995) 'Liberals Versus Neo-liberals: A Critical Look at Some Recent Writings on Civil Society', *Labour Focus on Eastern Europe*, No. 51.

Gowan, P. (1999) *The Global Gamble: Washington's Faustian Bid for World Dominance* (London: Verso).

Grigg, W. N. (2003) 'Rallying 'Round What Flag?', *New American*, Vol. 19, No. 8, 21 April.

Grugel, J. (2003) 'Democratisation Studies Globalisation: the Coming of Age of a Paradigm', *British Journal of Politics and International Relations*, Vol. 5, No. 2, pp. 258–283.

Guinier, L. (1995) *The Tyranny of the Majority: Fundamental Fairness in Representative Democracy* (New York: Simon & Schuster).

Haas, P. M. (1999) 'Social Constructivism and the Evolution of Multilateral Environmental Governance', in A. Prakash and J. Hart (eds) *Globalization and Governance* (London: Routledge).

Habermas, J. (1981) 'New Social Movements', *Telos*, Vol. 49, Fall, pp. 33–37.

Habermas, J. (1990) *Moral Consciousness and Communicative Action* (Cambridge: Polity Press).

Habermas, J. (1997) *Between Facts and Norms* (Cambridge: Polity Press).

Hall, S. (2003) 'Poll Shows Blair Losing Voters' Trust', *Guardian*, 19 August.

Halliday, F. (1986) *The Making of the Second Cold War* (2nd ed.) (London: Verso).

Hardt, M. and Negri, A. (2001) *Empire* (Cambridge, Mass: Harvard University Press).

Hardy, J. (2003) 'Four Days in Hell', *Guardian*, 15 April.

Hazboun, I. (2001) 'Volunteers Act as Human Shields', *Associated Press*, 2 August.

Hearn, J. (1999) 'Foreign Aid, Democratisation and Civil Society in Africa: A Study of South Africa, Ghana and Uganda', *Institute of Development Studies Discussion Paper*, No. 38 (Brighton: University of Sussex).

Hearn, J. (2000) 'Aiding Democracy? Donors and Civil Society in South Africa', *Third World Quarterly*, Vol. 21, No. 5, pp. 815–830.

Heartfield, J. (1996a) 'Marxism and Social Construction', in S. Wolton (ed.) *Marxism, Mysticism and Modern Theory* (Basingstoke: Macmillan).

Heartfield, J. (1996b) 'Rights and the Legal Subject'. Unpublished Freedom and Law discussion paper.

Heartfield, J. (2002) *The 'Death of the Subject' Explained* (Sheffield: Sheffield Hallam University Press).

Heartfield, J. (forthcoming) 'Contextualizing the Anti-Capitalist Movement', in G. Baker and D. Chandler (eds) *Global Civil Society: Contested Futures* (London: Routledge).

Heater, D. (1999) *What is Citizenship?* (Cambridge: Polity).

Heins, V. (2000) 'From New Political Organizations to Changing Moral Geographies: Unpacking Global Civil Society', *GeoJournal*, No. 52, pp. 37–44.

Heins, V. (forthcoming) 'Global Civil Society as Politics of Faith', in G. Baker and D. Chandler (eds) *Global Civil Society: Contested Futures* (London: Routledge).

Held, D. (1995) *Democracy and the Global Order* (Cambridge: Polity).

Held, D. (1998) 'Democracy and Globalisation', in D. Archibugi, D. Held and M. Köhler (eds) *Re-imagining Political Community: Studies in Cosmopolitan Democracy* (Cambridge: Polity).

Held, D. (2000) 'The Changing Contours of Political Community: Rethinking Democracy in the Context of Globalization', in B. Holden (ed.) *Global Democracy: Key Debates* (London: Routledge, 2000).

Held, D. (2002) 'Cosmopolitanism: Ideas, Realities and Deficits', in D. Held and A. McGrew (eds) *Governing Globalization: Power, Authority and Global Governance* (Cambridge: Polity).

Heraclides, A. (1992) 'The CSCE and Minorities: The Negotiations Behind the Commitments, 1972–1992', *Helsinki Monitor*, Vol. 3, No. 3, pp. 5–18.

Himmelfarb, G. (1999) *One Nation, Two Cultures* (New York: Knopf).

Hobden, S. and Hobson J. M. (eds) (2002) *Historical Sociology of International Relations* (Cambridge: Cambridge University Press).

Holbrook, J. (2002) 'Humanitarian Intervention and the Recasting of International Law', in D. Chandler (ed.) *Rethinking Human Rights: Critical Approaches to International Politics* (London: Palgrave Macmillan).

Holloway, J. (1998) 'Dignity's Revolt', in J. Holloway and E. Peláez (eds) *Zapatista! Reinventing Revolution in Mexico* (London: Pluto Press).

Holsti, O. (2000) 'Public Opinion on Human Rights in American Foreign Policy', in D. P. Forsythe (ed.) *The United States and Human Rights: Looking Inward and Outward* (Lincoln: University of Nebraska Press).

Honneth, A. (1993) 'Conceptions of "Civil Society"', *Radical Philosophy*, No. 64, pp. 19–22.

Hopgood, S. (2000) 'Reading the Small Print in Global Civil Society: The Inexorable Hegemony of the Liberal Self', *Millennium: Journal of International Studies*, Vol. 29, No. 1, pp. 1–25.

Hubert, D. (1998) 'Inferring Influence: Gauging the Impact of NGOs', in C. Ku and T. G. Weiss (eds) *Toward Understanding Global Governance: The International Law and International Relations Toolbox* (Providence, RI: ACUNS Reports and Papers, No. 2).

Hudock, A. C. (1999) *NGOs and Civil Society: Democracy by Proxy?* (Cambridge: Polity Press).

Hulme, D. and Edwards, M. (eds) (1995) *Non-Governmental Organisations – Performance and Accountability: Beyond the Magic Bullet* (London: Earthscan/ Save the Children Fund).

Hulme, D. and Edwards, M. (eds) (1997a) *NGOs, States and Donors: Too Close for Comfort?* (London: Macmillan/Save the Children Fund).

Hulme, D. and Edwards, M. (1997b) 'NGOs, States and Donors: An Overview', in *NGOs, States and Donors: Too Close for Comfort?* (London: Macmillan/Save the Children Fund).

Hulme, D. and Edwards, M. (1997c) 'Conclusion: Too Close to the Powerful, Too Far from the Powerless', in *NGOs, States and Donors: Too Close for Comfort?* (London: Macmillan/Save the Children Fund).

Hume, M. (2002) 'One War That Bush Has Already Lost', *Spiked Online*, 15 October. Available from: http://www.spiked-online.com/Articles/00000006DAB6.htm.

Hutchings, K. (2000) 'Modelling Democracy', in H. Smith (ed.) *Democracy and International Relations: Critical Theories/Problematic Practices* (Basingstoke: Palgrave Macmillan).

Hutchings, K. (forthcoming) 'Global Civil Society: Thinking Politics and Progress', in G. Baker and D. Chandler (eds) *Global Civil Society: Contested Futures* (London: Routledge).

ICISS (2001a) International Commission on Intervention and State Sovereignty, *The Responsibility to Protect* (Ottawa: International Development Research Centre, 2001).

ICISS (2001b) International Commission on Intervention and State Sovereignty, *The Responsibility to Protect: Research, Bibliography, Background* (Ottawa: International Development Research Centre).

Ignatieff, M. (2000) *Virtual War: Kosovo and Beyond* (London: Chatto & Windus).

IICK (2000) Independent International Commission on Kosovo, *The Kosovo Report: Conflict, International Response, Lessons Learned* (Oxford: Oxford University Press).

Jabri, V. (2000) 'Discourse Ethics, Democratic Practice and the Possibility of Intercultural Understanding', in H. Smith (ed.) *Democracy and International Relations: Critical Theories/Problematic Practices* (Basingstoke: Palgrave Macmillan).

Jackson, R. H. (1990) *Quasi-States: Sovereignty, International Relations and the Third World* (Cambridge: Cambridge University Press).

Jacques, M. (2004) 'The Interregnum', *London Review of Books*, 5 February, pp. 8–9.

Jessop, B. (1990) *State Theory: Putting Capitalist States in their Place* (Cambridge: Polity Press).

Josar, D. (2003) 'Voices on the Ground', *Stars and Stripes*, 15 October.

Kaldor, M. (1999a) *New and Old Wars: Organized Violence in a Global Era* (Cambridge: Polity, 1999).

Kaldor, M. (1999b) 'Transnational Civil Society', in T. Dunne and N. J. Wheeler (eds) *Human Rights in Global Politics* (Cambridge: Cambridge University Press).

Kaldor, M. (2001a) *Analysis*, BBC Radio Four, 29 March.

Kaldor, M. (2001b) 'A Decade of Humanitarian Intervention: The Role of Global Civil Society', in H. Anheier, M. Glasius and M. Kaldor (eds) (2001a) *Global Civil Society 2001* (Oxford: Oxford University Press).

Kaldor, M. (2003) *Global Civil Society: An Answer to War* (Cambridge: Polity).

Kaldor, M. (forthcoming) 'The Idea of Global Civil Society', in G. Baker and D. Chandler (eds) *Global Civil Society: Contested Futures* (London: Routledge).

Kampfner, J. (2003) 'Interview with John Reid', *New Statesman*, 3 March.

Kant, I. (1795) *Perpetual Peace: A Philosophical Sketch*. Available from: http://www.mtholyoke.edu/acad/intrel/kant/kant1.htm.

Kaplan, M. A. (1957) *System and Process in International Politics* (New York: Wiley).

Katzenstein, P. (ed.) (1996) *The Culture of National Security: Norms and Identity in World Politics* (New York: Columbia University Press).

Keane, J. (1998) *Democracy and Civil Society: on the Predicaments of European Socialism, the Prospects of Democracy, and the Problem of Controlling Social and Political Power* (London: Verso).

Keane, J. (2003) *Global Civil Society?* (Cambridge: Cambridge University Press).

Keck, M. E. and Sikkink, K. (1998) *Activists beyond Borders: Advocacy Networks in International Politics* (Ithaca: Cornell University Press).

Kenny, M. (2003) 'Global Civil Society: A Liberal-Republican Argument', *Review of International Studies*, Vol. 29, Special Issue, pp. 119–143.

Keohane, R. O. (ed.) (1986) *Neorealism and Its Critics* (New York: Columbia University Press).

Keohane, R. O. and Nye, J. S. (2001) *Power and Interdependence* (3$^{rd}$ ed.) (New York: Longman).

Klein, N. (2002) *Fences and Windows: Dispatches from the Front Lines of the Globalization Debate* (London: Flamingo).

Klein, N. (2003) 'Activists Must Follow the Money', *Guardian*, 12 September.

Klotz, A. (1995) *Norms in International Relations: The Struggle against Apartheid* (Ithaca, NY: Cornell University Press).

Klug, F. (2000) *Values for a Godless Age: The Story of the UK's New Bill of Rights* (London: Penguin).

Köhler, M. (1998) 'From the National to the Cosmopolitan Public Sphere', in D. Archibugi, D. Held and M. Köhler (eds) *Re-imagining Political Community: Studies in Cosmopolitan Democracy* (Cambridge: Polity).

Konrad, G. (1984) *Anti-Politics: An Essay* (New York: Harcourt, Brace and Janovich).

Korey, W. (1999) 'Human Rights NGOs: The Power of Persuasion', *Ethics and International Affairs*, Vol. 13, pp. 151–174.

Kratochwil, F. (1991) *Rules, Norms and Decisions: On the Conditions of Practical and Legal Reasoning in International Relations and Domestic Affairs* (Cambridge: Cambridge University Press).

Kratochwil, F. and Ruggie, J. (1986) 'International Organization: A State of the Art on an Art of the State', *International Organization*, Vol. 40, pp. 753–775.

Kumar, C. (2000) 'Transnational Networks and Campaigns for democracy', in A. M. Florini (ed.) *The Third Force: The Rise of Transnational Civil Society* (Washington, D.C.: Carnegie Endowment for International Peace).

Kumar, K. (1993) 'Civil Society: An Inquiry into the Usefulness of an Historical Term', *British Journal of Sociology*, Vol. 44, No. 3, pp. 375–395.

Laclau, E. and Mouffe, C. (2001) *Hegemony and Socialist Strategy: Towards a Radical Democratic Politics* (2nd ed.) (London: Verso).

Laxer, G. and Halperin, S. (eds) (2003) *Global Civil Society and its Limits* (Basingstoke: Palgrave).

Lewis, N. (1998) 'Human Rights, Law and Democracy in an Unfree World', in T. Evans (ed.) *Human Rights Fifty Years On: A Reappraisal* (Manchester: Manchester University Press).

Linklater, A. (1981) 'Men and Citizens in International Relations', *Review of International Studies*, Vol. 7, No. 1, pp. 23–37.

Linklater, A. (1998) *The Transformation of Political Community* (Cambridge: Polity).

Lipschutz, R. (1992) 'Reconstructing World Politics: The Emergence of Global Civil Society', *Millennium: Journal of International Studies*, Vol. 21, No. 3, pp. 389–420.

Lipschutz, R. (forthcoming) 'Global Civil Society and Global Governability', in G. Baker and D. Chandler (eds) *Global Civil Society: Contested Futures* (London: Routledge).

Lister, S. (2000) 'Power in Partnership? An Analysis of an NGO's Relationships with its Partners', *Journal of International Development*, Vol. 12, pp. 227–239.

Maina, W. (1998) 'Kenya: The State, Donors and the Politics of Democratization' in A. van Rooy (ed.) *Civil Society and the Aid Industry* (London: Earthscan).

Mann, M. (1988) *States, War and Capitalism* (Oxford: Blackwell).

Marcos, S. (2003) 'The Slaves of Money – and Our Rebellion', *Guardian*, 11 September.

Marcussen, H. S. (1996) 'NGOs, the State and Civil Society', *Review of African Political Economy*, Vol. 23, No. 69, pp. 405–423.

Martin, G. (2003) 'New Social Movements and Democracy', in G. Taylor and M. Todds (eds) *Democracy and Protest* (Sheffield: Sheffield Hallam University Press).

Mathews, J. T. (1997) 'Power Shift', *Foreign Affairs*, Vol. 76, No. 1, pp. 50–66.

McGrew, A. (1997) 'Conclusion: Democracy Beyond Borders?: Globalization and the Reconstruction of Democratic Theory and Politics', in A. McGrew (ed.) *The Transformation of Democracy? Globalization and Territorial Democracy* (Cambridge: Polity Press/Open University).

Melucci, A. (1985) 'The Symbolic Challenge of Contemporary Movements', *Social Research*, Vol. 52, No. 4, pp. 789–816.

Melucci, A. (1988) 'Social Movements and the Democratization of Everyday Life', in J. Keane (ed.) *Civil Society and the State: New European Perspectives* (London: Verso).

Melucci, A. (1989) 'Nomads of the Present: Social Movements and Individual Needs in Contemporary Society', in J. Keane and P. Mier (eds) *Nomads of the Present: Social Movements and Individual Needs in Contemporary Society* (London: Hutchinson Radius).

Mendel, J. (2003) 'Reading the 'War on Terror': Psychoanalysis and Beyond', paper presented at the British International Studies Association 28th annual conference, University of Birmingham, 15–17 December.

Mische, A. (1993) 'Post-communism's 'Lost Treasure': Subjectivity and Gender in a Shifting Public Place', *Praxis International*, Vol. 13, No. 3, pp. 242–267.

Monbiot, G. (2003) 'Rattling the Bars', *Guardian*, 18 November.

Morgenthau, H. J. (1993) *Politics among Nations: the Struggle for Power and Peace* (brief ed.) (New York: McGraw-Hill).

Mouffe, C. (1993) *The Return of the Political* (London: Verso).

Müller, H. and Risse-Kappen, T. (1992) 'From the Outside In and from the Inside Out: International Relations, Domestic Politics, and Foreign Policy', in D. Skidmore and V. M. Hudson (eds) *The Limits of State Autonomy: Societal Groups and Foreign Policy Formulation* (Boulder, Co.: Westview Press).

Najam, A. (1996) 'NGO Accountability: A Conceptual Framework', *Development Policy Review*, Vol. 14, pp. 339–353.

*New York Times* (2003) 'Pentagon's Heart Not in New York's Ticker Tape Parade', *New York Times*, 5 May.

Norton-Taylor, R. (2000) 'From Killing to Cuddling', *Guardian*, 17 August.

Nye, J. S. (1988) 'Neorealism and Neoliberalism', *World Politics*, Vol. 40, No. 2, pp. 235–251.

Nye, J. S. (2002) *The Paradox of American Power: Why the World's Only Superpower Can't Go It Alone* (New York: Oxford University Press).

Offe, C. (1987) 'Challenging the Boundaries of Institutional Politics: Social Movements since the 1960s', in C. Maier (ed) *Changing Boundaries of the Political* (Cambridge: Cambridge University Press).

O'Keefe, K. N. (2002) 'Back to Iraq as a Human Shield', *Observer Comment Extra*, 29 December. Available from: http://observer.guardian.co.uk/comment/story/0,6903,866254,00.html

Onishi, N. (2002) 'Nongovernmental Organizations Show Their Growing Power', *New York Times*, 22 March.

Onuf, N. (1989) *A World of our Making: Rules and Rule in Social Theory and International Relations* (Columbia: University of South Carolina Press).

Otto, D. (1996) 'Nongovernmental Organizations in the United Nations System: The Emerging Role of International Civil Society', *Human Rights Quarterly*, Vol. 18, pp. 107–141.

Palan, R. (2000) 'A World of their Making: An Evaluation of the Constructivist Critique in International Relations', *Review of International Studies*, Vol. 26, pp. 575–598.

Patel, S., Bolnick, J. and Mitlin, M. (2001) 'Squatting on the Global Highway: Community Exchanges for Urban Transformation', in M. Edwards and J. Gaventa (eds) *Global Citizen Action* (London: Earthscan).

Pender, J. (2001) 'From "Structural Adjustment" to "Comprehensive Development Framework": Conditionality Transformed?', *Third World Quarterly*, Vol. 22, No. 3, pp. 397–411.

Pender, J. (2002) 'Empowering the Poorest? The World Bank and the "Voices of the Poor"', in D. Chandler (ed.) *Rethinking Human Rights: Critical Approaches to International Politics* (Basingstoke: Palgrave Macmillan).

Perlstein, R. (2002) 'Goodbye to the Vietnam Syndrome', *New York Times*, 15 October.

Pianta, M. (2003) 'Democracy vs Globalization: The Growth of Parallel Summits and Global Movements', in D. Archibugi (ed.) *Debating Cosmopolitics* (London: Verso).

Pogge, T. (1994) 'An Egalitarian Law of Peoples', *Philosophy and Public Affairs*, Vol. 23, pp. 195–224.

Posner, M. (1997) 'Foreword: Human Rights and Non-governmental Organizations on the Eve of the Next Century', *Fordham Law Review*, Vol. 66, No. 2, pp. 627–630.

Pupavac, V. (2001) 'Misanthropy without Borders: The International Children's Rights Regime', *Disasters*, Vol. 25, No. 2, pp. 95–112.

Rawls, J. (1999) *A Theory of Justice* (rev. ed) (Oxford: Oxford University Press).

Raz, J. (1984) 'Right-Based Moralities', in J. Waldron (ed.) *Theories of Rights* (Oxford: Oxford University Press).

Reus-Smit, C. (2001) 'Constructivism', in S. Burchill et al (eds) *Theories of International Relations* (2nd ed.) (Basingstoke: Palgrave Macmillan).

Reus-Smit, C. (2002) 'Imagining Society: Constructivism and the English School', *British Journal of Politics and International Relations*, Vol. 4, No. 3, pp. 487–509.

Rieff, D. (1999) 'A New Hierarchy of Values and Interests', *World Policy Journal*, Vol. 16, No. 3, pp. 28–34.

Rieff, D. (2000) 'The Necessity of War', Book Reviews, *Los Angeles Times*, 3 September.

Rieff, D. (2002a) *A Bed for the Night: Humanitarianism in Crisis* (London: Vintage).

Rieff, D. (2002b) 'David Rieff, Author of *A Bed for the Night* talks with Robert Birnbaum'. Posted 20 November. Available from: http://www.identitytheory.com/printme/rieffprint.html.

Risse, T. (2000) 'The Power of Norms Versus the Norms of Power: Transnational Civil Society and Human Rights', in A. M. Florini (ed.) *The Third Force: The Rise of Transnational Civil Society* (Washington, D.C.: Carnegie Endowment for International Peace).

Risse, T. and Ropp, S. C. (1999) 'International Human Rights Norms and Domestic Change: Conclusion', in T. Risse, S. C. Ropp and K. Sikkink (eds) *The Power of Human Rights: International Norms and Domestic Change* (Cambridge: Cambridge University Press).

Risse, T. and Sikkink, K. (1999) 'The Socialization of International Human Rights Norms into Domestic Practices: Introduction', in T. Risse, S. C. Ropp and K. Sikkink (eds) *The Power of Human Rights: International Norms and Domestic Change* (Cambridge: Cambridge University Press).

Roberts, A. (2001) 'Intervention: Suggestions for Moving the Debate Forward', Round Table Consultation, London, 3 February, *Discussion Paper*. International Commission on Intervention and State Sovereignty, p. 2. Available from: http://web.gc.cuny.edu/icissresearch/london%20discussion%20paper.htm.

Robertson, G. (1999) *Crimes Against Humanity: the Struggle for Global Justice* (London: Allen Lane/Penguin Press).

Roniger, L. and Güneş-Ayata, A. (eds) (1994) *Democracy, Clientelism and Civil Society* (Boulder, CO.: Lynne Rienner).

Rosenau, J. N. (1992) 'Citizenship in a Changing Global Order', in J. N. Rosenau and E.-O. Czempiel (eds) *Governance Without Government: Order and Change in World Politics* (Cambridge: Cambridge University Press).

Roth, K. (1999) 'Human Rights Trump Sovereignty in 1999'. Human Rights Watch, 9 December. Available from: http://www.hrw.org/press/1999/dec/wr2keng.htm.

Ruggie, J. G. (1993) 'Territoriality and Beyond: Problematizing Modernity in International Relations', *International Organization*, Vol. 47, No. 1, pp. 139–174.

Ruggie, J. G. (1998) *Constructing the World Polity* (London: Routledge).

Sakamoto, Y. (1991) 'Introduction: The Global Context of Democratization', *Alternatives*, Vol. 16, No. 2, pp. 110–123.

Salamon, L. M. (1994) 'The Rise of the Nonprofit Sector: A Global "Associational Revolution"', *Foreign Affairs*, Vol. 73, No. 4, pp. 109–122.

Sali-Terzić, S. (2001) 'Civil Society' in Z. Papić (ed.) *International Support Policies to South East European Countries – Lessons (Not) Learned in Bosnia-Herzegovina*. (Sarajevo: Open Society Fund Bosnia & Herzegovina/Soros Foundations). Available from: http://www.soros.org.ba/en/dokumenti/ostali/book/014.pdf.

Sandel, M. (1998) *Liberalism and the Limits of Justice* (Cambridge: Cambridge University Press).

Schecter, D. (2000) *Sovereign States or Political Communities? Civil Society and Contemporary Politics* (Manchester: Manchester University Press).

Schmitz, H. P. (1999) 'Transnational Activism and Political Change in Kenya and Uganda', in T. Risse, S. C. Ropp and K. Sikkink (eds) *The Power of Human Rights: International Norms and Domestic Change* (Cambridge: Cambridge University Press).

Scholte, J. A. (2001) 'The IMF and Civil Society: An Interim Progress Report', in M. Edwards and J. Gaventa (eds) *Global Citizen Action* (London: Earthscan).

Scholte, J. A. (2002) 'Civil Society and Democracy in Global Governance', *Global Governance*, Vol. 8, pp. 281–304.

Schwarz, B. (2000) 'Round Three: Concluding Remarks'. Roundtable: Picking a Good Fight, *Atlantic*, 14 April. Available from: http://www.theatlantic.com/unbound/roundtable/goodfight/schwarz3.

Scott, M. J. O. (2001) 'Danger – Landmines! NGO-Government Collaboration in the Ottawa Process', in M. Edwards and J. Gaventa (eds) *Global Citizen Action* (London: Earthscan).

Seligman, A. (1992) *The Idea of Civil Society* (New York: Free Press).

Shaw, M. (1994a) *Global Society and International Relations: Sociological Concepts and Political Perspectives* (Cambridge: Polity).

Shaw, M. (1994b) 'Civil Society and Global Politics: Beyond a Social Movements Approach', *Millennium: Journal of International Studies*, Vol. 23, No. 3, pp. 647–667.

Shaw, M. (1996) *Civil Society and Media in Global Crises: Representing Distant Violence* (London: Continuum).

Shaw, M. (1999) 'Global Voices: Civil Society and the Media in Global Crisis', in T. Dunne and N. J. Wheeler (eds) *Human Rights in Global Politics* (Cambridge: Cambridge University Press).

Shaw, M. (2000) *Theory of the Global State: Globality as Unfinished Revolution* (Cambridge: Cambridge University Press).

Shaw, M. (2001) 'Hard Heads, Soft Liberals', Letters, *Guardian*, 1 November.

Shaw, M. (2002) 'Post-Imperial and Quasi-Imperial: State and Empire in the Global Era', *Millennium: Journal of International Studies*, Vol. 31, No. 2, pp. 327–336.

Sikkink, K. (1993) 'Human Rights, Principled Issue-Networks, and Sovereignty in Latin America', *International Organization*, Vol. 47, No. 3, pp. 411–441.

Smith, H. (2000) 'Why is There no International Democratic Theory?', in H. Smith (ed.) *Democracy and International Relations: Critical Theories/Problematic Practices* (Basingstoke: Palgrave Macmillan).

Smith, J., Pagnucco, R. and Lopez, G. A. (1998) 'Globalizing Human Rights: The Work of Transnational Human Rights NGOs in the 1990s', *Human Rights Quarterly*, Vol. 20, pp. 379–412.

Smith, S. (2001) 'Reflectivist and Constructivist Approaches to International Theory', in J. Baylis and S. Smith (eds) *The Globalization of World Politics: An Introduction to International Relations* (2nd ed.) (Oxford: Oxford University Press).

Stammers. N. (1999) 'Social Movements and the Social Construction of Human Rights', *Human Rights Quarterly*, Vol. 21, No. 4, pp. 980–1008.

Stirrat, R. L. (1996) 'The New Orthodoxy and Old Truths: Participation, Empowerment and Other Buzz Words', in S. Bastian and N. Bastian (eds) *Assessing Participation: A Debate from South Asia* (Delhi: Konark Publishers).

Straw, J. (2002) 'Failed and Failing States: A Speech given by Foreign Secretary Jack Straw at the European Research Institute, University of Birmingham', 6 September. Available from: http://www.eri.bham.ac.uk/jstraw.htm.

Taylor, C. (1991) 'Civil Society in the Western Tradition', in E. Groffier and M. Paradis (eds) *The Notion of Tolerance and Human Rights: Essays in Honour of Raymond Klibansky* (Ottawa: University of Carelton Press).

Thakur, R. (2001) 'Global Norms and International Humanitarian Law: An Asian Perspective', *International Review of the Red Cross*, Vol. 83, No. 841, pp. 19–44.

Tilly, C. (1990) *Coercion, Capital and European States, AD 990–1990* (Oxford: Blackwell).

Tremlett, G. (2004) 'Furious Voters Oust Spanish Government', *Guardian*, 15 March.

Tuckman, J. (2003) 'Zapatistas Go Back to the Grassroots', *Guardian*, 27 December.

Tussie, D. and Tuozzo, M. F. (2001) 'Opportunities and Constraints for Civil Society Participation in Multilateral lending Operations: Lessons from Latin America', in M. Edwards and J. Gaventa (eds) *Global Citizen Action* (London: Earthscan).

Tyson, A. S. (2002) 'Invading Iraq: Would the Public go along', *Christian Science Monitor*, 17 July.

UK (2000) United Kingdom House of Commons Foreign Affairs Committee, *Fourth Report*, Session 1999–2000, 23 May.

UK (2002) 'PM meets President Bush for Talks', Press Conference: Prime Minister Tony Blair and President George Bush, 6 April, Newsroom, 10 Downing Street. Available from: http://www.number-10.gov.uk/output/Page4757.asp.

UN (1991) United Nations Security Council resolution 688, S/RES/0688, 5 April.

UN (2000) *Report of the Panel on United Nations Peacekeeping Operations*, A/55/305–S/2000/809. Available from: http://www.un.org/peace/reports/peace_operations/.

US (2002) *The National Security Strategy of the United States of America*, 11 September, The White House. Available from: http://www.whitehouse.gov/nsc/nss.html.

van Rooy, A. (1998) 'Civil Society as Idea: An Analytical Hatstand?', in A. van Rooy (ed.) *Civil Society and the Aid Industry* (London: Earthscan).

van Rooy, A. and Robinson, M. (1998) 'Out of the Ivory Tower: Civil Society and the Aid System', in A. van Rooy (ed.) *Civil Society and the Aid Industry* (London: Earthscan).

van Tuijl, P. (1999) 'NGOs and Human Rights: Sources of Justice and Democracy', *Journal of International Affairs*, Vol. 52, No. 2, pp. 496–515.

Vaux, T. (2001) *The Selfish Altruist: Relief Work in Famine and War* (London; Earthscan).

Vidal, J. (2002) 'Odd Couple's African Tour Highlights Battle over Debt', *Guardian*, 22 May.

Vidal, J. (2003) 'Peasant Farmers Show Strength in Cauldron of Grassroots Politics', *Guardian*, 10 September.

Vincent, R. J. (1986) *Human Rights and International Relations* (Cambridge: Cambridge University Press).

Wagner, P. (2002) 'The Project of Emancipation and the Possibility of Politics, or, What's Wrong with Post-1968 Individualism?', *Thesis Eleven*, No. 68, pp. 31–45.

Walker R. B. J. (1993) *Inside/Outside: International Relations as Political Theory* (Cambridge: Cambridge University Press).

Walker, R. B. J. (1994) 'Social Movements/World Politics', *Millennium: Journal of International Studies*, Vol. 23, No. 3, pp. 669–700.

Walker, R. B. J. (1995) 'International Relations and the Concept of the Political', in K. Booth and S. Smith (eds) *International Relations Theory Today* (Cambridge: Polity).

Waltz, K. N. (1962) 'Kant, Liberalism and War', *American Political Science Review*, Vol. 56, pp. 331–340.

Waltz, K. N. (1979) *Theory of International Politics* (New York: McGraw-Hill).

Walzer, M. (1995) *Spheres of Justice: A Defence of Pluralism and Equality* (Oxford: Blackwell).

Wapner, P. (1995) 'Politics Beyond the State: Environmental Activism and World Civic Politics', *World Politics*, Vol. 47, pp. 311–40.

Watt, N. (2003) 'Americans Raise Hackles by Flying Stars and Stripes in Iraq', *Guardian*, 22 March.

Weber, H. (2002) Global Governance and Poverty Reduction: The Case of Microcredit', in R. Wilkinson and S. Hughes (eds) *Global Governance: Critical Perspectives* (London: Routledge).

Weiss, T. G. and Gordenker, L. (eds) (1996) *NGOs, the UN, and Global Governance* (Bolder, CO: Lynne Reinner).

Wendt, A. (1992) 'Anarchy is what States Make of it: The Social Construction of Power Politics', *International Organization*, Vol. 46, No. 2, pp. 391–425.

Wendt, A. (1999) *Social Theory of International Politics* (Cambridge: Cambridge University Press).

West, P. (2004) *Conspicuous Compassion* (London: Civitas).

Wheeler, N. J. (1992) 'Pluralist and Solidarist Conceptions of International Society: Bull and Vincent on Humanitarian Intervention', *Millennium: Journal of International Studies*, Vol. 21, pp. 463–487.

Wheeler, N. J. (1996) 'Guardian Angel or Global Gangster: A Review of the Ethical Claims of International Society', *Political Studies*, Vol. 44, No. 1, pp. 123–135.

Wheeler, N. J. (2000) *Saving Strangers: Humanitarian Intervention in International Society* (Oxford: Oxford University Press).

Wheeler, N. J. (forthcoming) 'Humanitarian Intervention after September 11', in T. Lang (ed.) *Humanitarian Intervention: The Moral Dimension* (Washington, D.C.: Georgetown University Press).

Wheeler, N. J. and Bellamy, A. J. (2001) 'Humanitarian Intervention and World Politics', in J. Baylis and S. Smith (eds) *The Globalization of World Politics: An Introduction to International Relations* (2nd ed.) (Oxford: Oxford University Press).

White, G. (1994) 'Civil Society, Democratization and Development. (1) Clearing the Analytical Ground', *Democratization*, Vol. 1, pp. 375–390.

White, M. (2003) 'Downing Street Rules Out Victory Parade', *Guardian*, 10 May.

White, M. and Borger, J. (2003) 'Blair Wins Time with Bravura Iraq Speech', *Guardian*, 16 January.

White, S. C. (1999) 'NGOs, Civil Society, and the State in Bangladesh: The Politics of Representing the Poor', *Development and Change*, Vol. 30, pp. 307–326.

Wight, M. (1991) *International Theory: The Three Traditions* (London: Continuum).

Wilkinson, R. and Hughes, S. (eds) (2002) *Global Governance: Critical Perspectives* (London: Routledge).

Williams, D. (1997) '"Good Governance" and the Ideology of Transformation', in W. Hale and E. Kienle (eds) *After the Cold War: Security and Democracy in Africa and Asia* (London: I. B. Tauris).

Wood, E. M. (1995) *Democracy against Capitalism: Renewing Historical Materialism* (Cambridge: Cambridge University Press).

World Bank (2000) *Consultations with Civil Society Organizations: General Guidelines for World Bank Staff* (Washington, D.C.: World Bank).

World Bank (2001) *World Bank-Civil Society Collaboration – Progress Report for Fiscal Years 2000 and 2001* (Washington, D.C.: World Bank).

Zaagman, R. and Zaal, H. (1994) 'The CSCE High Commissioner on National Minorities: Prehistory and Negotiations', in A. Bloed (ed.) *The Challenges of Change: The Helsinki Summit of the CSCE and its Aftermath* (London: Martinus Nijhoff).

Zizek, S. (2003) 'The Interpassive Subject', 20 May. Available from: http://www.lacan.com/interpass.htm.

# Index